New c

MW00623586

the
FUEL

&

the
FLAME

→ ←

ignite your life & your campus for
JESUS CHRIST

- Advanced Readers Copy -

steve shadrach & paul worcester

CMM Press is the publishing ministry of the Center for Mission Mobilization (CMM), an international Christian ministry.

Campus Ministry Today is a ministry of the CMM that is dedicated to helping train, equip and resource those involved in campus ministry. If you are passionate about college students, we are committed to helping you succeed. Our website, campusministry.org, houses a growing collection of resources we've researched, others we have developed, as well as our online journal written by experts in the field of collegiate ministry. We aim to be a leader for tools and training in college ministry.

For more resources, go to cmmpress.org or campusministry.org.

The Fuel and the Flame

CMM Press
PO Box 3556
Fayetteville, AR 72702
cmmpress.org

Second Edition, Advanced Readers Copy, 2020.
C: 05-08-20   : 05-14-20 4:25

ISBN: 978-1-947468-41-2

Printed in the United States of America

The Fuel & The Flame:

Ignite your life & your campus for Jesus Christ

The Fuel

Open Your Eyes: How's Your Vision?

Chapter 1: What's Your Story? 1
→ WILL'S STORY
→ GOD'S STORY
→ YOUR STORY

Chapter 2: The Real World Starts Now 9
→ WHY ARE YOU AT COLLEGE?
→ THE POWERFUL PERCENT
→ STUDENTS WHO CHANGED THE WORLD

Chapter 3: Jesus' Prayer Request 19
→ LOST SHEEP
→ LABORERS WANTED
→ THE POWER OF MULTIPLICATION

Dig Deep: Laying Your Foundation

Chapter 4: Groundwork 29
→ ALWAYS BEGIN AT HOME
→ BUILT ON LOVE
→ THE INVENTION OF THE WHEEL

Chapter 5: First Things First 37
→ UNSWERVING DEVOTION
→ SEEKING HIS KINGDOM & LIFE'S CONVEYER BELT
→ ONE DECISION I MADE IN COLLEGE

Chapter 6: Fully Charged 47
→ GOD IN US
→ WALKING IN THE SPIRIT
→ ENTERING THE BATTLE

Chapter 7: Living and Active 55
→ GREATEST BOOK EVER WRITTEN
→ KNOW HIM AND HIS HEART
→ GET A GRIP

Chapter 8: At His Feet 67
→ DAILY INTIMACY
→ "OUR FATHER"
→ TOUCH THE WORLD

Chapter 9: Contagious Community 77
→ CIRCLE UP
→ GET REAL
→ BODY PARTS AND BATTLESHIPS

Chapter 10: Landmines 85
→ LIVING THE "SAFE" LIFE
→ LOSING THE BATTLE AGAINST LUST
→ LOOKING FOR LOVE IN ALL THE WRONG PLACES

Chapter 11: Hustle Mode On 95
→ STAY FAITHFUL
→ LEARN TO SERVE
→ PURSUE WISDOM

The Flame

Show and Tell: Everyday Evangelism

Chapter 12: Who Cares? 109
→ THE BIG BAD "E" WORD
→ CHRIST'S LOVE COMPELS US
→ "BUT WHAT IF...?"

Chapter 13: Open Doors Everywhere 121
→ SEIZE OPPORTUNITIES
→ PRAYER, CARE, SHARE
→ NOT OUT OF THIS WORLD

Chapter 14: Just Do It 129
→ FILL YOUR TOOLBELT
→ SHARE YOUR STORY
→ ASK THE GOLDEN QUESTION

Chapter 15: Your "Mission Trip" to Campus 139

→ WHERE HAVE YOU BEEN SENT?

→ YOUR "PEOPLE GROUP"

→ PRAY, PLAN PROCEED

Chapter 16: Real Talk **149**

→ GETTING PERSONAL

→ EVANGELISTIC BIBLE STUDY

→ ONE-ON-ONE

Build Your Chain: *Disciple-making Links*

Chapter 17: Jesus Is a Genius **161**

→ THE MASTER'S PLAN

→ START HERE

→ DISCIPLE-MAKING 101

Chapter 18: Baby Steps **171**

→ THE DELIVERY ROOM

→ WET CEMENT

→ THE FIRST DAY, WEEK, AND MONTH

Chapter 19: Handcrafted **183**

→ HANG-OUT-OLOGY

→ DIRECTION AND AFFECTION

→ KNOWLEDGE, SKILLS, CHARACTER AND VISION

Chapter 20: Choosing Wisely **195**

→ THE UNBROKEN CHAIN

→ FOCUS ON THE FAITHFUL

→ NO DEAD-END DISCIPLESHIP

Chapter 21: Plugged In **205**

→ GROWING IN GROUPS

→ ONE AT A TIME

→ THE 5 CS

Chapter 22: Two Are Better Than One **215**

→ REPRODUCE YOURSELF

→ THE SYNERGY OF MINISTRY TEAMS

→ FROM THE CAMPUS TO THE WORLD

Go Global: *You Are a Missions Mobilizer*

Chapter 23: Let the Facts Inflame You **225**

→ GOD'S WORD

→ GOD'S WORLD

→ GOD'S WORK

Chapter 24: Your Most Strategic Role **233**

→ WHAT IS A WORLD CHRISTIAN?

→ GOING, PRAYING, SENDING

→ WELCOMING, MOBILIZING, FRONTIER MOBILIZING

Chapter 25: Not for College Days Alone . . . **245**

→ THREE POTENTIAL PITFALLS: JOB, MATE, LIFESTYLE

→ HAVE YOU BEEN "CALLED"?

→ KEEP FUELING THE FLAME

Chapter 26: Pass the Baton **257**

→ WHAT CAN ONE STUDENT DO?

→ THE DECISIVE HOUR

→ TAKE IT AND RUN!

About the Authors **263**

Welcome to the totally revised and updated version of *The Fuel and the Flame*! This one was written with students in mind. While we expect that ministry staff or recent grads will come across it as well, our hope is that you—a college student—feel like this book was written just for you. The original version was published in 2003 and quickly became the go-to book for a myriad of campus-based and church-based college ministries around the U.S. and beyond. However, it is high time we reexamined everything for this new generation of students in light of the challenges and opportunities that lie before you.

Our goal in this book is to focus on a few of the simple commands and modeling Jesus provided us. To be able to easily remember these commands, we will refer to them as EDM (evangelism, disciple-making, and mission mobilization). While we believe God is passionate about the pursuit of social justice, racial equality, and many other righteous causes in our day, those are outside of the scope of this book. We also know that every culture has its own set of ever-changing values, challenges, and injustices, and we are trying not to "Americanize" this material but instead make it easily adaptable in many other countries and languages. We hope that God uses the basics of EDM shared in this book to transform your everyday life and change your heart to be more like His own.

So, if you want to walk with God more closely, have a vision for your life and ministry, develop a practical plan for you to lead others to Christ and make disciples, and to impact the world for the glory of God…you've come to the right place! Read this on your own. Or take a small group through it. Encourage your whole college ministry to use it as their semester training tool or summer project book. Not everything in here will work for you and your group, but—as long as you are seeking to be an obedient (and teachable!) disciple of Jesus Christ—a lot will!

Lastly, I want to give credit for this book to four amazing people:

Our publisher, CMM Press, is led by John Patton, who is also the Chief Operating Officer for the Center for Mission Mobilization, the organization

I am on staff with. Over the last 20+ years, I may have had a few ideas and written them down on a napkin someplace, but John is the implementer of so many of our crazy, world-changing schemes. Couldn't do it without you, bro!

Over the last five years, I've built a friendship with an incredible campus ministry leader named Paul Worcester, the co-author of this book. After coming to Christ and being discipled under Max Barnett's Baptist Campus Ministry at OU, he spent the last decade doing major EDM with Christian Challenge at Chico State in California. He has a huge heart for helping the collegiate body of Christ around the world to embrace and fulfill the Great Commission. When it came time to choose a next generation leader to co-author this new version, Paul was at the top of my list. This book, in my humble opinion, is much better than the first; that is mainly due to Paul's vision, heart, experience, and jaw-dropping stories of changed lives!

Two others who have labored so long and hard on this project are Taylor Tollison and Heidi Loften. Taylor was a staff leader with Campus Outreach for years and had so consumed and utilized the original *The Fuel and the Flame* that I knew we had to get him involved in the creation of this edition. There is so much here that reflects his strategic thinking and his experience working with powerful, grassroots EDM ministries over the years. And finally, a special thank you to Heidi, the gifted (and long-suffering!) editor for this book who stuck with us through my procrastination and indecision. She came to Christ through our Student Mobilization ministry as a college student and has lived out the EDM model with her "campus-minister-turned-pastor" husband Charlie for decades. We can't thank Taylor and Heidi enough.

Now, enjoy!

—Steve Shadrach (Fayetteville, Arkansas)

the **FUEL**

Open Your Eyes:
How's Your Vision?

1

What's Your Story?

→ **WILL'S STORY**

Will grew up in a wealthy and well-known family from upper Chicago. When he graduated from high school, his parents sent him on a summer-long cruise around the world. As he traveled through Europe, the Middle East, and Asia, he saw so many different people groups that had no church or gospel. His burden for the lost became so great that he told his parents, "I want to give my life to prepare for the mission field." His best friend was shocked, and told him he would be "throwing himself away" as a missionary. That night Will wrote two words in the back of his Bible:

"No reserves."

When Will started at Yale University, he had fully surrendered his heart to Christ, and other students "leaned on him like a solid rock" because he was so full of vision and purpose. One reason may have been that Will's life motto was: "Say 'no' to self and 'yes' to Jesus every time." That fall, Will began a morning prayer and Bible study group that grew to 150 freshmen coming each week, and by the time he graduated, 1,300 Yale students were in small groups. During his time in college, Will started the Yale Hope Mission that helped widows, orphans, and addicts. He also hosted a large annual missions conference on campus to help other students catch a vision for reaching the world.

Although Will was worth millions, he lived a modest life, not even bringing a car to college and giving away large sums of money to various ministries. One student said, "It didn't matter that Will was fabulously wealthy; he

was always about his Father's business, not wasting time in trivial pursuits."
He felt a growing burden to plant a church among one of the hardest-to-
reach people groups of all: the Muslim Kansu in China. At graduation he
turned down several lucrative career opportunities. After one especially
tempting job offer, he went home and wrote two more words in his Bible:

"No retreats."

News services across the nation published articles about this wealthy and
gifted young man who turned his back on affluence and comfort to raise his
own support and risk everything to go to China as a missionary. On his way
there, he stopped first in Cairo, Egypt to learn Arabic, the language these
Chinese Muslims spoke. But while there, he contracted spinal meningitis,
and died a few weeks later in a hospital room—all alone.

As news travelled back to America that young Will had died, there was
a "wave of sorrow" across the country and beyond. One writer praised him,
saying the young man's sudden death was a "joyous and natural one that
seemed a privilege rather than a sacrifice for him." Many people, though,
didn't understand Will's choices. Why would someone who could have had
it all just throw his life away? When a couple of his old classmates came to
Cairo to pack up his belongings, they found his well-worn Bible next to
his hospital bed. In the back, underneath the words "No reserves" and "No
retreats," they were astonished to see their dying friend had scrawled two
final words:

"No regrets."

Although the life of William Whiting Borden (of the famed "Borden Dairy"
family) appeared to end prematurely in that lonely hospital room in 1913,
he had accomplished everything God had planned for him. In his heart of
hearts the young 25-year-old millionaire missionary must have reconciled
his destiny there on his deathbed, making peace with God—and himself.
The story of Will's life and early death became a rallying cry for thousands
of college students who ended up spending their lives on the mission field
because of Borden's time at Yale.

How about you? How about me? There are endless stories we could
write with our lives, numerous pursuits for which we could exchange it. But

how many of them will enable you to end your story with, "No reserves, no retreats, no regrets"?

→ GOD'S STORY

When a New York professional sports team wins a championship, they are honored with a huge ticker tape parade lined with millions of cheering fans. The athletes ride in a long line of convertibles that stretches out a mile, allowing each superstar to receive maximum adulation. The New Yorkers stand ten to fifteen people deep, hoping to catch a glimpse of their favorite athlete through the pressing crowd. Bit by bit the parade goes by, while each spectator only sees a small sliver of the action.

What if you were at the next parade and instead of wading into the mass of people, you were invited to view the mile-long procession from the top of the Empire State Building? You'd be thrilled because this time you could look down and see from the beginning to the end and every car and athlete in between. This kind of perspective, in a weak, human way, describes the view God has on this world and life.

History is passing by like a parade, and He does see the beginning to the end and every detail in between! We may only be able to view a tiny bit of today's events, but history is truly *His* story. The Lord is fulfilling His plan for the ages, and nothing will deter it. We can either get on board with Him and view things from His eternal perspective, or we can live out our quiet little lives, never reaching the God-ordained potential He has planned for us.

There are two stories you can live for: God's story or your story. Most people will opt to live for their own story, giving all their time, attention, money, and abilities to fulfilling their *own* dreams and desires. Few trade their story for God's. The Bible tells us God's story. Although it was written over a period of 1,500 years by more than 40 authors on three continents, and in three different languages, it has but one theme. One story. The story from Genesis to Revelation is about God's quest to redeem all nations back to Himself. Cover to cover, God has one plan—reaching all nations, and one method—using people. Since the creation of mankind, the Father has been on an epic mission of redemption. From the command to "be fruitful and multiply" in Genesis, to the Messiah discipling the twelve apostles in the Gospels, to believers from every tribe and tongue around the throne in Revelation, it's obvious our mandate is to join God in His worldwide, history-long mission to "make disciples of all nations." Everyone who has been rescued by Jesus' triumph over sin has a key role to play in the Lord's grand adventure of drawing people into the saving love of Christ.

So, here is our challenge to you. Don't settle for just writing your own life story. Be a part of *His* story!

→ YOUR STORY

Too often when we think about what we are going to do with our lives, we start at the wrong place—looking at ourselves. We are told to discover and develop *our* personality, passions, gifts, and abilities. Those things can play a helpful role in directing us, but our first question should not be what is *my* passion, but what is *God's* passion. Before we can even try to make our plan, we should have a firm grip on His plan. The Lord is redeeming people from every tribe, tongue and nation, and we get to play a part in it! In his excellent book, *It's All Backward*, Claude Hickman put it this way: "All the advice you have been given about your life is wrong. It's actually backward. I wish I were exaggerating. But seriously, after years of reading the books, listening to many seminars and sermons for helping people discover their life direction, they all have the same problem: they begin with the wrong person—you. God doesn't want to endorse your life; He wants to direct your life."

The last words of Jesus, known as the Great Commission, provide all the direction any of us will ever need. It's enough to keep you busy for a lifetime. And in fact, it was intended to!

> "Then Jesus came to them and said, "All authority in heaven and on earth has been given to me. Therefore go and make disciples of all nations, baptizing them in the name of the Father and of the Son and of the Holy Spirit, and teaching them to obey everything I have commanded you. And surely I am with you always, to the very end of the age" (Matthew 28:18-20, New International Version).

Speaking to His disciples between His resurrection and ascension, Jesus wanted to remind them one last time what the heart and soul of their life's work should be. The main verb in this passage is "to make" disciples. The other actions of "going," "baptizing," and "teaching" are all participles that hang their full weight on the mandate to *make disciples*. A paraphrase of this text might read: "I've provided you all of My power. So, wherever you go, you are always to be creating new followers of Me from every group on earth. First have them publicly identify with Me, and then show them how to apply all the truths that I handed to you. And be assured, My presence will be with you forever."

Imagine this passage like a sandwich you're making for yourself. Verse 18 is the top slice of bread, representing Christ's complete authority, or *power* that He provides you. Verse 20 is the bottom slice of bread, symbolizing His *presence* that He promises you through the end of the age. In between these layers of His power and presence is the main course, which is the command to "make disciples of all the nations." I'm certain that if I was supposed to try to fulfill this mandate in my own strength, I'd be paralyzed with fear; however, knowing His power and His presence are backing me to the hilt, I can proceed with confidence. Theologian John Stott puts it this way: "His authority on earth allows us to dare to go to all the nations. His authority in heaven gives us our only hope of success. And His presence with us leaves us no other choice."

> "There is no higher calling or greater privilege than being involved in helping fulfill the Great Commission."
>
> **—BILL BRIGHT, FOUNDER OF CRU**

> "The Great Commission is not an option to be considered; it is a command to be obeyed."
>
> **—HUDSON TAYLOR**

It is each of our jobs to "make disciples of all nations." How can I tell if you've taken personal responsibility for the Great Commission? Simple. You have a plan to fulfill your role in it. I'm sure you've taken personal responsibility for your studies, your finances, your exercise, your future, and for sure your love life. How do I know? You have goals and a plan for each of these areas, and you're working diligently to accomplish them.

For most Christians, the Great Commission is really the Great *Omission,* because they have no visible, tangible strategy to fulfill this mandate the Lord has given *every* believer. Too many of us are waiting for some sort of special call—a "warm fuzz" or a "liver quiver"—to join God on His mission. You don't need an emotional experience when you have a clear command. If you are a follower of Christ, you have been called by God to play a key role in the greatest cause on earth. The Lord is waiting for you to join Him in His mission. The Great Commission is *your* mission.

The Bible teaches there are only three things that last forever: God Himself, the Word of God, and the souls of people. Yet many people focus all of their energy on being successful or pursuing experiences in this life, as if this short stay on earth is all there is.

In 1 John 2:15-17 we're told: "Do not love this world nor the things it offers you, for when you love the world, you do not have the love of the Father in you. For the world offers only a craving for physical pleasure, a craving for everything we see, and pride in our achievements and posses-sions. These are not from the Father, but are from this world. And this world is fading away, along with everything that people crave. But anyone who does what pleases God will live forever" (New Living Translation).

If we're going to be in step with the eternal purposes of God, we had better see what He sees and value what He values. Vision comes from allow-ing the "vision Giver" to open your eyes and expand your heart. We don't just want to do good things for God by adding Christian activity to our already busy schedules. We want to co-labor with the Lord of the universe and flow into His stream, not demand that He flow into ours!

As you look at the Great Commission, your life, and the vast spir-itual needs and opportunities surrounding you, step back and ponder two questions:

> Am I spending my time and energy
> writing my story...or God's story?

> Have I fully embraced the Great
> Commission as my mission?
>
> If so, do I have a specific plan
> to fulfill my role in it?

Note: At the end of each chapter, we are going to include several questions for you to ask yourself and reflect upon. If you are going through this book in a small group, these can serve as discussion starters.

2

The Real World Starts Now

If you only knew.

If you only knew what God really wanted to do in and through your life during your college experience, your heart would be beating out of your chest and tears would be streaming down your face.

It's true.

The Lord wants to transform your life in such a dramatic way that by the end of your college years you will barely even recognize yourself. God wants to use you to change other students' lives for eternity and start a raging fire for Jesus Christ on your campus.

How can we say this?

It happened to us.

God completely transformed our lives in college and, to our amazement, used us in the lives of others to lead them to Christ and disciple them.

The question is not, "Does God want to change me and use my life during college?" The question is, "Will I let him do His work in and through me?"

→ PAUL'S STORY

I (Paul) came to know Christ at a young age. However, all through high school and into my first semester of college, the focus of my life was me. I was all about accumulating patches on my letterman jacket, skateboarding, surfing, snowboarding, and any "extreme sport" you could think of. When I wasn't jumping off of something, I was singing lead vocals for a painfully bad Christian punk band called Misplaced Cargo.

Once I moved into the dorms at the University of Oklahoma, I started to realize that no one cared about the patches on my letterman jacket or that I could kickflip down a set of stairs. They definitely didn't want to listen to a cheesy Christian punk CD.

That first semester I got involved in the Baptist Collegiate Ministry led by Max Barnett and started to notice a group of students who were different—in a good way. Their conversations were not focused on *their* problems or plans or even the next party that was coming up, but instead they were about what the Lord was saying to them from their time alone with Him and the Bible verses they were memorizing. They were talking about friends they were presenting the gospel to and dreaming about ways to reach more people on campus.

God started to open my eyes to His mission at a winter conference my freshman year. The speaker, Nik Ripken, author of the book *Insanity of God*, told story after story of followers of Christ who were enduring the most intense persecution imaginable in order to share Christ with others. One quote Nik shared from a persecuted Christian really stuck with me: "Never give up in freedom what others would not in persecution." I remember thinking, "If these people can risk their lives to share Christ, I can handle a little bit of rejection from presenting the gospel to the guys in my dorm hall."

The next semester my twin brother, David, and I decided to start a Bible study in our dorm to reach fellow freshmen. We got so jazzed about it that we actually ended up living in the dorms all four years of college so we could keep reaching out to freshmen. Being in the dorms enabled us to be in the lives of hundreds of lost students and provided endless opportunities to share Christ with them. As a result, the Lord changed many students' lives right in front of our eyes. Once we got a taste for God moving, the thrill I got from my extreme sports didn't quite measure up. I found so much joy being immersed in a cause greater than myself. My life was no longer about me. It was about being used by God to accomplish His mission of reaching the whole world with the love of Jesus!

→ WHY ARE YOU AT COLLEGE?

Walt Henrichsen, author of the classic *Disciples Are Made Not Born*, made this shocking statement: "If you are at college for *any* other reason than to be on mission for Jesus Christ, you are there for selfish, sinful reasons." Whoa!

I'm glad he said it and not me! Did this former pastor and Navigator representative go *too* far in his challenge to students, or had he found an open nerve that desperately needed to be uncovered and dealt with?

If you're currently a student, let's have a little chat:

"So, why *did* you come to college?" I ask in a laid-back, casual manner.

"Well," you say proudly, "I'm here because I want to get a *good* education."

Sitting up in my chair, I respond, "Okay…but *why* do you want to get a good education?"

"Mmm," you ponder. "Well…because I want to get a *good* job."

Now I lean toward you and say, "A good job, huh? Why is it that you want to get a *good* job?"

"Wait a minute," you shoot back. "I see where you're going with this! Okay, I admit it. I want a good job so I can get a better salary."

"Well, *why* would you want a better salary?" I slyly inquire.

If you and I are *really* honest, a big part of going to college is to get a good job, in order to make a better salary, so that we can…so that we can—*What? Say it!*—support the kind of comfortable lifestyle we have dreamed about! Maybe this is the exact motive your well-intentioned parents have drummed into your brain, but can you see why Henrichsen makes the statement he does? Ninety-nine percent of students, even "committed" Christians, are at college with an agenda that could very well be described as selfish, and yes, even sinful!

Before you beat yourself up too badly or march down to the admissions office to drop out, there are some great reasons for sticking around. The college years are the *best* time in life to build the essential knowledge, skills, character, and vision to prepare effectively for a life of walking with God, leaving a legacy of changed lives, and reaching the world.

> **college** (*Webster's* definition)—an independent institution of higher learning offering a course of general studies leading to a bachelor's degree

> **college** (my definition)—a four (or more!) year window in a person's life when God has maximum opportunity to build a foundation into a life lived for Him

If life is defined as the preparation for an eternity lived with one's Maker, then college is the ideal time of prepping for *this* life. It's a small time frame when the Lord can reach down into your heart and turn it toward Himself. College is the ideal season for this divine intervention because you're no longer under the protective wing of Mom or Dad, and you get a chance to figure out what *you* really believe. Because you don't yet have to face the rush of responsibilities that follow after graduation, it's the perfect period of time for God to lay down some long-term tracks in your life. I know you may think you are busy now, but you'll never have more time, flexibility, or opportunity to focus on laying this kind of foundation to become a disciple who is on mission with God to reach all nations.

Your Creator wants to use these formative years to build a strong, below-the-surface spiritual substructure for a life lived for His glory. You are studying and preparing to have a meaningful career. Maybe you hope to eventually meet someone, get married, and start a family. In some ways college can be seen as your last pit stop on your journey to the "real world." Sadly, many see it more as a waiting room where you can mess around, and the choices you make don't really matter. Nothing could be further from the truth. The real world starts now. Right here, right now, you have an unprecedented chance to not just get an education but to grow in your walk with Christ and make a real impact on reaching the world.

→ THE POWERFUL PERCENT

This is the right time, and you are in the right place! The college campus is one of the best venues in the world to reach people for Christ. God has positioned you exactly where you are for the purpose of reaching those around you. You may never have a better opportunity in life to share the gospel and make disciples of all nations. The only way you could be around as many other people and have a better chance to engage them with the gospel would be if you joined the military or went to prison. I don't recommend the latter, but my point is: not all opportunities are created equal. So, don't waste it!

> "The university is a clear-cut fulcrum with which to move the world. The church can render no greater service, both to itself and to the cause of the gospel, than to try to recapture the universities for Christ. More potently than by any other means, change the university and you change the world."
>
> —CHARLES MALIK, FORMER SECRETARY-GENERAL OF THE UNITED NATIONS

We don't have to look far to see the incredible potential of college students. Even though only a little more than one percent of the world's population are collegians, they are a powerful percent! This small sliver of humanity is, and will be, the leader of every facet of society. Every country sends their best and brightest to the university for education and training. Focusing our evangelistic and multiplication efforts on this one percent is a very strategic way to expand the kingdom of God and fulfill the Great Commission.

College students represent the most reachable, recruitable, trainable, and sendable category of persons on the planet. Many students on your campus are just one conversation away from giving their lives to following Christ. You don't have to wait to graduate college to become a missionary and start changing the world for Christ. You can start living on mission now.

In John 4:35 Jesus tells us not to waste one more second: "Don't you have a saying, 'It's still four months until harvest'? I tell you, open your eyes and look at the fields! They are ripe for harvest" (NIV).

→ THREE KINDS OF STUDENTS: WHICH ARE YOU?

In my years of making disciples on college campuses, I've observed three kinds of Christian students:

Busy

This student equates maturity with "Christian busyness." They are heading to a Bible study now, then a worship concert, afterward to help out at a homeless shelter, then off to mentor at the middle school. As great as these activities might be, many times they are packed into students' schedules out of boredom, or not being able to say no, or because they have no clear direction in life, or they are simply trying to impress others.

Effective

This person can say no to many exciting opportunities, but they aren't really sure what to say yes to. They've narrowed down their priorities to a few important things that may relate to reaching out to others for Christ, but have no specific Great Commission plan. They see God using them in the lives of people, but aren't sure if they are really making an eternal difference.

Strategic

There are a lot of busy Christians, some effective ones, but precious few who are truly strategic. This student looks at their campus from God's perspective and has singled out an affinity group they want to build relationships in to reach and disciple other students for the Lord. Some may view them as too intense, but in reality they are finding tremendous pleasure in saying no to their own agenda and joining God in His mission! This person will leave a lasting legacy behind, and is working to raise up other students who will join them in reaching the nations. This person says with John R. Mott: "Let us be satisfied with nothing less than the deepest mark on our generation."

→ STUDENTS WHO CHANGED THE WORLD

> "The fact is, no one thought up the strategy of fulfilling the Great Commission by reaching the college campus. Campus ministry is the result of the observation that God has chosen to use the university and college students as His primary vehicle in accelerating the evangelization of the world. To be involved in campus ministry is to be involved in God's primary missions strategy."
>
> —PATRICIA BURGIN, *THE POWERFUL PERCENT: STUDENTS AT THE HEART OF THE GREAT COMMISSION*

I (Steve) love history, students, and missions, and I've done a lot of reading and research in these three areas. I've concluded that the last 250+ years of Protestant missions from the West have been spearheaded and sustained primarily by college students. They have provided most of the impetus and manpower to fulfill the Great Commission from the eighteenth through the twenty-first century. Though not all were college students, this sampling of mostly college-aged revolutionaries from both sides of the Atlantic will stir your heart.

Nicolaus Ludwig Von Zinzendorf

Born in Germany in 1700, Count Nicolaus Ludwig von Zinzendorf attended the University of Wittenburg to study law. At age nineteen he was looking at a painting of Christ in agony on the cross and an inscription that read, "All this I did for you. What are you going to do for Me?" From that moment on, Ludwig committed himself to spreading the gospel throughout the world. He started a 24-hour prayer vigil focused on world intercession that continued unbroken for a hundred years. As a result, his mission society, the Moravians, sent out more missionaries in the next twenty years than all the Protestants had sent out in the previous two hundred years! This simple passion for Jesus and mobilizing workers to the ends of the earth was contagious. In his words, "I have but one passion: It is He, it is He alone. The world is the field and the field is the world; and henceforth that country shall be my home where I can be most used in winning souls for Christ."

Lottie Moon

Born and raised in a wealthy Virginia family before the American Civil War, Lottie Moon was a well-educated woman who measured all of four feet three inches. Sailing for China as a single 23-year-old female missionary was unusual but par for the course for this diminutive, yet bold, pioneer. She passed up a marriage proposal from a prominent seminary professor, justifying it by proclaiming, "God had first claim on my life, and since the two conflicted, there could be no question about the result!" At first her ministry was confined to teaching at a girls' school, but she finally struck out on her own to do evangelistic work in northern China. Despite tremendous opposition, nationals did come to Christ, a church was established, and thousands were baptized over the years.

Lottie is most known for her vigorous recruiting of volunteers and money for missions. She mobilized thousands of women in the United States to pray, volunteer, and give to foreign missions work. Severe drought broke out in China, and Lottie gave away *all* her money and food to help the starving. Other missionaries tried to rescue Lottie in time to save her life, loading her frail and famished body onto a ship headed for America, but she died on board late one December night in 1912—Christmas Eve. How appropriate that the Southern Baptist world missions funding effort, which has raised hundreds of millions of dollars over the years, is named for Lottie Moon and takes place at the same time each year—Christmas.

William Carey, Samuel Mills, and the "Haystack Five"

Englishman William Carey was a self-educated, college-aged believer when he wrote a small book that analyzed the need for world evangelization and convinced a few of his friends to form a tiny missions agency that sent him to India in 1793. Carey and his book ignited a bonfire of evangelistic activity that led to the formation of many mission agencies over the next twenty-five years. While Carey's bravado was making waves in England, his little book made its way across the Atlantic and into the hands of five students at Williams College in Massachusetts. On a rainy August afternoon in 1806, Samuel Mills and four other students were praying under a haystack to stay dry. They had been reading Carey's book and wanted to intercede for the world. As they finished their prayer, Mills turned to his friends and exhorted them, "We can do this if we will!" These five young collegians not only initiated the first nationwide student movement, but they also began the first six mission agencies in North America. The "Haystack Five" helped launch secret world prayer clusters called the Society of the Brethren on numerous other campuses.

Grace Wilder

Grace was born in 1863, the daughter of an American missionary to India who was a recruit of Samuel Mills of "Haystack" fame. As a student at Mount Holyoke College, Grace started a weekly Bible study for girls where she challenged them to sign a declaration stating: "We hold ourselves willing and desirous to do the Lord's work wherever He may call us, even if it be in a foreign land." Thirty-four girls signed it. At the same time, her brother Robert started a weekly meeting in their home for Princeton men. When word got out there would be a month-long summer project for Christian college men from around the country at Mount Hermon, Massachusetts, Grace recruited Robert to begin praying that a nationwide missionary movement would spring out of it. Indeed, by the final day of the July 1886 conference, a hundred men had signed a pledge to missions, and these "Mount Hermon 100" became the American pioneers of the Student Volunteer Movement. Over the next forty years, 100,000 students were recruited to reach the world!

C.T. Studd and the "Cambridge Seven"

In the early 1880s, God used a group of aristocratic college students in England, called the "Cambridge Seven," to ignite the most effective mobilization effort of all time: The Student Volunteer Movement (SVM). These seven young men helped catapult the little-known China Inland Mission agency (CIM) from obscurity and inspired hundreds of recruits for CIM and other mission societies. After a year-long tour of the British Isles speaking to packed audiences, Studd and the other six set sail for China in February of 1885. Their written story about giving up fame and fortune for a missionary call, *The Evangelization of the World*, was distributed to every YMCA and YWCA throughout the British Empire and United States.

> "Christ wants not nibblers of the possible,
> but grabbers of the impossible."
>
> — C.T. STUDD

The impact was amazing, and by the time the seven men arrived in China, CIM had already signed up 163 new missionaries. By 1890 that number had doubled, and by 1900 there were 800 missionaries at the ready. These totals represented over one-third of the entire Protestant missionary force across the planet.

Here is the golden thread that ties the various stories of these student firestarters together: their lives revolved around a passion for Christ which overflowed into obedience to Him. What about you? Have you decided whether or not you want to follow in the footsteps of these world changers? There's a tremendous cost, and yes, some of these pioneers lost their lives for the gospel. But today Jesus is asking you to do something much tougher than dying for Him. He is asking you to *live* for Him, and to make an unreserved commitment of all that you are to Christ and His purposes on earth. Will you put your "yes" on the table and let God use you as He sees fit?

"We can do this if we will!"

—SAMUEL MILLS

REFLECTION QUESTIONS:

→ Which of these world changers impressed you, and why?
→ Right now, according to our descriptions, would you say you are busy, effective, or strategic?
→ Why are you in college?
→ Fast forward in your mind. What would you like your life to be like at your graduation?

3

Jesus' Prayer Request

Alexa's time in high school was an insecure frenzy of ever-changing friend groups and efforts to escape her pain (cutting, guys, etc.). Her first few weeks at Baylor University were spent partying before she accepted an invitation to a small group for freshmen at Antioch Community Church. She attended multiple weeks and even showed up at a sleepover the leader was hosting. On that night, the leader, Courtney, shared the story of her fractured family and having a mother who had divorced, remarried a woman and brought lots of confusion into the home. Jesus met Courtney with His acceptance and grace in the midst of her brokenness, and as she recounted her story, she also shared her longing for the girls in her group to know that same love. Alexa sat there stunned. How could someone who was now a Bible study leader have lived a life that seemed as messy as hers? She pulled Courtney off to the side and asked her tearfully, "How can I know that Jesus?" That night Alexa surrendered her own struggling and mixed-up life to Jesus.

Courtney began leading Alexa and a group of girls, as well as individually discipling her each week. Alexa took advantage of every opportunity she could find to grow in her faith—including a mission trip to India, where she served the poor and learned to share the gospel boldly and pray for the sick. Eventually, Alexa became a leader herself and reached out to another girl, named Chelsea, whose story was almost identical to hers. When the time came for Alexa to graduate from the college ministry, she replaced herself by recruiting and training Chelsea to take on her leadership role.

What could have been a story too filled with devastation and shame for Courtney to share openly instead became a platform to raise up a chain of women who would allow Jesus to redeem their brokenness and use their lives for His glory!

→ LOST SHEEP

Our estimate is the average college campus is less than 5% followers of Christ. If so, that means 19 out of 20 of the thousands of students rushing to class alongside you don't have a relationship with Christ. These students are living without the full and eternal life Jesus died to give them. Many of these students are wondering if there is purpose beyond popularity and parties. They suffer from addiction, depression, and hopelessness. One-third of these students are binge drinking and at least 1 in 5 are regularly using some kind of drugs. According to a recent American College Health Association survey, 37% of students reported feeling so depressed within the last 12 months that it was difficult to function, and 21 percent felt overwhelming anxiety. Ten percent of full-time college students had serious thoughts of suicide in the past year. Even those who *seem* to have it all together on the outside have hidden fears and insecurities and are hopelessly enslaved to sin. The average student on your campus is hurting and broken, wandering through life without the direction or protection of God. Sorry to be so blunt here, but if nothing changes, they are headed for disaster—in this life, and the next.

The good news is Jesus sees every student on your campus. He knows their thoughts, secret sins and every struggle each of them is dealing with. When Jesus looks at the crowds of students rushing between classes, His heart breaks for them. Matthew 9:36-38 says this about Jesus: "When he saw the crowds, he had compassion on them, because they were harassed and helpless, like sheep without a shepherd. Then he said to his disciples, 'The harvest is plentiful, but the laborers are few; therefore pray earnestly to the Lord of the harvest to send out laborers into his harvest.'"

The Greek word for compassion in this passage is *splagchnizomai* which literally means "to feel it in your gut." When Jesus saw the crowds, He felt a deep and emotional pit in His stomach. Why? Those who were so precious to Him were lost and hopeless, wandering around in a daze without any guidance or someone to care for them.

Jesus' prayer request is for laborers in His harvest: people who share His heart of compassion and join Him in His mission to reach the lost and broken. He asks us to pray for laborers who will feel the "pit" in their stomach when they think about the thousands of students on campus stuck in sin and headed to a Christless eternity. It all starts with a love and burden for those without a relationship with God. Bob Pierce, founder of the Christian relief organization World Vision, famously prayed, "Let my heart be broken by the things that break the heart of God." God loves the students on your campus more than you and I will ever know. Why don't you take a moment and ask Him to break your heart for what breaks His. It's a prayer He loves to answer.

→ LABORERS WANTED

In Matthew 9, Jesus shares His compassion for the hordes of lost sheep, but then switches to a metaphor about harvesting crops: "The harvest is plentiful, but the laborers are few." The harvest represents people who are ready to follow Christ. God is currently at work in thousands of people's lives across your campus and around the world, preparing them to respond to the gospel *if only* a laborer will simply step into their lives, love them, and share Christ with them. A laborer is an obedient follower of Jesus Christ who continually seeks to win and disciple others. Laborers give their time and energy to helping others follow Christ and grow as His disciples. That's why we often refer to laborers as "disciple-makers."

The problem is not with the harvest; the harvest is plentiful. The issue is a lack of laborers. What a tragedy! Think about it. There are myriads of people who are ready right now to respond to Christ, but there are not enough laborers to go share with them. I don't know what could possibly be a more urgent dilemma. The good news is, God didn't leave us to figure this one out on our own. He gave us a master plan.

He says our first response to this overwhelming problem should be to "pray earnestly to the Lord of the harvest." God is the Lord of this harvest. When I am tempted to despair or get discouraged about the state of my campus or the state of the world, it's helpful for me to remember it's not my harvest. No, it's God's world, and He has a plan to raise up and send out laborers. He is the "Great Connector," and as He draws people to Himself, He simultaneously calls laborers to go share the gospel with them. So when we pray earnestly for God to raise up laborers, we are reminded this is God's work, and He will answer your prayer. I call this Mt. 9:36-38 passage the sneakiest verse in the Bible, because when you obey Jesus by praying for more laborers, *you* are likely going to be the answer to your prayer!

Prayer is God's main way to mobilize you. Personally, I have never met someone who faithfully prayed for laborers and *wasn't* burdened by the Lord to become a laborer themselves. God is inviting you to become a disciple-maker and join Him on His mission to labor in the harvest and make disciples of all nations!

> "Tell the students to give up their
> small ambitions and come eastward to
> preach the gospel of Christ."
>
> —FRANCIS XAVIER, MISSIONARY TO INDIA,
> THE PHILIPPINES, AND JAPAN

→ THE POWER OF MULTIPLICATION

We have watched hundreds of ordinary college students go from lost to laborer during their college experience. It starts with passionately pursuing God and building the foundation of your life on Him. Then it's all about taking what you are learning and passing it on, introducing others to Jesus, teaching them to walk as His disciples, and training those you teach to pass on what you teach them.

Think of it like holding the ends of two ropes, one in each hand. With one rope you are being pulled along by those who are teaching you to follow Jesus. They are modeling for you what the life of a disciple looks like. As they are helping you lay the foundation for your life, you are also learning what it looks like to help someone else follow Christ. Then you invite others to grab onto the loose end of the rope in your other hand, sharing with them about the life Christ offers and asking if they would like to join you in following Jesus. Once someone takes you up on your invitation and grabs hold of the rope you are pulling, you provide the momentum and determine the direction, leading them to follow Jesus and training them to look for someone to grab hold of the rope in their other hand. Continuing to grow as a disciple, while teaching someone else to be a disciple—each hand holding one end of a rope—is the lifestyle of a laborer.

People, being used by God to labor in the harvest and make disciples, are His method of reaching the nations. We get the incredible opportunity to leave our mark on the world by imparting our life to someone else. When you lead another student to Christ, then help them grow in their relationship with God to the point where they now lead another student to Christ and start to disciple them...this is multiplication. You have literally multiplied your life into another person who can do the same for someone else. This process of multiplication was modeled and taught in the life of Jesus and the apostles and is the most strategic, effective, and biblical way of reaching the world for Christ. Do you want to be a world changer? Then believe in, practice, and get addicted to the vision of multiplication!

Below is a visual comparison between the typical way of thinking about reaching the world through simple addition and the process of multiplication we are describing. If a great evangelist were to win 10,000 people a day to Christ, we would all be amazed and full of praise to God. Even though we might stand on the sidelines and cheer them on, it would still take them 1,200 years to win the world to Christ at *today's* population. But suppose I were to lead you to the Savior and then spend a year building deep into your life, and then we both turn around and do the same for someone else the following year? Now that there are four of us, we would begin this third year of ministry by each finding another person to win and disciple. If the chain remained unbroken, the enormous power of multiplication would kick in, and the world would be won to Christ in an incredibly short thirty-two years!

	Evangelist	Disciple-Maker
Year 1:	365,000	2
Year 2:	730,000	4
Year 10:	3,650,000	512
Year 20:	7,300,000	210,994
Year 30:	10,950,000	190,406,656
Year 38:	13,870,000	8,124,017,323

Making disciples is a powerful way to multiply your life. I know pouring yourself into just one other student may seem like an insignificant way to begin changing the world for Jesus, but it is the best place to start. As you can tell from the chart above, although the process of multiplication (disciple-making) starts out very slow in comparison to addition (i.e. doing only evangelism), we can see that eventually it overtakes it in *quantity* and has been higher in *quality* all along.

→ STARTING TO BUILD YOUR OWN CHAIN

We are going to walk through and unpack this disciple-making chain step by step, helping you learn to build your foundation as a disciple of Jesus and how to take your passion for loving Christ and making Him known and pass it on to others. Investing in reproducing more laborers who share your desire to go make disciples of all nations is your part to play in God's plan to reach the ends of the earth. Here's the process and progression:

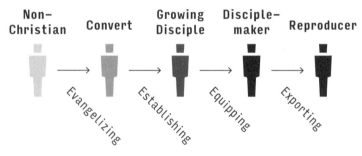

There may be various churches and campus ministries on or near your campus that draw large groups of students to their weekly meetings, but don't mistake that for disciple-making. I'm sure there is great teaching, worship, and fellowship in many of those gatherings, but they cannot replace the impact of one student helping another student receive Christ into their life, spending months following them up to establish them in their new faith, and many more months (or years) showing the new disciple how to repeat this process. So plug into a great church and campus ministry, serve and lead when opportunities arise, bring your Christian and non-Christian friends along—but never sacrifice the one-on-one influence you can have on other students.

The Apostle Paul modeled the concept of making disciples who make disciples. In 2 Timothy 2:2, Paul documents how he brought his young disciple, Timothy, to many group teaching sessions over the years they ministered together. But in his final words, the soon-to-be-martyred apostle exhorted him: "The things you have heard from me in the presence of many witnesses, entrust them to faithful men who will be able to teach others also." Here's what that looked like:

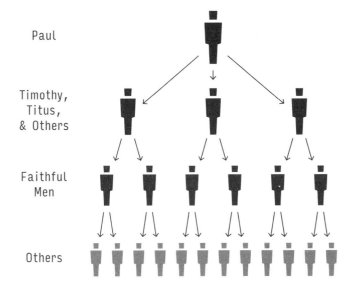

Wouldn't it be awesome to look back on your life, including your college years, and know God used you to raise up and leave behind fully devoted disciples of Jesus who were actively engaged in continuing your disciple-making chain? This is what it means to begin taking *personal* responsibility for the Great Commission in Matthew 28 to "make disciples of all the nations." And if you can do it at least one time as a student, there is a much better chance you will continue to reproduce yourself into others once you graduate and on through the decades of your life. Impacting life after life for the glory of God and the reaching of the nations...that, my friend, would be a life well lived!

But, stop! You need to know that before you can *make* a disciple, you must *be* a disciple. A disciple builds their life on a foundation of loving God with all that they are and loving others as themselves. Let's begin by digging deep into our hearts and motivations and rooting out sin that can knock us off course. So, put on your hard hat and start your own personal excavation project. Better yet, grab a fellow believer and the two of you team up to become (and accomplish) all that God has for you!

REFLECTION   QUESTIONS:

→ What is a disciple-maker?
→ Where and why did Jesus command us to be one?
→ Is someone discipling you right now? If not, why not?
→ Are you discipling someone right now? If not, why not?

Dig Deep:

Laying Your Foundation

4

Groundwork

Although Katherine came from a fairly moral and religious home, she had secretly decided to become a sorority party girl when she hit college. Sure enough, she was able to accomplish that goal as she spent her weekends in drunken stupors and in the beds of accommodating upperclassmen. By Christmas, though, life had become empty and boring, and she began searching for more. Soon after, one of her friends invited her to a worship event a local church was sponsoring on campus where several believers shared their testimonies. She had never seen people so real, so vulnerable, and so accepting. That night she bowed her head to ask the Lord to come in and save her, a sinner.

Her decision appeared to be genuine because everyone observed such immediate changes. Her vast network of friendships now presented opportunities for bold witness. Some turned her away, but many responded to her testimony of a transformed life. Different Christian groups on campus recruited her to give her testimony at their meetings, and the church even asked her to sing on the worship team. Katherine was on a spiritual high when a group of her sorority sisters asked her, a freshman and new Christian, to lead a house Bible study for them.

However, trouble was on the horizon for this girl who sprang up quickly but had no real roots to draw from. In place of laying a deep personal foundation, she became prideful about the newfound celebrity status she received from the Christians on campus. A turning point took place one Monday morning in late April. After a glorious time of Bible study and praise the evening before, she woke up and felt nothing—no joy, no sense of God's presence, no desire to pray or witness. Absolutely nothing. Had she lost her salvation? Had God left her? Was she really a Christian, or was this all an act? Thoughts of doubt and betrayal flooded her mind. Katherine didn't have a spiritual leader she could go to, and she was embarrassed to admit this to any of her Christian friends, so she decided to go it alone. One day of no fellowship with the Lord turned into two, three, a week and then two weeks.

Three weeks later she snuck out to a party of one of her old boyfriends, looking to find some kind of high to replace the one she had lost that Monday morning. Not only did her testimony fall apart in the ensuing weeks, but her life began to unravel as well. By July she had married one of her old bedmates, denied any Christian commitment she once had, and decided not to return to college. A tragic story of a girl who had incredible potential but whose spiritual life was a mile wide and an inch deep. She had deceived herself and others by learning the "Christian" things to do and say. And in the midst of trying to add all of those new religious activities to her schedule, she hadn't taken the time to truly understand the gospel and build a deep, lasting foundation, powered by the Holy Spirit and grounded in the truth of the Word.

→ ALWAYS BEGIN AT HOME

Here's how Jesus tells us to prepare ourselves: "Everyone who comes to me and hears my words and does them, I will show you what he is like: he is like a man building a house, *who dug deep and laid the foundation on the rock.* And when a flood arose, the stream broke against that house and could not shake it, because it had been well built. But the one who hears and does not do them is like a man who built a house on the ground *without a foundation.* When the stream broke against it, immediately it fell, and the ruin of that house was great" (Luke 6:47-49, English Standard Version).

I (Steve) grew up in Dallas but went to college in Fayetteville, Arkansas. Whenever I went home for a visit, I would cruise through downtown just to see the new buildings that were going up. One day I heard a lot of heavy earth-moving equipment. I got out to look but could not see anything due to the tall, wooden wall the construction workers had built around the site. The only thing I could be sure of was they were digging a hole—a very deep hole.

On one visit, my curiosity got the best of me, and I pulled over to peer down through the crack in the fence where I could stand on my tiptoes and see the huge hole. For almost a year they did nothing but dig a deep foundation for that building. In fact, I think it took them longer to lay the foundation than to construct the entire ninety-story skyscraper!

In the midst of my fascination, I realized the taller the building, the deeper the foundation it needed. If I had been the contractor, having no knowledge of construction, I probably would have scratched my head, looked to see if the ground was level, turned to the work crew, and said, "Okay boys, let's get started on the first floor." I might be proud of completing my edifice of steel and glass until the first gust of wind came along and the whole building toppled over!

The question I pose to you today is, do you want to be a flimsy little hut or giant skyscraper for Christ? If you want to have a deep and abiding lifelong walk with the Lord, drawing many others to the Savior, and joining God in making disciples of all nations, then begin at once on your personal excavation project. So, if you are definitely a born-again believer in Jesus, then this is your season to become established as a growing disciple. You will *never* again have as much time and opportunity to lay the groundwork required to become the disciple-maker and reproducer you ultimately desire to be. The depth of the foundation you build in college will determine the strength and height of your spiritual "building" in the years to come.

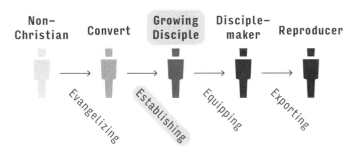

"The higher your structure is to be,
the deeper must be its foundation."

—SAINT AUGUSTINE

Now is the time to focus. *Now* is the time to get as much spiritual training as possible. Jesus spent three decades allowing the Father to prepare Him for three short years of ministry. If the Son of God needed that much time to build a foundation from which to launch His life's work, how much more do we mortal humans need?

→ BUILT ON LOVE

Our lives were designed to glorify God and reflect His values. We have looked at the Great Commission, Jesus' last words to His followers. The Bible also gives us the Great Commandment—Jesus' response when asked, "Teacher, which is the greatest commandment in the Law?" He didn't reply to this question with His favorite "thou shalt not" from the original Ten Commandments, but rather a mandate to build our lives on love: "'Love the Lord your God with all your heart and with all your soul and with all your mind.' This is the first and greatest commandment. And the second is like it: 'Love your neighbor as yourself.' All the Law and the Prophets hang on these two commandments" (Matthew 22:36-40, NIV).

Jesus didn't just give us one greatest commandment. He emphasized two, which together summarize *all* the commands in the Bible. A life established on loving God above all else and loving others as yourself will be "well built," undergirded by strong relationships and able to withstand the floods of life. A life on mission with God—a life of fulfilling the Great Commission—must flow from obedience to the Great Commandments. Wholehearted love for Jesus which spills into selfless love for others is the foundation for a life of laboring in His harvest and reaching the nations.

→ THE INVENTION OF THE WHEEL

The Wheel illustration, originally introduced by the Navigators, provides a model of what it looks like to live a life centered on devotion to Christ and flowing out into love for Jesus and others. It has been used by many Christians over the years to evaluate and grow their own spiritual lives—and to help others do the same. Faithfully growing in these areas is key to building a life on the foundation of the Rock, Jesus Christ, and being usable by God in His mission to redeem the world. Let's break it down:

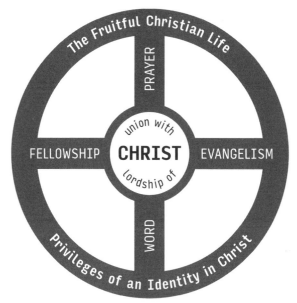

The Fruitful Christian Life

PRAYER

FELLOWSHIP **CHRIST** union with / lordship of **CHRIST** EVANGELISM

WORD

Privileges of an Identity in Christ

Modified from the Navigators. Used with permission.

Lordship of Christ and Obedience

(Galatians 2:20; 2 Corinthians 5:17)

Loving Christ with all our heart, soul, mind, and strength forms the hub of our wheel, where all the power originates and connects to our lives. According to God's math, love doesn't equal feelings; love equals obedience (John 14:21). Your daily willingness to say no to sin will show and strengthen your love for Christ. No one can live the obedient Christian life in their own strength, but *only* through the daily filling and empowerment of the Holy Spirit. Put Him at the center of your life now...and every day.

The Word (2 Timothy 3:16-17; Joshua 1:8)

There are four spokes on this wheel that connect the person and power of the Lord Jesus Christ (the hub) to us (the rim). The two vertical spokes deal with our relationship with God, while the two horizontal ones deal with our relationships with others. The foundational spoke is the Word of God, the pillar that all the others are based upon. Trust God to use His Word to grow your knowledge of and love for Him and to radically transform your life from the inside out (Romans 12:1-2). Students of the Word are drawn into God's mission as they see His heart for all people revealed from Genesis to Revelation!

Prayer (John 15:7; Philippians 4:6-7)

If the Bible is how God talks to us, prayer is how we talk to Him. Set up a daily time with God in which you can build intimacy and consistency in your relationship with Christ. If you will make prayer and the Word a priority in your daily schedule, you'll have a much better chance of surviving the storms of life and following through on the commitments you have made to the Lord. Prayer changes lives, including yours!

Fellowship (Ecclesiastes 4:9-10; Hebrews 10:24-25)

The key to success in the horizontal spokes of our Wheel is to make the vertical spokes the priority in our lives. God made us to be worshipers and workers—but in that order! The importance of teaming up with other believers to keep fueling the flame is described in Ecclesiastes 4:9-10: "Two are better than one, because they have a good return for their labor. For if either of them falls, the one will lift up his companion. But woe to the one who falls when there is not another to lift him up." Keep building lots of relationships with non-believers, but make sure your very best friends are those who are running towards God, not away from Him.

Evangelism (Romans 1:16; Matthew 4:19)

Start learning how to share your personal conversion testimony and a simple gospel illustration. Begin to pray and look for opportunities to dive into those life-changing discussions with people all around you. Jesus promised His disciples, "Follow Me and I will make you fishers of men." Let's lay our lives down like Jesus did and not be ashamed of the gospel, knowing full well it is truly the "power of God for salvation." Stop now to think of the first (or next) person you could share with.

→ YOUR BUILDING BLOCKS

If we want to build a life God can use to labor in His mission, the building blocks in our foundation must be values and convictions from God's quarry, not man's. Paul referred to himself as a wise master builder and exhorted the Corinthians to use the right materials in their spiritual foundation. He wrote in 1 Corinthians 3:11–13: "For no man can lay a foundation other than the one which is laid, which is Jesus Christ. Now if any man builds on the foundation with gold, silver, precious stones, wood, hay, straw, each man's work will become evident; for the day will show it because it is to be revealed with fire, and the fire itself will test the quality of each man's work."

Paul is telling us that the foundation is Christ Himself. We must be careful how we build upon that base, using precious and enduring materials rather than worthless ones that will quickly perish. All of us are trading our lives for something, aren't we? We exchange ourselves for what we *believe* is valuable. You spend your time, energy, and money, but what are you hoping to gain in return? Wealth and possessions? A comfortable life? The right relationships? Achievements your parents can be proud of?

> "God is more concerned about the person you are becoming than what you are accomplishing."
>
> **—DALLAS WILLARD**

Whether we would like to admit it or not, the answers to these questions show us what we care about the most and ultimately what we are building our lives on. Giving your all to secure what the world says is happiness or success, or pursuing the approval from others, will always be a recipe for a wasted life.

Talk is cheap. I can fool you, and you can fool me. I can tell you that I believe Bible study and prayer are important. I can say, "Amen, brother" when you speak of personal holiness or servanthood. However, the proof of my Christian maturity is whether the things I say I believe in have trickled down from my mind and mouth into my spiritual bloodstream to become a reality in my life. If I'm not ordering my life around the things I *say* I believe are valuable, then I must not really believe that they are.

Bottom line: to ignite yourself for Jesus Christ, fueling a fire that will be a light to your campus and the world, you must build your foundation on Him—and Him alone.

R E F L E C T I O N   Q U E S T I O N S :

→ How deep and strong is your spiritual foundation right now?
    Why?
→ What can you do to deepen and strengthen it?
→ Draw out The Wheel diagram and rank the six areas it describes
    from strongest to weakest in your life: Lordship, Word, Prayer,
    Witnessing, Fellowship, and Obedience.
→ Share something specific you could do *this* week to begin grow-
    ing in one of these six areas.

5

First Things First

When I was a freshman in college, I (Steve) slept on the top bunk in my fraternity room. On the ceiling, I taped one verse that I would look at each morning and night. It was Luke 6:46, where Jesus cried out, "Why do you call me 'Lord, Lord' and do not do what I say?" A translation might be, "Don't insult me with your phony flattery. Don't say you're a sold-out follower unless you're going to obey me in *all* things!" Meditating on that verse kept my mind on Christ and His purposes as I daily did battle with the enemy of my soul. Each day I stepped out of that room, there were sixty of my fraternity brothers watching and waiting for me to trip and fall. I had a choice to either fully obey my Lord Jesus or fade right into the woodwork of mediocrity and compromise.

→ UNSWERVING DEVOTION

Allegiance to Jesus is the bedrock conviction everything else in your Christian life is built on (1 Corinthians 3:11-13). If you ever try to leave this behind, you won't be living a Christian life anymore but a legalistic form of slavery where you are trying to appease God through your good morals and religious performance. Imagine what would happen to that skyscraper we described if you tried to remove the foundation out from underneath it. It would collapse! It is the same with our Christian life. We can't live it apart from Christ, the chief cornerstone (Acts 4:11; Ephesians 2:20). Devotion to the person of Jesus Christ is the heartbeat, joy, and the power source for a Christian's life and ministry.

> "If there is no passionate love for Christ
> at the center of everything, we will only
> jingle and jangle our way across the
> world, merely making a noise as we go."
>
> **—WILLIAM WILBERFORCE,
> ABOLITIONIST (1759 - 1833)**

One definition of devotion is "an unswerving adherence to." Why should we have an *unswerving* adherence to Christ? If we legitimately understand His death on the cross and what He accomplished for us there, we will want to respond with our lives and, like Paul, say: "For the love of Christ controls us, because we have concluded this: that one has died for all, therefore all have died; and He died for all, that those who live might no longer live for themselves but for Him who for their sake died and was raised" (2 Corinthians 5:14-15, ESV).

Do you have an *unswerving* adherence to the person of Jesus Christ? Is your life, like Paul's, a response to what Jesus did on the cross for you? The fruit of devotion to Christ is obedience to Him. If we are thankful for Jesus as Savior, we will be obedient to Him as Lord. These two aspects of His person cannot be separated. You don't get to pick and choose which aspects of Jesus you want. He is Savior *and* Lord and you either bow down to the Jesus of the Bible...or you don't.

Know this for sure, if *you* do not choose the center of your life, the inertia of life will choose it for you. You can't just live life on autopilot and by default be devoted to Christ and reaching the world with the gospel. No, our hearts are too sinful and the world is too deceitful for us to ever be able to "accidentally" glorify Christ with our lives. We will always gravitate towards putting ourselves at the center. We must (with God's help) intentionally *choose* each day to be devoted to Him and not live for ourselves, but for Him who died and was raised for our sake.

Imagine every area of your life put into a pie chart. You have your dating relationship (or lack thereof!), your family, friends, future, money, school, work, and free time—including your social media and web surfing. Most people give God a slice of their life. This is the spiritual area of life where they might pray or go to church or a Bible study, but that's not what it means to recognize Jesus as Lord of your life. For Jesus to truly be your Lord, you must invite Him to *rule* your life, to guide and empower you to live every "slice" of your pie in the way that honors Him and fulfills His plans, not yours. No exceptions. He is at the center and controlling *all* areas! Jesus is king, but we need to personalize it by inviting Him to sit on the throne of our heart as our king.

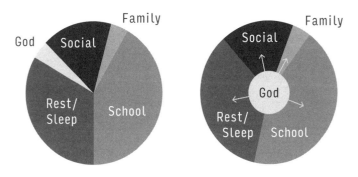

"If Jesus is not Lord of all then He is not Lord at all."

—A.W. TOZER

→ SEEKING HIS KINGDOM

Most students would say their whole lives are wrapped up in getting through college, but where in the Bible does it say to go to college? George Washington, Abraham Lincoln, Harry S. Truman, and Ernest Hemingway never went to college. Bill Gates and Steve Jobs were dropouts! And where in the Scriptures are we commanded to make good grades? Some people (or parents) say, "Well, if God has called you to be in school, that means you need to do your very best." They might even go so far as to say that making A's is your life "calling" right now. If that's true, why shouldn't this concept apply to your job after college, where you will work all the time, possibly doing *whatever* it takes to climb the ladder at the expense of your devotional life, family, or personal ministry? The question is, "When does following God on His mission take priority over school or vocation?"

I'm not saying it's bad to go to college (it can be very good!), but let's try to determine the Lord's reason to have you there. One definition of wisdom is "looking at life from God's perspective," and Matthew 6:33 gives us a glimpse into the mind of Christ: "But seek first His kingdom and His righ-teousness, and all these things will be added to you." Many college students are notorious for seeking everything *but* the kingdom of God. In fact, they seem to major in the S's: studies, sports, social life, and social media. The only problem with giving your time and energies to these four S's is that God is silent about these things in the Scriptures. As valuable or enjoyable as they appear to be, nowhere does He tell us to make our studies, sports, social life or "technological entertainment" a priority!

In contrast, there are some areas God *clearly* says we should give our-selves to. The W's consist of worship, the Word, walking in the Spirit, and our witness to others. The ironic (and tragic) thing is we spend almost all of our time on temporal things He is silent about and neglect the very disci-plines and priorities He clearly commands.

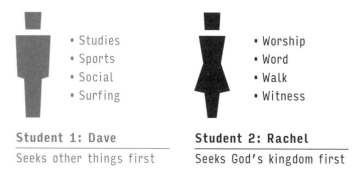

• Studies	• Worship
• Sports	• Word
• Social	• Walk
• Surfing	• Witness

Student 1: Dave   **Student 2: Rachel**

Seeks other things first   Seeks God's kingdom first

How do you see the "6:33 Principle" at work in Dave and Rachel's schedules?

Dave tries to squeeze in a quiet time or share his faith with a friend as long as it doesn't conflict with a date or studying for a test. He seeks other things first by locking into his daily routine priorities like studies, work-ing out, and social outings. Every minute of downtime is spent scrolling through social media platforms liking, commenting, and making sure he doesn't miss anything.

Rachel, on the other hand, seeks God first. She has blocked out major chunks of her schedule to spend time reading and studying the Word, learning to follow God's lead and walk with Him. She then uses wisdom about how to use her discretionary time. She studies (and makes pretty good grades!), plays intramurals, and goes out with her friends, but even in those pursuits she is engaged for the glory of God and the opportunity to share Christ.

What do you think? Can you call yourself a Matthew 6:33 man or woman? If not, what needs to change?

Years ago, I (Steve) stepped into a collegiate pastor position where all the students were caught up in a "making A's in school is my calling" philosophy. As we explored what the Scriptures taught about this, one of the pre-med students who was set free from this self-imposed legalism created the doctrine of "good 'nuf." He wanted to do well in his studies, but not at the expense of obeying God in his life and ministry. Whatever amount of preparation he could do before tests was just going to have to be "good 'nuf!" At the heavenly gates, the Lord is not going to check your GPA. Even here on earth, where I've earned my bachelor's, master's, and doctorate degrees, I've never once been asked my GPA. Whew!

→ LIFE'S CONVEYER BELT

Whatever you exchange your time and money for is what you value. Let me take a look at your schedule and your bank statement, and I'll tell you exactly what's important to you. You might say, "I don't have a schedule." No, everyone has a schedule. It may not be a good one, but everybody has one! The way in which you use your time will reflect your priorities. Our earthly existence is a little like standing in front of a huge conveyor with all kinds of choices, options, and opportunities on the rapidly moving belt, each one yelling out to us, "Pick me!" "No, pick me!" "Over here! Hey, I'm the best; look at me!" How in the world are we to discern what we are to do and what we are not to do? Most end up allowing the tyranny of the urgent to dictate their priorities and schedule.

> "Your greatest danger is letting the urgent things crowd out the important."
> —CHARLES E. HUMMEL, *TYRANNY OF THE URGENT*

God has created us for a purpose. He has also given us a limited amount of time on this earth to fulfill that purpose. We want to be good stewards of this precious gift of life and time. However, to use your time wisely, you must first know what is important to you (priorities) and the way to live your life according to your priorities (objectives and goals). Maybe you've been to a talk or listened to a podcast on "discerning the will of God," where you heard tips on unlocking the secret plans God has for your future. It may sound oversimplified, but I believe the Word of God is the will of God. I'm not saying don't listen to the Lord or be sensitive to His leading, but if He has *already* given us His marching orders right there in black and white, why are we waiting for an emotional experience to tell us what He *really* wants us to do? To me, that appears as just thinly disguised disobedience, and the truth is, many of us claim that we are "waiting on God" when, in fact, He is waiting on us!

Jesus told this simple and profound parable: "The kingdom of heaven is like treasure hidden in a field. When a man found it, he hid it again, and then in his joy went and sold all he had and bought that field" (Matthew 13:44, NIV). Most people are not willing to "sell everything" to gain Jesus. Some are willing to try to add God into their busy schedules and maybe even make some minor changes to clean up their act in certain areas. But seeking Jesus first means making sacrificial choices until He becomes greater than every other thing in your life.

Deitrich Bonhoeffer, in his classic book *The Cost of Discipleship,* says, "When Christ calls a man, He bids him come and die." The call to follow Christ is a call to die to self. "For whoever wants to save their life will lose it, but whoever loses their life for me will save it" (Luke 9:24). When you seek to put God first in your life, He promises to bless you with spiritual fruit and a deeper experience of His presence. "Whoever has My commands and keeps them is the one who loves Me. The one who loves Me will be loved by My Father, and I too will love them and show Myself to them" (John 14:21).

The more obedient I am to the Lord, the more I experience Him working in and through my life. My intimacy and devotion to Jesus are deepened, bringing an inexpressible joy that can only be found in full surrender. In his sermon "The Weight of Glory," C.S. Lewis put it this way: "If we consider the unblushing promises of reward and the staggering nature of the rewards promised in the Gospels, it would seem that our Lord finds our desires not too strong, but too weak. We are half-hearted creatures, fooling about with drink and sex and ambition when infinite joy is offered us, like an ignorant child who wants to go on making mud pies in a slum because he cannot imagine what is meant by the offer of a holiday at the sea. We are far too easily pleased."

"When you obey My commandments, you remain in My love, just as I obey My Father's commandments and remain in His love. I have told you these things so that you will be filled with My joy. Yes, your joy will over-flow!" (John 15:10, NLT). Wow! Overflowing joy. If we only knew the deep and satisfying delight of living in full obedience to Jesus, we would never go back to half-heartedly following Him!

→ ONE DECISION I MADE IN COLLEGE

It seems like it was just yesterday that I (Steve) was a freshman in love. Yes, I was a Christian, as was she, but our emotions were more wrapped up in each other than in Jesus Christ. I kept getting a gnawing feeling the Lord wanted us to break up with each other, but I wouldn't listen. I thought, "Most of my Christian friends have girlfriends, and certainly all of my fraternity brothers do; why shouldn't I?" I carried this heavy load of rationalization around with me until the end of fall semester. We finally got enough courage to bring up the subject, talk about it, and make a decision. We broke up because both of us felt it was God's will.

That night I went and hid out in an empty classroom and wept for three hours. I didn't feel sad or jilted—instead I felt like 100-pound weights had been taken off my shoulders. I don't cry easily, but that night I had a steady stream of joyous tears signaling I was finally free! I had fully obeyed and was now willing to do *any*thing and *every*thing God wanted me to do. This gave me enough backbone to make another important decision that night. I resolved that for the rest of my college years I would develop only friendships, not romances, with girls. Making a commitment not to date may sound radical and unrealistic for some, but for me, it was one of the best decisions I ever made. I'm not prescrib-ing this step as God's will for you, but I am saying that you may have to make some fundamental changes in your priorities to make room in your life for what's really important.

Even though I'd been a Christian for over nine months, it was at this juncture that my spiritual life really accelerated. I had fully submitted my life to the lordship of Jesus Christ, and I could now pursue Him with unhindered zeal. My love for Christ and my desire to spend time with Him took massive steps forward! I searched for gaps in my schedule where I could steal away for some intimate fellowship with the Lord and drink deeply from the Scriptures. Early each morning I found a dark, lonely place among the discarded furniture in the third-floor attic of my fraternity house to get on my knees, worship God, and intercede for the souls of all the men in my chapter.

On Friday and Saturday nights, while the other guys were out with their dates, I would lock my door and click off the overhead lights, turn on my little desk lamp, spread out my Bible and study helps, and spend huge chunks of time just soaking in the Word. It may sound weird or fanatical, but God and I were spending hour after hour, month after month, digging a deep foundation in my life. I was finding a secret joy and fulfillment in my ever-increasing love relationship with the Lord and Savior of my life. Understanding that He was all I would ever need, I sought to find my satisfaction in Him—and in Him alone.

Late night prayer walks on campus became my routine. Many times, I would cry out to God, "Whom have I in heaven but You, and besides You, I desire nothing on earth" (Psalm 73:25, New American Standard). Yearning to be abandoned to His purposes, I sensed God was preparing me and wanted to use me, a lowly college student, to impact the world for Jesus Christ.

Guess what? God also wants to work in and through *you* to bring the light of Christ to a lost and dying world. Evangelist D.L. Moody once said, "Let God have your life; He can do more with it than you can." God used Moody's life to lead literally millions of people to Christ, but it all started with a total and unreserved commitment to Christ.

> "The world has yet to see what God can
> do with a man fully consecrated to Him.
> By God's help, I aim to be that man"
> —D.L. MOODY

R E F L E C T I O N   Q U E S T I O N S :

→ What could God do in and through your life if you fully surrendered to His lordship?
→ Using the pie chart, what are the current areas of your life and
   which one is at the center?
→ Is there some decision you need to make right now to really set
   you free to grow spiritually?
→ While in college, how can you discern and prioritize the temporal and the eternal?

Fully Charged

We all know the feeling when we hear that dreaded beeping sound or see that ominous warning screen, our laptop or phone alerting us its battery is almost drained. Panicked, we dig for a charger or scour the room for an outlet. Keeping our devices powered up is a high priority to most of us because they are key to our productivity and connection with the world. Our spiritual lives are often the same way. Like our trusted electronics, we have trouble holding a charge. We must constantly be filled up by our power source—the Holy Spirit—in order to live the life God is calling us to. When D.L. Moody was asked why he said he needed to be filled continually with the Holy Spirit, he replied, "Because I leak!"

Jesus gave us supernatural power and abundant life by sending us the Holy Spirit. When He was preparing His followers for His departure, He made this statement about the Holy Spirit to comfort them: "Nevertheless, I tell you the truth: it is to your advantage that I go away, for if I do not go away, the Helper will not come to you. But if I go, I will send him to you" (John 16:7, ESV).

If I had been one of those who was with Jesus at that moment, I would have been tempted to argue with Him. What could possibly be better than walking and talking with Jesus in the flesh? But according to the God-Man Himself, it was better to have the Spirit come and live inside of us. The sad reality, however, is most followers of Christ are living drained, defeated, and powerless lives due to lack of understanding and experience with the Holy Spirit.

> "The Spirit inside you is better
> than Jesus beside you."
>
> —J.D. GREEAR

→ GOD *IN* US

"The Spirit-filled life is not a special, deluxe edition of Christianity. It is part and parcel of the total plan of God for His people," says author and pastor A.W. Tozer. When we receive Jesus Christ into our life, the Holy Spirit comes and takes up permanent residence in us. Our task then becomes *allowing* Him to control and empower us for godly living and service. The Christian life He has called us to live is not difficult, it's impossible! The good news is that the Holy Spirit has more than enough power to help us live God's way and fulfill His mission. "The Spirit of God, who raised Jesus from the dead, lives in you. And just as God raised Christ Jesus from the dead, he will give life to your mortal bodies by this same Spirit living within you" (Romans 8:11, NLT).

Do you realize what you just read? The same Spirit who raised Christ from the dead lives inside of you! That is a mind-blowing amount of power. The reason we struggle spiritually or get stuck in sin is not because of a lack of power, but because we are not filling up or regularly charging our lives with His power. If we want authentic supernatural energy to live holy lives and make disciples of all nations, we had better plug into the power source—God Himself through the person of the Holy Spirit.

> "When believers live in the power of
> the Holy Spirit, the evidence in their
> lives is supernatural. The church
> cannot help but be different, and the
> world cannot help but notice."
>
> **—FRANCIS CHAN**

The Holy Spirit is not like Casper the Friendly Ghost, even though some refer to Him as the Holy Ghost. He's not an impersonal "Force" to wield like in Star Wars. God's Spirit is not the granter of wishes like Aladdin's blue genie. He is not even an experience or tingling goosebumps on your arms during a great set of worship music. He is God. He is a person to fully obey and follow. Learning to cooperate with the Spirit is one of the greatest joys and privileges of life.

Anna, a Christian student at Boston College, had been dating Chad happily for almost six months when the bomb dropped that he was secretly seeing Christy, one of her sorority sisters. The betrayal of knowing their relationship had begun after Christy started sending Chad pictures of herself pierced Anna's heart and attacked her self-esteem. In her quiet time one morning, Anna came across Ephesians 4:31: "Get rid of all bitterness, rage and anger." This was followed by verse 32: "Be kind and compassionate to one another, forgiving each other, just as in Christ God forgave you." At that moment she knew exactly what the Holy Spirit was telling her to do: release the anger and bitterness she held toward Chad and Christy.

As the tears flowed, Anna felt the shackles fall off and the cleansing of Christ's forgiveness wash over her. With a new freedom and perspective, she set out to show kindness and compassion, especially to Christy, who she was pretty sure was not a Christian. A few weeks later, a devastated Christy came to Anna's room after Chad had dropped her and moved on. Christy was different though, asking for forgiveness and seeking solutions for her shattered life. God had used Anna's unconditional love to show Himself to her, and late that night, Christy bowed her head and invited Christ to come into her heart as Savior and Lord. Anna and Christy became best friends, growing together spiritually by leaps and bounds. These two girls experienced the supernatural love and forgiveness of Jesus Christ in the face of a cruel and undeserved betrayal, and their lives would never be the same. Yielding her will to the Holy Spirit, Anna allowed the person (and personality!) of Christ to flow through her and, in turn, draw Christy to the Savior.

When we turn from our sin and embrace the Sin-bearer, we become a Christian or "Christ one." Because the Spirit of God lives in and works through us, we each are now a walking, talking mirror, continually reflecting more and more of the character of Jesus to the people we interact with and the world as a whole.

One list of the qualities we are to exhibit is found in Galatians 5:22–23: "The fruit of the Spirit is love, joy, peace, patience, kindness, goodness, faithfulness, gentleness and self-control" (ESV). As you build your foundation in life, these are the kinds of materials that construct a life of love for God and others. This fruit begins to characterize our lives when we, like Anna, surrender the sinful thoughts, actions, or feelings we are holding on to and allow the Spirit to take control of our hearts, minds, and lives and lead us toward godliness. Not only will others be drawn to you because they see these fruits in you, but these traits are the very Christlike qualities you are to pass on to others.

→ WALKING IN THE SPIRIT

Sin hinders the flow of the Holy Spirit in your life. Just like dirt can clog up a tube, sinful thoughts, attitudes, and actions clog up the Spirit's work in your life. If you are not experiencing the fruit of a Spirit-filled life, start by examining your heart for any disobedience or apathy toward the Lord. Ask God to specifically show you what you need to confess, and turn away from it immediately. You can use this prayer: "Search me, God, and know my heart; test me and know my anxious thoughts. See if there is any offensive way in me, and lead me in the way everlasting" (Psalm 139:23-24, NIV). Don't rush this process. Allow the Lord to show you what thoughts, attitudes, and actions are displeasing to Him. Or maybe He puts something on your heart that you need to clear up with another person. But don't overanalyze or become paranoid. God is more concerned about the attitude of your heart than you remembering every single sin you have ever committed.

Once you have repented of all known sin, you can simply ask the Holy Spirit to fill you by faith. God commands you in Ephesians 5:18 to "be filled with the Spirit." He would never command you to do something He would not empower you to do. Trust Him to fill you when you ask in faith. The final step is to boldly *do* whatever the Lord is calling you to do. This is what it means to walk in step with the Spirit (Galatians 5:16). Trust that God's Spirit has got your back and will help you walk in obedience to Him. The process of being filled with the Spirit is not a magic formula. It's more about *choosing* to sync your heart attitude up with God's. The goal is to empty your life of your sin and pride. God can't fill you up if you're full of yourself. Andrew Murray, in his challenging book *Humility*, puts it this way: "Just as water seeks to fill the lowest place, so the moment God finds you humble and empty, His Spirit flows in."

I (Paul) remember being floored the first time I read "How You Can Be Filled with The Spirit" by Bill Bright, founder of Cru. The simple yet profound concept of spiritual breathing I learned from this booklet changed my life.

Here's how I practice spiritual breathing:

I identify the anger or lust or jealousy I've allowed to enter my mind and heart, then specifically confess it to God. Like our physical breathing, this is exhaling the bad air followed by inhaling a big dose of the fresh, clean air. I do this by thanking Him for forgiving and cleansing me with the purifying blood Jesus shed on the cross for my sins. Then I pray, "Now fill me with Your Spirit. Control me. Help me abide in Christ. Work in me and through me today, that I can walk in faith and obedience." I may or may not *feel* forgiven or filled, but we can trust Jesus' promise that "If we confess our sins, he is faithful and just and will forgive us our sins and purify us from all unrighteousness" (1 John 1:9). And if the devil tries to whisper doubts into your ear, remind yourself of God's promise that you stand before Him "holy and blameless" in Ephesians 1:4.

→ ENTERING THE BATTLE

The Lord wants to use you mightily to labor among the nations, but He needs a clean vessel to work through. Here's how Paul describes the kind of person He can use: "In a large house there are articles not only of gold and silver, but also of wood and clay; some are for special purposes and some for common use. Those who cleanse themselves from the latter will be instruments for special purposes, made holy, useful to the Master and prepared to do any good work" (2 Timothy 2:20-21).

Picture yourself home for the holidays, and the big turkey feast is spread out on the table for everyone to gorge themselves on. Your mom sets the table with the nice china and tells everyone to grab one of the fancy goblets from the cabinet to fill with her special sweet tea. You make your way to the glass shelf and pick up the last goblet, only to jump back when you see a roach crawling around in it. "Eww!" you shriek. You wouldn't dare think about drinking from it, so what do you do? You set it aside and look around on the shelf for something that *is* clean. You see one of the emptied glass peanut butter jars your mom likes to wash and hang on to. No problem. You don't really care what the glass looks like or how much it costs, only that it's clean. You hold it up to make sure it really is usable, fill it with some tasty iced tea, and you are ready to chow down!

Sometimes we look at someone who is good-looking, smart, talented, or popular and say to ourselves, "Wow, if *that* person ever became a Christian, think how much God could do through their life." But God doesn't look at the outside; He looks at the heart. And He isn't as interested in someone's *ability* as He is their *availability*. Are they willing to empty themselves of their own self-reliance and look to and rely totally upon the grace that is in Christ Jesus? (2 Timothy 2:1). God can only fill a vessel that is empty, and as long as we are full of ourselves and our own agendas, He will set us aside like the fancy, but dirty, goblet. One way to get in the right frame of mind each day is to pray the prayer John the Baptist did after He baptized the Messiah: "You must increase. I must decrease." Jesus doesn't want to just be *present* in our lives, or even *prominent* in our lives. No, if we are going to truly be used by God, Jesus Himself must be *preeminent*—above anything and everything else—in our lives.

As you trust the Holy Spirit and choose obedience, you will notice God changing your character and using you to love and lead others. The Lord is looking for people to fill with His Spirit and use in mighty ways to advance His Kingdom. If you become usable, God will wear you out! And if you're being used by Christ to bring people from darkness to light, fully engaged in "kingdom warfare," you're not only a strategic officer in God's army but also a prime target of Satan, our enemy. In 1 Peter 5:8, we see that Peter was fully aware of this: "Be alert and of sober mind. Your enemy the devil prowls around like a roaring lion looking for someone to devour." At this very moment, is the devil prowling around your campus, your ministry, your dorm, or house searching for someone just to distract? To discourage? No! To *devour*! He doesn't just want to sidetrack or trip you up; his objective is to rip you limb from limb, grind you up, and eradicate you. Sorry for the graphic detail, but that is what the passage teaches.

If you're going to get serious about leading other students to Christ, discipling them, equipping them for personal ministry, and launching them out to join you as world changers, you are in a heap of trouble! You have moved up to Public Enemy #1 on Satan's hit list, and don't be surprised if all hell breaks loose as you begin to take the Great Commission seriously. He doesn't waste his time on inward-focused, self-absorbed, "bless me Lord" kind of Christians, but if you really get down to business for God, Satan will work night and day in order to pierce and purge you from the ranks of God's mighty men and women.

→ THE ARMOR OF GOD

So, how do you plan on winning this battle the Lord has placed you in? Will you depend on your great intellect, dynamic personality, or dazzling good looks? For me (Steve), my foolishness and self-deception were on full display when I started my very first Bible study in college. Looking back, it was obvious my confidence was in myself rather than God, and I fell flat on my face. The guys in the group could see right through my motives of exalting myself rather than the Lord, and the group quickly disintegrated. God humbled me, but then drew me back to the Scriptures. Ephesians 6:10-13 tells us where our strength comes from as well as who our real enemy is: "Finally, be strong in the Lord and in His mighty power. Put on the full armor of God, so that you can make your stand against the devil's schemes. For our struggle is not against flesh and blood, but against the rulers, against the authorities, against the powers of this world's darkness, and against the spiritual forces of evil in the heavenly realms."

> "Global evangelism does not take place
> in a demilitarized zone but on the
> battleground of spiritual warfare."
>
> —ED STETZER

Continuing on, verses 14-18 are a daily instruction manual, teaching us how to put on and utilize the various defensive and offensive equipment the Lord has provided us as we run to the battle: "Therefore take up the full armor of God, so that when the day of evil comes, you will be able to stand your ground, and having done everything, to stand. Stand firm then, with the belt of truth buckled around your waist, with the breastplate of righteousness arrayed, and with your feet fitted with the readiness of the gospel of peace. In addition to all this, take up the shield of faith, with which you can extinguish all the flaming arrows of the evil one. And take the helmet of salvation and the sword of the Spirit, which is the word of God."

Finally, verses 19-20 share the ultimate weapons we as believers possess to claim spiritual victories in our life and ministry: "Pray in the Spirit at all times, with every kind of prayer and petition. To this end, stay alert with all perseverance in your prayers for all the saints. Pray also for me, that whenever I open my mouth, divine utterance may be given me, so that I will boldly make known the mystery of the gospel, for which I am an ambassador in chains. Pray that I may proclaim it fearlessly, as I should." Intercession and the gospel are two of the most potent weapons the Lord has entrusted us with. Let's get them off the shelf and use them!

John Piper issues an important challenge to fight our spiritual battles by praying in the power of the Holy Spirit: "Life is war. That's not all it is. But it is always that. Our weakness in prayer is owing largely to our neglect of this truth. Prayer is primarily a wartime walkie-talkie for the mission of the church as it advances against the powers of darkness and unbelief. It is not surprising that prayer malfunctions when we try to make it a domestic intercom to call upstairs for more comforts in the den. God has given us prayer as a wartime walkie-talkie so that we can call headquarters for everything we need as the kingdom of Christ advances in the world. Prayer gives us the significance of frontline forces and gives God the glory of a limitless Provider. The one who gives the power gets the glory. Thus, prayer safeguards the supremacy of God in missions while linking us with endless grace for every need."

Will you fully suit up each morning with the holy armor the Lord has provided you, to prayerfully run to the battle in the power of the Holy Spirit? The most tangible offensive weapon God has provided us warriors for Christ is a sword. A very powerful one. Continue on and read all about it!

REFLECTION QUESTIONS:

→ Who is the Holy Spirit and what does it mean to "be filled with the Spirit"?

→ Describe "spiritual breathing" and how you can practice that each day.

→ Are you engaged in God's spiritual battle here on earth? If so, how?

→ What are the components of the "armor of God" and how can you put them on each morning?

7

Living and Active

Marcus was an angry teenager who escaped the violence of inner-city Canton, Ohio, to attend the University of Akron. He immersed himself in the college party life, and after one night of heavy drinking, a friend turned to Marcus and said, "You need to read the Bible." Although Marcus hadn't given any credence to the Scriptures, he began to read passages each night. He found his eyes were opened to the truth. He dug deeper and started studying the Word, sitting for hours "reading, believing, doubting, crying, smiling, and all the while being convicted of sin." The repentance was so thorough that he yearned to expose others to the truth God had revealed to him, so he began small group Bible studies through the ministry of Coalition for Christian Outreach. Later, Marcus went on staff with CCO and continued to saturate himself with the Word and help hundreds of students do the same. The "sword of the Spirit, which is the Word of God" was the tool Marcus' loving God used to fight through the hardness of his heart and win him to the truth (Ephesians 6:17).

→ GREATEST BOOK EVER WRITTEN

The Bible is the only book that is "alive" and able to move in people's hearts and minds with the very power of God! With so much debate today about the legitimacy of the Scriptures, we want to clearly state that we believe the Bible to be the true and authoritative Word of God. "All Scripture is God-breathed and is useful for teaching, rebuking, correcting and training in righteousness, so that the servant of God may be thoroughly equipped for every good work" (2 Timothy 3:16-17). Here's what we mean by that: if God has literally "breathed out" or inspired the Scriptures, then we can view the words in the Bible as coming directly from Him, as if He penned them. Being His words, they must be absolutely perfect and without error, just as He is perfect (Matthew 5:48).

> "The Word of God is like a lion. You don't have to defend a lion. All you have to do is let the lion loose, and the lion will defend itself."
>
> **—CHARLES SPURGEON**

It also follows that these words must carry with them His authority as the Creator of the universe. So, when we are reading the words of the Bible, we should be hearing them and viewing them as having just as much authority over our lives as if God was speaking to us directly. Because it carries His authority, the Bible holds a power beyond any other book. The Bible was given to us not to increase our knowledge but to change our lives. It's even described as *living* and *active*: "For the word of God is alive and active. Sharper than any double-edged sword, it penetrates even to dividing soul and spirit, joints and marrow; it judges the thoughts and attitudes of the heart" (Hebrews 4:12). God says His Word will accomplish His purposes: "So is my word that goes out from my mouth: It will not return to me empty, but will accomplish what I desire and achieve the purpose for which I sent it" (Isaiah 55:11). I (Steve) have watched in awe as my wife has spent the last forty years recruiting college girls to small group studies and then trusting God to use His Word to radically transform them.

There are millions of "changed life" stories of how the Word of God has impacted people's lives for good, but now you have a decision to make. Do you truly believe the entire Bible is from God? Is He powerful and sovereign enough to give us a book without error to tell His story, share His heart for mankind, and teach us how to follow Jesus? To doubt the authority of the Scriptures is to doubt God Himself. Settle in your heart today that the Lord has given us a book of truth that is to be read, studied, taught, and applied to *all* areas of our lives. When you turn that lion loose in and through your life...watch out!

→ KNOW HIM AND HIS HEART

We talk to God through prayer, and His Word is His means of talking to us. In his book *The Pursuit of God*, A.W. Tozer puts it like this: "The Bible is not an end in itself, but a means to bring men to an intimate and satisfying knowledge of God, that they may enter into Him, that they may delight in His presence, may taste and know the inner sweetness of the very God Himself in the core and center of their hearts."

From cover to cover, the Bible not only shows God's character but also tells of the Father's heart to reveal His goodness and glory to the whole world. So don't let your study of the Bible be simply an academic endeavor; make it a pursuit of personally knowing the God of the universe! You learn what the Lord is like and what He values by what He reveals about Himself in the Bible. If you want to get to know Him, get to know His Word.

Would you say you have a thirst for knowing the person and purposes of God? "As the deer pants for streams of water, so my soul pants for you, my God. My soul thirsts for God, for the living God. When can I go and meet with God?" (Psalm 42:1-2). Time alone with the Lord can be an acquired taste at first. But if you fight to build this habit into your life, you will quickly discover the more you taste sweet fellowship with God, the more you will yearn for it. Our soul's deepest longing is connection with God. It's impossible to spend time with the Lord without wanting more of Him!

→ HE ALREADY KNOWS YOU

Since God is our creator, He knows everything about us (Psalm 139). If anyone has insight into what would lead us toward a joyful and fulfilling life, it is God, our Maker. Knowing the words of the Bible are His, we ought to be searching and devouring them to find out from Him how we ought to live! If you were to analyze your life, how much do you live according to what you've read in God's Word? Do you make decisions about dating or social activities the way you do because of something you've read in Scripture? Is the Word of God your main influence in how you spend your time or money? If you are looking for God's will for your life, dig for answers in the Scriptures.

"Don't say God is silent when
your Bible is closed."

— MATT BROWN

With all this in mind, we need to figure out how we can get God's Word into our lives so we can gain His view of the world, find the answers we seek in life, and develop and maintain a growing and intimate relationship with Him.

→ GET A GRIP

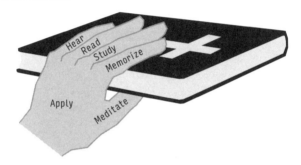

Modified from the Navigators. Used with permission.

Years ago, the ministry of the Navigators came up with the "Hand Illustration" which shows the importance of utilizing six methods to "get a grip" on God's Word in your life. When trying to hold something with your hand, the more fingers you use, the more securely you can hold on. Understanding the Bible is similar. The four fingers represent hearing the Bible taught, reading it for yourself, studying God's Word, and committing verses to memory. The thumb represents meditating on the Scriptures. Lastly, you have the palm of the hand, which represents the application of all you've heard, read, studied, memorized, and meditated on. Let's look at each of these aspects:

Hear: (1 Timothy 4:13; 1 Thessalonians 2:13)
Although it may seem the easiest of the five to do, the importance of hearing God's Word should not be overlooked. Sitting under good teaching at a local church is high on God's list for your growth plan. If you will commit to hearing the Word taught, taking notes, and asking your pastor or mentor

questions afterwards, you will be amazed how much stronger a grasp on God's Word you will have. We also have access to thousands of sermon podcasts, allowing us to listen to world-class Bible teachers while walking to class or driving to work.

Common Barrier:
We have grown accustomed to zoning out when someone is speaking up front. "Listening" to professors, teachers, and pastors is quite a challenge for today's over-entertained culture. Don't let yourself sit through and merely *hear* what is being said in church while your mind is preoccupied with other concerns. Zero in and focus on His Word, pushing yourself to really *listen* to what God is trying to say to you.

Where to Start:
Find a church that is committed to teaching Scripture and join it with the intention of soaking in the pastor's teaching. Hearing is usually where it stops for most people. They like to go and listen to the Bible being taught but don't take much personal responsibility to get the Word into their lives past that. Most people forget 95% of what they hear after 24 hours. Try taking notes in a journal and making at least one application to your life each week.

Read: (Revelation 1:3; Matthew 4:4)

Reading for enjoyment has almost entirely become a thing of the past. Few people want to put in the work of reading even for entertainment, much less dive into an ancient book they are afraid will go over their heads. However, reading the *whole* Bible, not just studying certain chapters or books, will give you a better understanding of the overarching message and plan of God's redemption of people from all nations. The perspective you will discover on God, history, mankind, and yourself will blow your mind!

Did you know if you sat down and focused, you could read the entire Bible in about 72 hours? Think about how much time you spend online across a span of 3 weeks. I bet it gets pretty close to 72 hours! What if you used that time to read God's Word instead? Can you imagine the grip you would have on the Bible after reading it cover to cover?

Common Barrier:
A lot of people try to start out reading in Genesis, but they may get discouragement when the long lists of descendants start appearing. Understanding Genesis is extremely important, but it is probably not the best place to start if you have never read the Bible.

Where to Start:
Try beginning with the Gospel of Mark. It is relatively short, easy to read, and action-packed with Jesus' life and ministry. This will help you get accustomed to reading and set you up for success. Eventually, find a daily plan that will take you through the entire Bible in a year—about 4 chapters a day. The *Bible App* has many great plans you can download, even audio versions, so you can listen to the Bible while you workout, do laundry, or trek across campus.

If reading the Bible is like flying over a city at 30,000 feet, then studying the Bible is like walking on the streets of that city. There are tons of advantages to each, but you must do both in order to really take in and *know* the entire city. Let's look at what studying the Bible will require:

Study: (Acts 17:11; 2 Timothy 2:15)
For some, two of the most unattractive words in the English language may be "Bible" and "study." It might seem like torture to the uninitiated, but if we really want to get a grip on God's Word and build our foundation for walking with Him for the rest of our lives, then we must start *studying* the Bible on a regular basis. Author Jerry Bridges says, "Reading gives us breadth, but study gives us depth." Let's not be content to stay in the shallow end, but instead choose to dive deep into the mind and heart of God!

> "Nobody ever outgrows Scripture; the book
> widens and deepens with our years."
> **—CHARLES SPURGEON**

One big difference between simply reading the Bible and studying it is a pen and a sheet of paper. When you are studying, you are trying to define words, pay attention to grammar, and understand the context of the passage you are studying.

Common Barrier:

The most common barrier that keeps college students from studying God's Word is the "want to." Most 18- to 22-year-olds don't have the best attention spans, so trying to sit and study a book written thousands of years ago doesn't happen easily. I would challenge you to set a time in your schedule, and do the hard work of "disciplining yourself for godliness" (1 Timothy 4:7). You may have to *commit* to doing Bible study before you fully *want* to do it, but trust us when we tell you it is 100 percent worth the effort! No one ever regrets time spent digging deep in Scripture.

> "A Bible that's falling apart usually belongs to someone who isn't."
>
> —CHARLES SPURGEON

Where to Start:

Purchase a good study Bible and dive into the book of Ephesians. Take it a couple of verses a day from beginning to end. Record as many observations as you can about each verse. Develop your curiosity and interpretive skills by asking various "what," "why," and "when" questions about the passage. Look up cross references that might give you insight and answers to your questions. Making specific personal applications to your life based upon a truth you discover in your study will transform your thoughts and behaviors. But don't do all this alone! Commit yourself to a solid group of believers to dig deep and study the Word together. It provides great accountability for this discipline and allows you to learn from others' insights as well.

If we hear, read, and study the Word, we are making a lot of progress toward getting the Scriptures into our *lives*. However, the primary way we get God's Word into our *hearts* is by memorizing portions of it.

Memorize: (Psalm 119:9-11; Colossians 3:2)

Philosopher Dallas Willard describes Bible memorization this way: "[It] is absolutely fundamental to spiritual formation. If I had to choose between all the disciplines of the spiritual life, I would choose Bible memorization, because it is a fundamental way of filling our minds with what it needs." Think about all the numbers you've memorized: phone numbers, social security, student ID. Or what about all of the ridiculous song lyrics you know by heart? If we can hold on to so much data long after we need it, we can certainly memorize a few verses!

By committing portions of God's Word to memory, we are adding His words into our thought life rather than just the sinful things our minds typically run to. This is what the psalmist is getting at when he says, "How can a young man keep his way pure? By keeping it according to your word...I have stored up your Word in my heart, that I might not sin against you" (Psalm 119:9, 11). The verses I have memorized have become the Holy Spirit's vocabulary in my life, ready and available for Him to bring into my mind at just the right time. The way you can win this spiritual battle to keep sin, anxiety and hopelessness from consuming you is to keep your "sword" handy at *all* times through Scripture memory!

Common Barrier:
It's hard to fathom the untapped power of simply hiding God's Word in your heart. Start small and try it out! Experience victory as God brings to mind a verse you've memorized in order to instantly overcome a temptation. Investing even a small amount of time memorizing produces huge spiritual results.

Where to Start:
I would start with Romans 6:23. It contains essentially the entire story of the Bible wrapped up in one sentence. Memorize it, and share it with one of your friends who doesn't know Jesus. Then get a simple plan to memorize at least one verse a week. Check out the Topical Memory System by The Navigators. Your smartphone can also be a great tool; there are lots of Scripture memory apps available, or you could easily use any regular flashcard app.

As you memorize God's Word, it will roll around in your mind during your free time and begin trickling down into your heart and soul. That is essentially what meditation is.

Meditate: (Joshua 1:8; Psalm 1:1-3)
To really get the most out of God's Word, you need to meditate on *everything* you hear, read, study, and memorize. Meditating on Scripture is when

the Holy Spirit is able to move these principles you've learned from simple knowledge to real change in your life. This kind of meditation is opposite of what Eastern world religions refer to as meditation. We are not talking about emptying our minds; instead, the goal is to fill our minds with the truth of God's Word.

You can think deeply about words, phrases, or concepts you've read or studied and benefit greatly in your understanding of them. Slowly read verses over and over, taking turns emphasizing each word in the passage. Don't let yourself read or study God's Word and then move on as if nothing happened. Like cows that chew and re-chew their food over and over to ingest and digest their food, we need to make opportunities to meditate over and over on God's Word.

> Blessed is the one
> who does not walk in step with the wicked
> or stand in the way that sinners take
> or sit in the company of mockers,
> but whose delight is in the law of the Lord,
> and who *meditates* on his law day and night.
> That person is like a tree planted
> by streams of water,
> which yields its fruit in season
> and whose leaf does not wither—
> whatever they do prospers.
>
> (PSALM 1:1-3)

Common Barrier:
Most of us don't take the time to meditate because we feel too rushed. We think we need to get our devotional time done as quickly as possible so that we can move on to other "more important" tasks.

Where to Start:
A simple method for reading and meditating on Scripture is the S.O.A.P. method designed by Wayne Cordeiro. I (Paul) don't get on social media until I do my S.O.A.P for the day. I want the first thing I open every day to be the Bible, not my email inbox or Instagram!

Here is how to have a **S.O.A.P.** quiet time:

Scripture: Choose a book of the Bible to read. Try to read one to four chapters a day. A daily Bible reading plan can be very helpful to provide structure. As you read, look for a verse that particularly impressed you and write it out in your journal.

Observation: What in this passage stuck out to you? What do you think God is saying to you from this scripture? Simply write down your thoughts about the verse in your journal.

Application: How should I live differently? Write down a specific application based on this passage.

Prayer: Spend some time praying about what you learned from the passage and surrendering your life to follow Christ today. Try writing out a prayer in your journal.

Try this for a month. Set your alarm at least 30 minutes earlier to spend some time with Jesus. Pound a couple cups of coffee beforehand if you must. The first few days it may be difficult to get started, but the perk of having your time with God early in the morning is there are fewer distractions. What's stopping you from trying this out for 30 days and seeing what the Lord does? "Taste and see that the Lord is good; blessed is the one who takes refuge in him" (Psalm 34:8).

> "I saw more clearly than ever, that the first
> great and primary business to which I ought
> to attend every day was, to have my soul
> happy in the Lord. The first thing to be
> concerned about was not how much I might serve
> the Lord, how I might glorify the Lord; but
> how I might get my soul into a happy state,
> and how my inner man may be nourished."
> **—GEORGE MUELLER**

One of the natural things that starts to happen as you meditate on the Word is you begin to think about ways you can apply it to your life as you go through your day.

Apply: (James 1:22-25; John 13:17)

Once you are regularly practicing each of the fingers in this illustration, the next step is to keep learning how to effectively *apply* what you've heard, read, studied, memorized, and meditated on. James 1:22-25 compares a man who listens to God's Word and doesn't do what it says to a man who looks in the mirror but walks away and forgets what he looks like. I know college freshmen pretty well, and most of them spend a good amount of time in front of the mirror before going to their first class of the day. Why? They want to be able to make any necessary changes before heading out to impress all of their friends. Would any of them ever look in the mirror, see some food stuck in their teeth or that their shirt is on inside out, and not make the fixes they need to? Absolutely not! Applying God's Word is exactly the same. If we come away from the Bible and don't make the adjustments we see we need to after comparing ourselves to the truth it teaches, then we are just as ridiculous as that freshman who doesn't remove the lettuce in their teeth staring back at them in the mirror!

Common Barrier:

Why don't people apply God's Word to their life? Because they don't know where to start. Most of them see so many things they need to change that they feel overwhelmed and defeated. And deep down, sometimes we don't *want* to change, repent, or admit we are wrong and need help.

Where to Start:

Just writing down an "application" in a notebook isn't an actual application to our life. Instead, based on what you read, ask yourself these questions:

> Is there a sin I need to confess or an attitude I need to change?

Is there a command I need to obey or an example I need to follow?

Does this verse teach me something about God or myself?

Avoid nebulous applications that are too open-ended to be effective, such as "I want to be a better Christian." When making applications from the Word, make sure they are "SPAM": Specific, Practical, Achievable, and Measurable. For example, "Beginning tomorrow at 7:00 a.m., I will get up, set my phone aside, and spend 20 minutes doing a S.O.A.P. quiet time, starting in Mark 1." Get into God's Word, and let His Word get into you through *aggressive* application of what you read and study.

Consistency in these basics will begin to give you victory over sin. Famous evangelist D.L. Moody put it well: "Either the Bible will keep you from sin, or sin will keep you from the Bible." Absorb God's Word into your life and you will become a different person. This unconditional commitment to the Word will serve as the unbending standard of truth in your personal life and ministry, slicing through your own sinful thoughts and guiding you into a deep knowledge of God. If you are going to ignite others on your campus for Christ, it must be your daily instruction and training manual!

REFLECTION QUESTIONS:

→ How and why did God give us the Bible?

→ Read 2 Timothy 3:16-17 again and put it in your own words. In light of that passage, how would you respond to someone who says the Bible is not from God, has errors, or is only inspired in certain sections?

→ List the six parts of the "Hand Illustration" and rank each from your strongest to weakest.

→ What does your daily "quiet time" look like, and how could the S.O.A.P. approach help you?

At His Feet

Peter was a freshman involved with InterVarsity Christian Fellowship at the University of Wisconsin- Madison when he and some of his Christian buddies decided to get serious about reaching others for Christ. Rick, an IVCF staffer in Madison at the time, was diligently praying that Peter and other believers would take personal ownership of the ministry there. God answered his petitions, and Peter and six other freshmen began meeting every Tuesday at 5:30 p.m. to pray, confess their sins, and intercede for the campus and other students. The Lord began to burden them for their lost friends, and Peter, without knowing any better, invited one of them to join the group for prayer. This wasn't just any non-believer. According to Rick, he was a "cosmic consciousness, pot-smoking, drug- and alcohol-abusing student, who had sampled Marxist and New Age thinking and decided to embrace atheism." Although everyone was a little uncomfortable with the new addition to the group, they proceeded as usual with the worship, confession, and intercession. But as the meeting concluded and the students began exiting, Alex, the non-Christian, raced over to confront Peter with a question.

"What was that?" Alex demanded.

"What was what?" Peter responded nervously.

"I don't even believe in God, but God was in that room. What happened?"

Overhearing the conversation, Rick asked Peter and Alex if he could join the two of them for a Coke and some conversation.

After Alex spent three hours hearing Rick and Peter explain the gospel, this outspoken atheist bowed in prayer to begin a personal relationship with Jesus. What convinced this hardened scoffer? Rick says it was simply a group of "struggling, authentic, accepting freshmen, who had learned how to be people of the Presence."

Alex had encountered the presence of God in a genuine, Spirit-filled community and would never be the same. When the story of his radical conversion got back to the other six freshmen in the prayer group, they immediately began inviting their non-Christian friends to the meetings. Over twenty-five students found the Savior that year through the IVCF freshmen prayer gathering. Looking back, it was obvious Peter was anxious for God to use him to impact other students on campus, but he wisely chose to prepare by constantly pouring his heart out at the feet of Jesus. He and his friends were determined to seek God's face until He showed up in very tangible ways. And show up He did!

→ DAILY INTIMACY

Prayer is the direct communication of our thoughts, feelings, and desires to our Heavenly Father. Through prayer we show our dependence on and trust in God, and He reveals Himself to us. What can be more important than spending daily time with the God of the universe, the Savior of our souls, the Lord of our lives? Nothing!

Prayer builds our intimacy with God. Your time with the Lord is not about accomplishing something—it's about *being* with someone. The last thing we want to do is quickly mumble a list of words and call that "prayer." No, we yearn to actually, specifically, and personally communicate with the living God.

Is prayer important to you? Of course you know it should be theoretically, but if someone spent a week with you, would they say prayer is important to you?

Most of us feel some measure of regret when it comes to prayer. We know we should pray, but that knowledge doesn't translate into action. Guilt over not praying enough may even keep us from praying more. Our Heavenly Father is not waiting for us to approach Him so He can scold us for all of the times we haven't come to Him. He wants us to lay our requests before Him with the utter sincerity and simplicity of beloved children. "Let us then approach God's throne of grace with confidence, so that we may receive mercy and find grace to help us in our time of need" (Hebrews 4:16).

The motivation for spending time in prayer should not be guilt or obligation, but love. If someone told you they love you but never wanted to spend time talking to you, would you believe them? We shouldn't be asking, "What's the bare minimum I can pray and still have God bless me?" Our question should be, "What's the maximum amount of time my schedule will allow me to spend talking to the Lord?" Loving God with all of our heart, soul, and mind draws us to the foot of our good Father's throne in prayer.

The best way to grow in your prayer life is to block out focused time every day to simply pray. A.W. Tozer says, "The key to prayer is simply praying." The most productive time of the day is your time alone with God. Like Jesus, we must fight to get away and spend time alone with God. "But Jesus often withdrew to lonely places and prayed" (Luke 5:16). The simple habit of blocking out 15-30 minutes to spend in prayer every day could be the most life-changing decision you will ever make. As my mentor, Max Barnett, always tells me, "If you are too busy to spend unhurried time alone with God every day, then you are more busy than God intended you to be." Missionary hero, Adoniram Judson, gave this bold challenge to younger Christian leaders: "Arrange your affairs, if possible, so that you can leisurely devote two or three hours every day not merely to devotional exercises but to the very act of secret prayer and communion with God…Be resolute in His cause. Make all practical sacrifices to maintain it. Consider that your time is short, and that business and company must not be allowed to rob you of your God."

Prayer also moves the hand of God. We can approach the Lord in prayer authentically, humbly, and with this reality: "If you remain in me and my words remain in you, ask whatever you wish, and it will be done for you" (John 15:7). God's power and promises are limitless. There are blessings in life the Lord wants to give you if you will simply ask Him. A challenging statement in Scripture is: "You do not have because you do not ask" (James 4:2). We may not always understand why God chooses to do or not do certain things. His ways and thoughts are beyond our comprehension (Isaiah 55:8-9). But even when we have prayers that seem to go unanswered, we can continue to ask confidently, knowing with certainty that He is a generous Father who loves to give good gifts to His children and has already blessed us with the greatest gift in Christ. We may not always understand His hand, but we can always trust His heart.

"Which of you, if your son asks for bread, will give him a stone? Or if he asks for a fish, will give him a snake? If you, then, though you are evil, know how to give good gifts to your children, how much more will your Father in heaven give good gifts to those who ask him!" (Matthew 7:9-11)

"He who did not spare his own Son, but gave him up for us all—how will he not also, along with him, graciously give us all things?" (Romans 8:32)

→ "OUR FATHER"

> "The greatest thing anyone can do for God
> and man is pray. It is not the only thing;
> but it is the chief thing. The great people
> of the earth today are the people who pray.
> I do not mean those who talk about prayer;
> not those who can explain about prayer; but I
> mean those people who take time and pray."
>
> **—S.D. GORDON**

So what does a biblical prayer life look like practically? When Jesus' disciples asked Him to teach them how to pray, He gave them the Lord's Prayer:

Our Father in heaven, may your name be kept holy.

May your Kingdom come soon. May your will be done on earth, as it is in heaven.

Give us today the food we need, and forgive us our sins, as we have forgiven those who sin against us. And don't let us yield to temptation, but rescue us from the evil one. (Matthew 6:9-13, NLT)

Jesus gave us an example which highlights the major elements we should include in our prayer lives. These include: proclaiming the glory of God, praying for His kingdom (salvation) to reach the whole earth as it is around the throne in heaven (Revelation 7:9), daily provision, forgiveness and the grace to forgive, and protection.

There are lots of models for prayer, and one of the most used is ACTS where you spend time each day in adoration, confession, thanksgiving, and supplication. But, if there is sin in my life that I am already aware of, that is always the place I like to begin—to repent and confess it to God *before* I proceed. So, I like to make a slight adjustment to this tool and call it "CATS" instead:

CATS

C – Confession: (Psalm 66:18, 1 John 1:8-10, Proverbs 28:13)

Use this time to specifically identify and acknowledge any sin in your life. Go through your day or the past couple of days. Ask Him to show you any areas of disobedience. Ask for forgiveness for sins you may be unaware of.

A – Adoration: (Psalm 96:1-4)

Continue by fixing your mind on God and who He is. Adoration is a time to focus on God's character. If you are unsure of what to say, think of His attributes: His unfailing love, His mercy, His grace, His beauty. Or open up the Psalms; they are full of God's praises!

T – Thanksgiving: (1 Thessalonians 5:16-18, 1 Chronicles 16:34)

Use this time to express gratitude for all the ways He is at work in your life. Thank Him for answered prayers, for daily provisions, for all of the ways He is blessing you, and even for the trials that come your way. Jesus' sacrifice for us on the cross is always a great starting point for thankfulness.

S – Supplication: (Philippians 4:6-7, 1 Timothy 2:1-4)

Finish your time by presenting any specific requests you may have to Him. These asks can be for yourself or for others. Pray for daily needs, for others' needs, for the salvation of friends/family, or for current world events.

Prayer List

Another helpful tool is to simply have a list of things you want to pray for. Some of the things on that list could be:

- Specific needs of friends, family members, people you lead
- Your church, campus ministry, and leaders
- Nations of the world without the gospel
- Specific people who need Jesus
- Your goals, relationships, and finances
- Large and small decisions and opportunities

Keep your prayer list in a journal where you can record the things you see God do in response to your prayers. Cross things off the list as they are answered. It is so faith-building to keep track of the Lord's answers to prayer.

Pick a day of the week to pray for an extended time

When I (Paul) was in college and just getting started reaching out to others for Christ, I began to see my desperate need to spend time asking God to save the people I was sharing the gospel with. I realized that on Tuesday mornings I didn't have class until 11:00 a.m. and could utilize that time beforehand to bring these souls before God and ask Him to draw them to Himself. Maybe you too have a gap in your schedule where you could make the most of your time (Ephesians 5:15-17) and intercede for individuals who don't know Jesus? I would also encourage you to think about finding a day or half-day a month to spend in prayer.

Pray in Groups

We as Christians are always more effective when we are unified. What better to be unified around than praying and asking God to save people on your campus and in the world? If there isn't currently a weekly prayer meeting for you to attend, start one. Start a prayer group specifically for your dorm, team, or sorority. You won't regret meeting together with other like-minded believers and begging God to draw people to Himself.

Prayer Walks

Lastly, one of the most enjoyable things I do is take prayer walks around the campus with students to build a deeper burden for prayer and evangelism. Usually in the early morning or late night, and sometimes in multiple pairs, we will create a prayer circuit where each twosome stops in front of every dorm, Greek house, athletic facility, office, and classroom building to inter-cede for that group as well as individuals.

Pray in the morning. Pray late at night. Pray with other students. Pray by yourself. Pray without ceasing (1 Thessalonians 5:17)! The more you lift your heart up to the Lord, and the more you position your-self in intercessory prayer between God and others, the more you will sense His going before you to touch and prepare the hearts of students. Saturate your campus with prayer and watch your good Father begin to work miracles.

→ TOUCH THE WORLD

Dawson "Daws" Trotman, founder of the Navigators, came to Christ in his early twenties and immediately began to grow, memorize Scripture, witness, and pray. He challenged a friend to meet him for two hours of prayer every morning at 4:30 for six weeks. For the first few days, they prayed only for individuals in their church and city. But God expanded their vision, and, armed with a U.S. map, they began praying that God would use them in the lives of men in all fifty states. In the final weeks, they were moved to pour their hearts out over a world map, realizing the Lord wanted to use their prayers and lives to redeem people from nations beyond the U.S. to Himself. This foundation of intercession not only launched the Navigators ministry but galvanized Daws and his men as lifetime prayer warriors.

After reading the excellent biography *Daws* as a student, I (Steve) decided to ask five men to get up at 5:30 a.m. (we weren't quite as com-mitted!) and pray together for two hours every morning. We divided up the campus into every imaginable affinity group to pray for the students' salvation, that laborers would be raised up to go *to* them, and that labor-ers would be raised *from* them. It seemed like we would always end up in front of a world map, praying for the nations and giving special atten-tion to the unreached millions in China. In the subsequent months and years, we saw God do marvelous works in response to our petitions. Two men from the early morning prayer group have now been ministering in China for over forty years, along with many of their disciples who followed them there!

"Do you know why I often ask Christians,
'What's the biggest thing you've asked God for
this week?' I remind them that they are going
to God, the Father, the Maker of the universe.
The One who holds the world in His hands. What
did you ask for? Did you ask for peanuts, toys,
trinkets, or did you ask for continents?"

—DAWSON TROTMAN

As disciples of Jesus Christ, we need to care about what He cares about. He is burdened with a desire for *every* person across the planet to have a chance to know and experience His love and forgiveness. In my little prayer hut next to my house, I have a table, a chair, a lamp—and a world map spread out. It's where I go to pray for the nations, to intercede for the leaders and people who don't have access to the gospel, to pour out my soul to a great and powerful God who died on the cross for these precious ones. Yes, prayer definitely changes *me*, but it also moves the hand of God. Do I understand it fully? No. Do I feel supremely privileged to partner with the Lord of the universe to see our intercessions be used of God to reach the nations? Oh yes.

A.W. Tozer, in his classic book *The Pursuit of God*, shares the following prayer. We challenge you to pray it with us now and join us in the life-long pursuit of knowing God better.

"O God, I have tasted Your goodness, and it has both satisfied me and made me thirsty for more. I am painfully conscious of my need for further grace. I am ashamed of my lack of desire. O God, the Triune God, I want to want You; I long to be filled with longing; I thirst to be made more thirsty still. Show me Your glory, I pray, so that I may know You indeed. Begin in mercy a new work of love within me. Say to my soul, 'Rise up my love, my fair one, and come away.' Then give me grace to rise and follow You up from this misty lowland where I have wandered so long.

REFLECTION   QUESTIONS :

→ Have you prayed (or memorized) the Lord's Prayer in Matthew
   6? Take time to read it out loud and pray it back to God slowly,
   thinking deeply about each phrase and opening your heart as
   you speak.

→ Go through the C-A-T-S progression again and write down at
   least one thing in each category you could bring to the Lord.
   Consider sharing these prayer points with your peers.

→ If God answered *all* your prayers this week, how would your life
   be different? How would the world be different?

→ Pick one non-Christian country of the world you are famil-
   iar with and lift them up in prayer, specifically asking God to
   send laborers there. (You may want to download the "World
   Christian" app to get current info.)

Contagious Community

During freshman orientation at the University of Florida, Stephen met Kevin, a Chinese American who came to all of the Baptist Collegiate Ministry's Welcome Week activities and immediately clicked with the community. Kevin's family was culturally Buddhist, and his only experience with Christianity had been a girl he liked in high school. Stephen shared the gospel with him, but Kevin admitted he wasn't ready to accept Jesus. "That's fine! You don't have to be a Christian to hang out with us," Stephen assured him.

Kevin continued to attend ministry events, and Stephen kept inviting him to join him and his friends to play ball or get pizza. He also came regularly to the worship service and dorm Bible study, asking questions and seeking answers. Two months later, on their way to play ultimate frisbee, Kevin confessed Jesus Christ as his Savior and Lord and asked Stephen if he would disciple him.

Kevin and Stephen are now roommates and have moved right back into the same dorm where they met last year, building relationships with this year's freshmen and inviting them to connect with their "contagious community!" The love of Christ flowing through a community of His followers is like a divine magnet for the lost and lonely all around us. It's also a haven of encouragement and protection for believers, drawing strength from each other to continue as bright lights to a desperately dark world.

> "A new commandment I give to you, that you love one another: just as I have loved you, you also are to love one another. By this all people will know that you are my disciples, if you have love for one another."
>
> —JOHN 13:34-35

Jesus says in the verse above, "All people will know that you are my disciples if you have love for one another." When you love God supremely, that same love will naturally overflow to other people. As we see in The Wheel diagram, the well-rounded Christian life is centered on Christ and is lived out in relationships with God and others. Each of us should have a vibrant personal relationship with the Lord, but if you isolate yourself and don't share that relationship with others, you are going to miss out on one of the primary purposes of your life.

When you become a follower of Christ, you are officially and instantly adopted into the family of God. "His unchanging plan has always been to adopt us into his own family by bringing us to himself through Jesus Christ" (Ephesians 1:5, NLT). Being part of a family means you are now connected together. It is crucial that every follower of Christ is involved in *genuine* community. Bonding with other committed believers is a vital building block in our foundation. It provides the gentle (and sometimes not so gentle!) push we need to live out all of the other building blocks of the Christian life.

→ CIRCLE UP

It breaks my heart to see so many students going through their college experience without a truly authentic Christ-centered community. If you are so busy working at your part-time job, studying, investing in a dating relationship, or pursuing extracurricular activities that you never make significant time to get networked into a biblical community, you will struggle spiritually. These other areas may be important, but not more vital than getting deeply connected with other believers.

I have watched too many students come to college and immediately get so stressed out about all the papers, tests, and projects that they start to see Christian community as an optional add-on. It can be easy to keep thinking, "I'll just get connected *next* semester when things settle down." The problem with this idea is that life never settles down! You must intentionally choose to pursue and join a tight-knit network of committed believers—*now*. You are deceived if you think you can follow Christ on your own. I've observed too many "youth group all-stars" with grand ambitions crash and burn spiritually their first semester. The reason? They bounce from one campus ministry large group meeting to the next, searching for the coolest crowd or the best experience but failing to ever get deeply connected to genuine Christian community.

One of the enemy's primary strategies is to get believers isolated so he can take them out. If you have ever watched the Discovery Channel, you know that lions prey on those that have become detached from the rest of the herd. Dietrich Bonhoeffer once said, "Sin demands to have a man by himself. The more isolated a person is, the more destructive the power of sin is over him."

I once saw a video of a pack of wolves trying to attack a baby musk ox that was separated from its herd. As the wolves started to head for the calf, the herd noticed and charged straight toward the action, forming a circle around the baby. They continued circling until the wolves decided to leave. Every follower of Christ needs a community like that. The best way to overcome temptation is to have a group of like-hearted people to run with. "Flee the evil desires of youth and pursue righteousness, faith, love and peace, along with those who call on the Lord out of a pure heart" (2 Timothy 2:22).

Every year, numerous students die due to drug- or alcohol-related issues at parties where they are desperately trying to fit in. I (Paul) remember trying to reach out to a guy and invite him to our meeting, only to find out later that year he had passed away. His "friends" took him out for 21 shots on his 21st birthday and ended up leaving him in a pile of his own vomit. He died later that night. You may think nothing like that would ever happen to you, but if you do not *intentionally* choose a group of godly friends to run with, the world will provide you with some substitutes who will end up taking you places you do *not* want to go. You pick your friends, you pick your future. "He who walks with the wise grows wise, but a companion of fools suffers harm" (Proverbs 13:20).

> "The next best thing to being wise...is
> to live in a circle of those who are."
>
> —C.S. LEWIS

Joining a small group Bible study can be a great first step towards building biblical community. I know of students in our ministry who treat our weekly small group Bible studies like a night class. They have made a decision to be there *every* week—no exceptions. The writer of Hebrews challenges followers of Christ to fight for their times of fellowship together: "And let us consider how we may spur one another on toward love and good deeds, not giving up meeting together, as some are in the habit of doing, but encouraging one another—and all the more as you see the Day approaching" (Hebrews 10:24-25). Would you say you are *fiercely* protecting your times each week with other committed believers?

→ GET REAL

If we want to individually grow as Christians, one of the best things we can do is be open with other believers about our sins and failures. The gospel produces genuine honesty and transparency in relationships with people. The cross has already exposed us. If your sin problem was so bad that it took the Son of God to die for you in order for you to be forgiven, your worst is already known. There is no need to try to hide your private or public transgressions from other sinners. Be open with your community!

Being scared to reveal our weaknesses, temptations, or sins to others slows down our sanctification. But bringing the darkest parts of our lives into the light as we confess our disobedience to others frees us from slavery. Don't be hardened by the deceitfulness of your sin. Confess it and enjoy living in a community of people who also know they desperately need Jesus and what He has done for them on the cross. "Therefore confess your sins to each other and pray for each other so that you may be healed" (James 5:16). You taking the initiative to be vulnerable will give them the courage to do so also. It's hard to do at first, but you'll be so glad you did.

→ LOCK ARMS

You need community not only for spiritual protection but also to accomplish your purpose in life. God designed us to depend on one another to make progress in our growth and advance His mission together. The Christian life is a team sport. Imagine if we put just one of the biggest and best pro football players in the world up against an average high school football squad. How would he do? He would be defeated easily. As we are seeking to advance the purposes of Jesus on earth and make disciples of all nations, the only way to do it effectively is in the context of community.

> "After we have done our best to
> communicate truth to a lost world,
> still we must never forget that the
> final apologetic which Jesus gave is the
> observable love of true Christians."
>
> **—FRANCIS SCHAEFFER**

When Christians regularly have a blast together and invite those who don't know Jesus to be a part of that, students experience the love we have for one another and the unconditional love we have for them. Non-Christians start to belong before they even believe. Evangelism works best when it is show and tell—not just tell. A verse that has become central to our ministry is 1 Thessalonians 2:8: "Because we loved you so much, we were delighted to share with you not only the gospel of God but our lives as well." Invite people into your loving and welcoming community and watch the gospel transform them.

→ JOIN A CHURCH

Dietrich Bonhoeffer, a German pastor who stood up to the Nazis during World War II and was martyred in a concentration camp, understood the absolute need for believers to band together: "Christian brotherhood is not an ideal which we must realize; it is rather a reality created by God in Christ in which we may participate. The more clearly we learn to recognize that the ground and strength and promise of all our fellowship is in Jesus Christ alone, the more serenely shall we think of our fellowship and pray and hope for it." Bonhoeffer did not take Christian fellowship lightly. Neither should we.

It is essential for you to find a local church where the Scriptures are taught as the Word of God and there is godly leadership, genuine worship, and a caring congregation. When you find a church like that, plug into it, find ways to serve, and bring other students along with you.

When I (Steve) was a student, we would see how many of our church's front rows we could pack with eager college students. Week after week our pastor filled our minds and hearts with the wonder of knowing and following Jesus Christ. He's easily one of the five men who has most influenced my life. Not only was he solidifying *my* walk with Christ and evangelistic zeal each service, but he was also reinforcing all the convictions I was trying to instill in the men I was discipling.

Beyond Sunday mornings, I brought guys to church retreats, prayer meetings, and early morning men's breakfasts. I helped with Sunday school and the youth ministry. Even though I was also involved in a campus ministry, I could clearly see how valuable it was to honor, serve, build up, and give to my local church. Besides, once students get through college and move on, the only real options for spiritual nurturing in most communities are local churches. College is the time to learn how to pick a good church and become a blessing to its leaders and members. Your future spouse and family will thank you someday!

→ BODY PARTS AND BATTLESHIPS

You play an essential role in the body of Christ. If you don't fulfill your role, then it will be missed forever. "Just as there are many parts to our bodies, so it is with Christ's body. We are all parts of it, and it takes every one of us to make it complete, for we each have different work to do. So we belong to each other, and each of us needs all the others" (Romans 12:4-5, Living Bible). God has specifically made you for a job that *only* you can do. "If your foot says, 'I'm not a part of the body because I'm not a hand,' that doesn't make it any less a part of the body. And if your ear says, 'I'm not part of the body because I'm only an ear and not an eye,' would that make it any less a part of the body?" (1 Corinthians 12:15-16, NLT). You have a vital part to play that only you can fulfill. How has God designed you to serve the body of Christ and help advance His mission? Immerse yourself in serving and reaching out to others, and the Lord will show how He has gifted you.

John Piper encourages believers to see our Christian communities as battleships rather than cruise ships. A cruise ship is designed for comfort and convenience. When you shop for a cruise, you look for great restaurants, cool nightclubs, and maybe even a waterslide! A battleship, however, is not filled with passengers lounging by the pool but with crew members who each have a crucial job to do. It is not designed for the comfort of the crew. It's *all* about the mission. Our churches and college ministries are most healthy when they, like battleships, are laser-focused on the mission of making disciples of all nations. The greatest community I have ever experienced has been in the context of serving together to advance God's mission. There is nothing better than being abandoned to a cause greater than yourself with a team of like-hearted people.

I am struck by the affection Paul has for the Philippians: "I thank my God every time I remember you. In all my prayers for all of you, I always pray with joy because of your partnership in the gospel from the first day until now" (Philippians 1:3-5). The Greek word that is translated as "partnership" in this passage is *koinonia*, which is the word most often translated as "fellowship" in the New Testament. It means "one who participates with another in some enterprise or matter of joint concern." Biblical fellowship is not just watching movies or talking sports with friends. No, genuine fellowship is actually more about being outward-focused than inward-focused. It's a battleship, not a cruise ship!

When Cru was founded, they had the rally cry, "Come help change the world!" This call to action was used by God to sweep thousands of students into God's grand story. What started as a handful of students on the campus of UCLA in 1951 multiplied into a worldwide movement with 25,000 staff in 190+ countries. When a group of people decide to band together to advance the mission of Jesus, they are relentless. What kind of personal responsibility do you need to take to help your community of believers become an unstoppable force for advancing God's kingdom around the world? If not you, who? If not now, when?

Just like a log separated from the fire begins to burn out, so will you if you try to separate yourself from other Christians. Whether it is your church and/or campus ministry, find a group of believers who have a strong plan of evangelizing and discipling students to reach the nations and who you can join with to light a fire for Christ on your campus that can spread to the ends of the earth. The time to "circle up" is now.

REFLECTION   QUESTIONS:

→ Who are your closest friends right now? Are they running
toward God or away from Him?

→ Do you have someone in your life you've given full permission to
speak hard truth to you when needed? Who is it and how have
they played that role?

→ Have you joined a Bible-believing local church in your college
town? How did you choose that church and how are you serving there?

→ What can you do now to insure you will never isolate yourself
but always be closely and genuinely connected to a committed
body of believers?

10.

Landmines

You are at war. Whether you know it or not, there is a battle raging for your soul. "Dear friends, I warn you as temporary residents and foreigners to keep away from worldly desires that wage war against your very souls" (1 Peter 2:11, NLT). In this passage Peter is warning believers in the strongest possible terms to avoid sin at all costs. Each one of us has worldly desires or "passions of the flesh" that we are naturally drawn towards. It's not *if* you will have these sinful desires but *when* you will have them. In wartime, the enemy will hide landmines on the battlefield in hopes you will step on one and be killed by the explosion. Ignoring the danger or effects of Satan's landmines can have devastating effects on the foundation you are building. The good news is that in Christ you have a power far greater than your temptations. Jesus saved us not only from the *penalty* of sin but also from the *power* of sin.

> "Sin will take you farther than you want to
> go, keep you longer than you want to stay,
> and cost you more than you want to pay."
>
> —RAVI ZACHARIAS

Sin is not simply a mistake or oversight; it is a direct violation of the holiness of God. If you do not address a sinful habit, you can bring destruction and pain into every area of your life. I have watched friends almost destroy themselves and even consider taking their own lives as a result of a pattern of disobedience to God. I've also seen some of these same people come back from dark places as the Lord restored them gloriously. Sin is not something to mess around with. Our own fleshly nature is our greatest enemy, so know this for sure: your fight against sin is literally a fight for your life.

Don't be discouraged, though; God has given us everything we need to overcome temptation and walk in obedience. "For if you live according to the flesh, you will die; but if by the Spirit you put to death the misdeeds of the body, you will live" (Romans 8:13). Think for a moment. What is the sin you need to put to death? Everyone has something they struggle with. There are two types of Christians: those who are struggling with sin...and those who are lying!

Unchecked sin can dangerously erode the life of devotion to Christ you are building. Let's identify and discuss some of the areas of sin or distraction most likely to wreak havoc on your foundation.

→ LETTING FEAR CONTROL YOU

Even though there are hundreds of "Fear nots" in the Bible, we still sometimes choose that which is safe and comfortable and avoid those things that are difficult or intimidating to us. Rick Warren says, "Fear is a self-imposed prison that will keep you from becoming what God intends for you to be. You must move against it with the weapons of faith and love."

Prior to his execution in Rome, Paul left young, timid Timothy in big, bad Ephesus to develop the fledgling church there. Timothy was struggling and close to allowing his opponents inside and outside the church to dominate him when Paul's letter arrived. In this final letter Paul would ever write, the tear-stained pages gave his frightened co-laborer a jab: "For God has not given us a spirit of fear and timidity, but of power, love, and self-discipline" (2 Timothy 1:7, NLT). In verse 8, though, he delivers the knockout punch, getting right in the face of his long-time disciple. He ordered him not to be ashamed of:

- Jesus: "So never be ashamed to tell others about our Lord."
- Paul: "And don't be ashamed of me, either, even though I'm in prison for Him."
- The gospel: "With the strength God gives you, be ready to suffer with me for the sake of the Good News."

If God has given us *His* power, love, and discipline, what are we doing relying on our own resources, or even worse, pathetically backing down from a little worldly opposition? The real issue is not how to escape our fears, but how to walk *toward* them in the power of the Holy Spirit.

These verses in 2 Timothy became real to me (Steve) when I started to hang out with Vic, the main individual who discipled me in college. He was a senior ROTC student who doubled as a resident assistant in a men's dorm. From all appearances his primary goal in life was to show me how ashamed I was of the gospel! One night as I was coming over to his dorm for our weekly small group, Vic hopped on the elevator right as the door closed. Instead of greeting me, though, he leaned up against the side of the crowded elevator and, acting like he didn't know me, said, "Hey, buddy. What's that in your hand?"

Of course, everyone had their eyes glued to the lit floor numbers above, pretending they weren't listening to *every single word* exchanged between Vic and me. I paused to catch my breath and sheepishly responded in a low voice, "It's a Bible, Vic."

"A Bible?!" Vic shouted. "That's not that stuff that talks about Jesus Christ being the *Son of God*, is it?"

After turning eighteen shades of red, I finally lowered my head and whispered, "Yeah, Vic. That's what it says."

The elevator door finally (and mercifully) opened as Vic was finishing me off with a riveting, "You don't *really* believe that stuff, do you?"

Even though at the time I wanted to vanish from the face of the earth, I was later grateful to Vic, who exposed my unwillingness to openly and totally identify with:

- Jesus Christ (who is to be the *only* One I'm seeking to please)
- Vic (who was like the apostle Paul on our campus)
- The gospel (which is contained in the Bible I was carrying)

Like a modern day Dr. Jekyll and Mr. Hyde, I wanted to be cool and accepted by my fraternity brothers but then appear spiritually radical to the other Christians on campus. I can remember the exact day and place when I made the decision once and for all that I would be one person, not two! I'd been playing both sides of the fence and was determined not to allow others'

opinions to control me any longer. I was ashamed of the two-faced hypoc-
risy I was living and was more than ready for some authenticity in my life.

> "How very little can be done
> under the spirit of fear."
> —FLORENCE NIGHTINGALE

What about you? Decide now to walk *toward* your fears, forsaking your
"esteemed reputation" in favor of suffering for the gospel. Why? Because
you desire to love and obey God, and your heart burns with a passion to see
every student on your campus and every person who has never heard His
name come to faith in Jesus Christ. And even if a so-called "friend" ditches
you, thinking you are weird or fanatical, know for sure that any sacrifice you
make will be well worth it.

→ LIVING THE "SAFE" LIFE

Besides tempting you to sin or inserting fear into your life, the enemy has
another very potent weapon in his arsenal—persecution. Paul warned
Timothy about this in 2 Timothy 3:12: "Indeed, all who desire to live a godly
life in Christ Jesus will be persecuted" (ESV). This is a clear promise that if
we're not being persecuted, then we must not desire to live godly lives in
Christ Jesus. According to the Voice of the Martyrs ministry, there are more
believers (over 165,000) being martyred for their faith each year than ever
before in history. If we haven't found something in life worth dying for, then
we really don't have anything worth living for!

Although my life was never actually in danger, I (Steve) faced tremendous
opposition during the three years I lived in the fraternity house. Yes, it was
an incredible spiritual battle, but it also caused me to go through the greatest
season of spiritual growth in my life. I prayed daily for each man's salvation,
started small group Bible studies, and had a goal to share the gospel with
every pledge each semester. It felt strange, but I was the most loved guy in
the house...and the most hated! Besides the nasty notes and being shouted
down in meetings, I was occasionally awakened with a senior's blazing eyes,
bulging veins, and scowling face one inch away from mine, shrieking about
killing me if I ever tried to cram my religion down one more pledge's throat.

But when I felt lonely and outcast, I would think about Jesus; although He is definitely the most loved man who ever walked our planet, his life also attracted murderous hatred. During times of intense rejection, Paul the Apostle yearned to feel what Jesus felt and to experience "the fellowship of His sufferings" (Phillipians 3:10). You're certainly not trying to be an obnoxious agitator in your Greek house or your dorm floor, but no matter how winsome your witness is, living out and speaking the gospel boldly will bring opposition. For three full years, in order to survive the daily onslaughts in my house, I would get up each morning and mentally put on God's "spiritual armor" piece by piece (see Ephesians 6:10-18). Desperate men do desperate things; I was fully aware that if I was going to walk with the Lord that day and truly be an ambassador for Him, I was going to have to totally forsake my own strength in order to absolutely rely on His! Some days there was failure, and some days, victory.

→ LOSING THE BATTLE AGAINST LUST

Sexual sins often leave the biggest scars in people's lives. We can be forgiven of any sin, but these "sins of the flesh" remain seared into our minds for many years to come. Whether it's premarital sex or the cheap substitutes we find in TV, movies, or pornography, they rob of us of our innocence, purity, self-esteem, and, worst of all, fellowship with the Lord.

For me (Paul), the addiction to lust started as a young teenager. It crippled my spiritual life and caused more pain than I like to think about. It was a spiritual cancer eating away at every part of me. Having this secret area of my life caused me to constantly feel guilty, insecure, and fearful of what others would think if they found out who I *really* was. I felt trapped. I am so grateful to God for leading me through a process towards freedom from this enslaving addiction.

The first step of freedom for me was just being honest about my sin. I remember staying up late one night at my parents' house listening to one of my favorite Christian punk bands, Slick Shoes. I know it seems crazy that any good could ever come from Christian punk, but one of the lyrics, "I can't do it on my own," struck me about my need to get help. Late that night, I confessed my shameful habits to my father. I was really scared because, let's be honest, who wants to confess that kind of stuff to their dad? To my shock, he didn't act surprised or disappointed in me at all. Instead he gave me grace and hope. I asked him to start keeping me accountable in this area. James 5:16 says: "Confess your sins to each other and pray for each other so that you may be healed" (NLT). That night was the first time I confessed this struggle to anyone. It felt like a huge weight was lifted off my shoulders. After being honest with my dad, I was free to be honest with my brother and other close friends. This was a scary step, but it helped me more than any other.

If you are struggling in this area, you need to find someone you can be completely honest with. The darkness hates the light (1 John 1:7-9). God longs to forgive you and heal you, but you must commit to start walking in the light. People will not be shocked if you are honest about your struggles. In a recent anonymous survey of Christian college students involved in campus ministries across the U.S., ninety percent of males and fifty percent of females admitted to regular porn use. Look at those numbers again. These percentages aren't of *all* the students on your campus; they are the percentages of students in your Bible study, large group meeting, and leadership team. You are not alone. "The temptations in your life are no different from what others experience. And God is faithful. He will not allow the temptation to be more than you can stand. When you are tempted, he will show you a way out so that you can endure" (1 Corinthians 10:13). Our honesty helps us gain freedom and encourages others to ask for help as well. I would challenge everyone reading this to have someone you can have regular, honest accountability with.

The next thing that really helped me was to start developing biblical convictions on lust. I began memorizing verses on the topic of purity, like Ephesians 5:3: "But among you there must not be even a hint of sexual immorality, or of any kind of impurity, or of greed, because these are improper for God's holy people" (NIV). I would quote these verses (sometimes even out loud) when faced with temptations. In Mark 4, Jesus was tempted three times by Satan. Each time He answered with, "It is written...." If Jesus needed to memorize and use Scripture to fight temptation, we would be wise to do so as well.

The last step for me was to take drastic measures to get free. I couldn't gain true freedom until I was willing to do whatever it took to overcome lust. I was challenged by Matthew 5:27-29: "You have heard that it was said,

'Do not commit adultery.' But I tell you that anyone who looks at a woman lustfully has already committed adultery with her in his heart. If your right eye causes you to sin, gouge it out and throw it away. It is better for you to lose one part of your body than for your whole body to be thrown into hell." It looks like Jesus is saying we need to do *whatever* it takes to pursue holiness. No eye gouging today please, but His point was: what drastic measures do *you* need to take to be free from lust? Starting an accountability group? Signing up for accountability software such as Covenant Eyes? Switching from a smartphone to a "dumb phone"? Enrolling in an online recovery program like The Freedom Fight? If this is a stronghold in your life, you will not gain freedom by taking half measures. Do whatever it takes!

We know there is not a person reading this book who has not struggled with lust. Romans 8:1-2 says "Therefore, there is now no condemnation for those who are in Christ Jesus, because through Christ Jesus the law of the Spirit of life set me free from the law of sin and death." God can forgive you and provide you a fresh start. Decide right now to live a pure and holy life before Him. Then take it a day at a time to totally rely on God's strength to walk in victory, not your own.

→ LOOKING FOR LOVE IN ALL THE WRONG PLACES

Tamara loved spending time digging deep into God's Word. She was excited to pass her passion for Scripture on to others, so she offered to host a Bible study in her dorm room and recruited her friends to join her. Always faithful to campus prayer times, you could sense Tamara's longing to see her lost friends come to faith and for Christ to be made known to the world. The girl who was helping Tamara grow in her relationship with Christ would have described her as a dream disciple, except for one thing: Tamara's relationship with Brad. High school sweethearts, Brad and Tamara came to college as a couple, and nothing—not Brad's rejection of the gospel on numerous occasions, pleas from her Christian friends, or the fact that it was ruining her witness on campus—would break them up. Not only was Tamara dating Brad, a vocal atheist, but she was openly sleeping with him every night in his dorm room. She didn't try to hide it and wasn't willing to change it. Giving up this aspect of their relationship might mean losing him, and she couldn't let that happen.

This bright, winsome friend to so many could have been an incredible light for fellow students at this spiritually dark liberal arts college. But, unwilling to let Christ be Lord of every part of her life, she eventually stopped hanging out with the small band of other believers on campus. "I just don't want to hear about it anymore," she declared as she walked away from fellowship, opportunities to grow, and the chance for God to use her life to impact others for Christ.

Who and how you choose to date is one of the most important decisions you'll ever make. Besides your choice to follow Christ, there is actually no life decision more important than choosing the right person to date and marry, if and when God leads you to do either. If you compromise in this area, it has the potential to crack wide open the deep and enduring foundation for life and ministry you are working to build. It pays to be picky. Is the person you are considering dating a committed follower of Christ? "Do not be yoked together with unbelievers. For what do righteousness and wickedness have in common? Or what fellowship can light have with darkness?" (2 Corinthians 6:14). Marriage is the ultimate way to be "yoked together" with another person. I know it sounds obvious, but you will marry *someone* you date. I have yet to hear a valid reason for a Christian dating a non-believer. As you might guess, we don't recommend the "flirt to convert" strategy!

In addition to following Christ, I would encourage you to ask yourself if a person you are considering dating has the values and character you would want in a spouse—and the future parent of your children. I have met a lot of well-meaning Christian students who look at the first person they are attracted to who happens to be a "Christian" and assume it is destined for them to be together. If you want to date someone who will help and not hinder you in building your foundation, they must currently and actively be investing in their own relationship with the Lord and growing in Christlikeness. Start asking God to lead you to someone who shares your convictions of wholeheartedly following Christ, fulfilling the Great Commission, and making lifelong sacrifices to make sure the name and fame of Jesus is exalted throughout the world. But don't be fooled: you can tell whether they are just talkers or doers based upon their track record. There are no guarantees, but the best way to tell what a person is going to do and be like in the *future* is simply to look at their *past*!

Once you find the right person to start spending time with, my best advice is to make a strategic plan for your dating relationship with specific goals and boundaries. You can date the right person in the wrong way and cause yourself a lot of unnecessary pain. Ask a mature leader to give you some wisdom and help you make your plan. Decide how much time you will spend together alone and establish physical boundaries you both agree on. I recommend even considering what you talk about and express to one another in your plan. Who can help you make a God-honoring plan and hold you accountable to stick with it?

What if you took it a step further and thought about this whole thing in a different way? Do *you* possess the character and convictions your dream guy or girl would be attracted to in a potential spouse? Take stock for a moment. Are you looking for qualities in a future spouse that you need to focus on building more deeply into your *own* life right now? Here's the best advice we can give you in this critical area: spend more time and effort on *becoming* the right person than on *finding* the right person.

REFLECTION   QUESTIONS:

→ Like Steve, have you ever been embarrassed or ashamed to fully and openly identify with Jesus, the gospel, or committed believers? How so?

→ Have you ever been persecuted for your Christian life or testimony? If so, when and how? If not, why not?

→ What has been your track record with sexual impurity and lust in your life? What steps do you need to take to have consistent victory in this area?

→ Describe the character and convictions you want in your spouse someday. What can you do now to insure they (and you!) will possess those?

11

Hustle Mode On

I'm hoping by now you have begun making radical decisions, setting challenging goals, and embracing life-shaping activities in the personal and essential "foundation building" project we've been describing for you. In the final chapter of this "Laying Your Foundation" section, we want to begin to transition you from the minor leagues to the majors. As my Dad was trying to help me move from childhood to manhood, he would say, "Steve, are you ready to put your 'big boy' pants on now?", lovingly provoking me to aspire to grow in maturity and take on greater responsibilities. I won't ask you that question, but I *will* inquire whether you are ready to progress from simply reading a Christian book with some cool stories and interesting questions to an all-out commitment to specifically *doing* all that the Lord is calling you to be and do.

Let's review, then do a quick heart check at this juncture. We sought to help you gain an eternal vision for your life and learn the necessity and the ingredients of building the deep foundation required to live a life of glorifying Christ and impacting the world for Him. So, put the book down for a moment and look into your soul. If you sense you are just going through the motions, "ho-humming" your way through the chapters and not really soaking all this in, you may just want to put this book in the recycle bin or give it to someone else. Why? Because you are not going to like these next three sections. We are going to challenge you right to the core of your being, prodding you to live for the person and purposes of Jesus Christ like never before.

On the other hand, if you are re-reading portions, underlining or highlighting poignant phrases, or making all kinds of notes and revolutionary plans in the margins, you are going to eat up the next sections. If the material thus far has...

- Caused you to dream about how God might use your life to change your campus and the world for His glory
- Motivated you to get in spiritual "hustle mode" like never before
- Galvanized you to specifically and powerfully live out and apply what you've learned to your personal life and ministry

...then hang onto this book and prepare for impact!

If you want to keep going, let's begin by attempting to peer into the future and work our way back. What is it going to cost you to become a world changer for Jesus Christ, and what kind of deep, long-term convictions will you need to develop to stay in the saddle during your college years—and for the rest of your life? We list a few in this chapter.

→ STAY FAITHFUL

The sad reality is many of you may not be actively following Christ ten years from now. The reason? It's the little things. Jesus tells us in Luke 16:10, "He who is faithful in a very little thing is faithful also in much" (NASB). Little things include choosing to be honest with your accountability partner instead of saving face, opening the Bible app rather than your favorite social media, hanging out with a lonely freshman instead of your bros, or giving to missions rather than buying more designer clothes. These seemingly small choices will either build strength into your Christian foundation...or add up to a life not really grounded in Christ at all.

There are no shortcuts to becoming the person the Lord is calling you to be. God may have put a big dream in your heart to live for His story and help advance His kingdom. But the Father's first concern is developing *you* into the kind of person He can use. Faithfulness in the "little things" of life develops the kind of unshakeable convictions you will need for a life of incredible impact. Building a life God can use happens one day at a time and one decision at a time. Are you faithful in the small things? Do you want God or others to give you big responsibilities? Start with the ones you've got and complete them all with integrity and excellence.

Are you faithful in the tough times? King David challenges us to follow through on our commitments in Psalm 15:4, in which he describes a godly man as someone who "swears to his own hurt and does not change." Keeping your word even when it costs you will prove just how reliable and credible you really are. "Many a man proclaims his own steadfast love, but a faithful man who can find?" is a sad testament from Proverbs 20:6 (ESV) that faithfulness is in short supply. Make a decision right now to allow God to build strong and abiding beams of faithfulness into the invisible, below-the-surface depths of your character, enabling you to spend a lifetime being faithful in little things and suffering alike.

→ HUMBLE YOURSELF

As a cocky young freshman, I (Steve) was walking along one cold day with the senior who was discipling me. Impressed by how many students I was influencing, I subtly boasted, "I'm really struggling with pride." He stopped, looked at me, and said, "What do *you* have to be proud about?" Having my arrogance totally exposed, I stuttered and stammered, "I...I...I guess, nothing?" Some people say pride is the opposite of humility, but I believe being humble is not thinking *less* of yourself, it's not thinking of yourself *at all*! Focusing on giving God glory, rather than trying to steal it for ourselves, is the key according to Isaiah 42:8: "I am the Lord, that is My name; I will not give My glory to another" (NASB).

> "For by the grace given to me I say to everyone among you not to think of himself more highly than he ought to think, but to think with sober judgment, each according to the measure of faith that God has assigned."
>
> —ROMANS 12:3, ESV

I (Paul) have noticed students in our ministry face three main challenges as they grow into a laborer. It starts with overcoming a lack of *vision*. Most students don't come into college with a strong vision for what God can do in their lives. They need to be taught and inspired to live for a cause bigger than themselves. The next hurdle is a lack of *discipline*. It's one thing to know what habits you need to develop, but it's another to build those habits into your life on a consistent basis. Once someone gains a strong vision and starts to get traction in their spiritual disciplines, the new struggle is often a lack of *humility*. It can be easy at this point to start "believing your own press" as others tell you how godly you are and what a great leader you are becoming.

The marks of pride are like bad body odor—evident to everyone except ourselves. Pride reeks! It raises its ugly head in the forms of defensiveness, prayerlessness, comparison, and unteachability. Here is a question to check your arrogance levels. In what ways are you tempted to cut corners? I had seasons as a student leader where I thought, "Yeah, having a daily quiet time is essential for those cute little new believers, but I am on to bigger and better things." What I didn't understand is that you *never* move on from the basics. I don't care how many conferences you attend or commentaries you own, there will always be a stark difference between reading books *about* God and spending time *with* God. Let me warn you: as you grow to lead others, be careful to keep living out the basics of following Christ yourself. You never outgrow that!

We need to ask ourselves this question: Can I follow well? The reason Jesus was the greatest leader of all time was because He was the greatest follower of all time and "only did the things He saw and heard from the Father." If the Son of God felt the need to humble Himself to spiritual authority, how much more should we? You'll never become a great leader until you learn how to be a great follower. A humble person is willing to learn from the ministry and leaders God has provided for them, no matter how imperfect those leaders may be. Become a humble, teachable disciple. If you don't have someone discipling you (helping you grow spiritually), pray about who you could ask to encourage, disciple, and, yes, even rebuke you when necessary. Rarely have I met anyone who was discipling others who hadn't themselves first been discipled.

→ LEARN TO SERVE

Missouri's Kanakuk Kamp has become one of the largest summer camps in the world, and I (Steve) had the privilege of being their head counselor for the two summers following my graduation from college. Even though I had previously been a counselor there and knew all the ropes, coming back to lead their staff of big, strong varsity athletes from campuses around the country was quite intimidating. This small, pudgy, fair-skinned 23-year-old (whose claim to fame was second place in intramural ping-pong) was now called upon to be the visionary leader for huge linebackers, wrestlers, and triathletes. Instead of trying to "fake it 'til I made it," I chose a different route, modeled by the leaders of the camp, father and son Spike and Joe White.

They called it servant leadership, where the organizational chart was turned upside down and the objective was to care for and serve the people who report to them instead of the other way around. I learned the only way I could ever lead or influence these superstar counselors was to lovingly pray for and serve them. I wrote down four words on a card and put it by my bed so I could be reminded of my priorities every morning: pray, serve, love, and build. Getting up at 5:20 a.m. and interceding for each counselor prepared me to spend the day encouraging and caring for them, always on the lookout for personal and spiritual needs I could meet. At first, I sensed some resistance toward me, but by midsummer the unity, mutual respect, and presence of the Lord was stronger than I'd ever felt. Because I chose to pray and serve versus acting like the big shot, their hearts were softened to my leadership. They became very teachable and receptive toward me as I sought to build into them a heart for God, for making disciples, and reaching the *whole* world with the gospel.

> "We are settling for a Christianity that revolves around catering to ourselves when the central message of Christianity is actually about abandoning ourselves."
>
> —DAVID PLATT

In a much greater way, Jesus came to the earth not "to be served, but to serve" (Mark 10:45). If the Son of God humbled Himself to put others' needs ahead of His own, how much more should we? He illustrated in living color the path to greatness is not up, but down. I believe if Jesus were asked to give a one-word definition of a leader, He would simply say "servant." Embracing the attitude of a humble servant will protect you against pride when God starts to ignite your campus for Christ. Jesus addressed this issue in Luke 17:10: "So you too, when you do all the things which are commanded you, say, 'We are unworthy slaves; we have done only that which we ought to have done'" (NASB). Humble obedience. Nothing more. Nothing less.

What if you made the decision now to spend your life serving others rather than being served? What if you began to define success by how well the people around you are doing rather than how well you are doing? The question remains: who will look out for "Number One" if you are spending all your time trying to help those around you maximize their potential for God? Humanly speaking, it feels backwards, but if you will spend your life getting excited about making *other* people successful, I predict you will end up being one of the most "successful" people on the planet!

→ PURSUE WISDOM

"A wise person is hungry for knowledge, while the fool feeds on trash" (Proverbs 15:14, NLT). So much of what we encounter in this world is garbage. We must learn to turn from the destruction and, instead, hunger for the mind of Christ. The problem is that pursuing wisdom is not the easy option. It doesn't come from mindlessly scrolling through your newsfeed, reading the worldly posts of celebrities, or keeping track of all the sporting events. God wants to give us real wisdom—*His* wisdom—but we have to intentionally pray for and work towards gaining it.

Here is a truth you need to embrace. You don't know what you need to know to live the life God has called you to live. I am not talking about head knowledge; I am talking about a deep understanding of God and how life really works. Wisdom is much deeper than mere intelligence. The book of Proverbs was written to encourage people to pursue wisdom. Let's check out Solomon's introduction:

"These are the proverbs of Solomon, David's son, king of Israel. Their purpose is to teach people wisdom and discipline, to help them understand the insights of the wise. Their purpose is to teach people to live disciplined and successful lives, to help them do what is right, just, and fair. These proverbs will give insight to the simple, knowledge and discernment to the young. Let the wise listen to these proverbs and become even wiser. Let those with understanding receive guidance by exploring the meaning in these proverbs and parables, the words of the wise and their riddles. Fear of the Lord is the foundation of true knowledge, but fools despise wisdom and discipline." —Proverbs 1:1-7

The book of Proverbs gives knowledge and discernment to the young. If you are a college student, you definitely fit in this category. There is a built-in disadvantage to being young; you have simply not lived long enough to even know what questions you should be asking. Have you ever heard the phrase "wise beyond your years?" There is a reason people take note of that—because it is rare. Wisdom doesn't necessarily come with age though. Just because someone is older doesn't automatically make them wiser. People who don't make the intentional decision to follow God and pursue wisdom often run increasingly harder and faster down the foolish pathways they have chosen. College is the perfect time to get a jump start on gaining wisdom. Let me challenge you to constantly be filling your mind with great audio resources like the audio Bible, sermon podcasts, or an audiobook while you are walking to class or working out. Use the time other people waste to grow in wisdom.

"Buy the truth and do not sell it—wisdom, instruction and insight as well" (Proverbs 23:23, NIV). Growing in wisdom doesn't happen by passively pursuing it; you must go out of your way to get it. "My child, listen to what I say, and treasure my commands. Tune your ears to wisdom, and concentrate on understanding. Cry out for insight, and ask for understanding. Search for them as you would for silver; seek them like hidden treasures. Then you will understand what it means to fear the Lord, and you will gain knowledge of God" (Proverbs 2:1-5, NLT).

Four principles gleaned from this passage are:

- "Treasure My commands." If you find something worth learning, it is worth remembering. Always be taking notes and capturing what God is teaching you.
- "Tune your ears to wisdom." Have your ears dialed into the frequency of wisdom. If there is biblical insight or a life lesson to be gained from a person or situation, make sure to take hold of it. Be on the lookout for opportunities to learn and grow.
- "Cry out for insight, and ask for understanding." The first person we should be asking for wisdom is God. "If any of you lacks wisdom, you should ask God, who gives generously to all without finding fault, and it will be given to you" (James 1:5, NIV). If you ask God for wisdom,

He promises to give it to you. Why don't you stop and ask Him right now to help you pursue wisdom in your life?

- "Search for them as you would for silver; seek them like hidden treasures." I know very few people who I would say truly obey this verse. Can you imagine the intensity of searching this verse is calling for? Once you start to experience the fruit of wisdom in your life, you will understand why someone would want to pursue it with such fervency. "Then you will understand what is right, just, and fair, and you will find the right way to go. For wisdom will enter your heart, and knowledge will fill you with joy. Wise choices will watch over you. Understanding will keep you safe" (Proverbs 2:9-1, NLT).

> "Teachability is the only shortcut
> to success in life."
> —HAROLD BULLOCK

Becoming firmly grounded in Christ will require you to be "aggressively teachable." A person seeking this level of teachability becomes an expert at asking good questions. Some of the most life-changing advice I (Paul) have gotten over the years has come from simply asking advice of wise people. My counsel to you is this: if you have a mentor or someone discipling you, always come to your time together with at least one question. It's a habit you can develop over time. Great questions usually get great answers. Whenever I go to a conference to speak or learn, I try to write out a list of questions I can ask wise people I might run into. I intentionally set up times with key leaders to make sure I have maximum opportunity to learn and grow from their experience and insight. Often those unofficial conversations have a deeper impact on my life than the conference itself. Jesus was a master at asking questions. We can be, too!

→ DEVELOP DISCIPLINE

"The lazy person craves, yet receives nothing, but the desires of the diligent are satisfied" (Proverbs 13:4, ISV). We all know being lazy is bad, but it feels so good. It is much easier to binge-watch a show than it is to review your Scripture memory verses. Here is a sad reality: most people have comfort and convenience as one of their main goals in life. We would never say it out loud, but our actions show this is our heart. "For, as I have often told you before and now tell you again even with tears, many live as enemies of the cross of Christ. Their destiny is destruction, their god is their stomach, and their glory is in their shame. Their mind is set on earthly things" (Philippians 3:18-19, NIV). Most people live with "their god as their stomach," meaning they are driven by their emotions and physical desires. Yet Jesus promised following Him would require saying no to what we want: "If anyone would come after me, let him deny himself and take up his cross daily and follow me" (Luke 9:23, ESV). When many were leaving Jesus because His sayings were too hard, He turned to His disciples one day and asked, "Would you like to leave too?" It is purely a volunteer army Jesus is creating. But if you want to follow Him...it will cost you everything.

Many students feel like they are overwhelmed by too many responsibilities to also have a vibrant walk with Christ and develop a personal ministry on campus. I do remember trying to juggle classes, studying, having a part-time job, and being active in our ministry on campus. I remember pulling the "all-nighters," studying for tests and wondering how in the world was I going to be able to balance it all. But believe it or not, as life moves forward after college, it gets even more complicated. The stress of having to prioritize and manage time is simply one of the realities of life. The good news is that effectively organizing and utilizing your time is a skill you can grow in, and taking steps in this area now can increase your capacity in college and benefit you for a lifetime.

> "Sow a thought, reap an action; sow an
> action, reap a habit; sow a habit, reap a
> character; sow a character, reap a destiny."
> —STEPHEN COVEY

Becoming the person God wants you to become will require you to embrace discipline in your life. Fight to develop the daily habits that will build the life the Lord wants you to live. Your life is actually the sum total of your habits. Change your habits, and you will change your life. Paul admonished young Timothy: "Have nothing to do with irreverent, silly myths.

Rather train yourself for godliness; for while bodily training is of some value, godliness is of value in every way, as it holds promise for the present life and also for the life to come" (1 Timothy 4:7-8). Anyone who works out understands that in order to get stronger you must consistently exercise your muscles to the breaking point, regularly pushing yourself beyond where you've been before.

A few years ago, I (Paul) was watching the Olympics and was becoming quite the fanboy of Michael Phelps as he won his 7 gold medals in swimming. The TV network did a special that described Michael's training regimen. All he did was eat, sleep, and swim. They showed the insane amounts of food he would consume each day, constantly "carbing up" for his next workout. And whenever he was not in the gym lifting weights or swimming, he was resting. Every aspect of his life totally revolved around winning those gold medals.

As I watched, I sensed one of the most clear times I have ever experienced of God speaking to me. A verse of Scripture I was memorizing flashed through my mind: "Everyone who competes in the games goes into strict training. They do it to get a crown that will not last, but we do it to get a crown that will last forever. Therefore I do not run like a man running aimlessly; I do not fight like a man beating the air. No, I beat my body and make it my slave so that after I have preached to others, I myself will not be disqualified for the prize" (1 Corinthians 9:25-28, NIV).

It was as if in that moment the Lord was saying: "I want to see you pursue Me with the same passion and dedication Michael Phelps has for winning gold medals." This may sound extreme, but I believe that is the logical implication of this passage. What would happen if followers of Christ had the same level of commitment to spiritual disciplines that Olympic athletes have to their workout goals and routines? What we are living for is far more important than Olympic gold medals. Very few even remember who won medals in the last Olympics, but a life of obedience before God will be a legacy that lasts for eternity. It starts with saying "yes" to Jesus day by day, hour by hour, moment by moment—and doing whatever it takes to get the basic spiritual disciplines into your life.

> "Successful people do consistently
> what others do occasionally."
>
> —CRAIG GROESCHEL

Pursuing spiritual disciplines doesn't earn God's favor. "He saved us, not because of righteous things we had done, but because of His mercy. He saved us through the washing of rebirth and renewal by the Holy Spirit" (Titus 3:5). God doesn't love you more if you had your quiet time today. Spiritual discipline is not about checking off boxes but about connecting with the Lord. We want to get to know the God who saved us. We want to experience the love and grace only He can give—and in turn be able to pass that on to others.

Before we move into the *Flame* section of the book, which focuses on your outreach and ministry to others, we want to ask you to first ignite the *Fuel* in your life. Radical, total abandonment to obey Jesus in all things is the spark God uses to set us on fire for Him. I've found no better way to do that than to continually pray a prayer that Luther Wishard prayed soon after graduating from Princeton College in 1878. He had heard about the Haystack Prayer Meeting that had taken place at Williams College, Massachusetts in 1806, and he wanted to go back to its exact location to consecrate his life to God. Kneeling in the snow, he prayed, "Lord, I am willing to go anywhere at any time to do anything for Jesus."

How about you? No need to travel to Massachusetts or kneel down in the snow, but in your heart of hearts, can you look up to the Lord and not hold anything back from Him? Lay everything on the table and go "all in." No reserves. No retreats. No regrets. If so, God will use you mightily to start and fan a bright flame for Jesus Christ on your campus that will spread across the nations.

> "Lord, I am willing to go anywhere...
> at any time...to do anything for Jesus."

REFLECTION   QUESTIONS :

→ Luke 16:10 teaches that before God will entrust us with bigger
things, He wants us to be faithful with the smaller ones. What
has the Lord entrusted to you right now that you can seek to be
completely faithful to?

→ Why is a servant's attitude one of the greatest qualities any
leader can have? How can you grow in your servanthood?

→ Being teachable is one of the main ways to stay humble and
gain true wisdom. How do you respond when others correct or
confront you with something?

→ Which spiritual disciplines would you like to grow in and what is
your plan to do so?

the
FLAME

Show and Tell:
Everyday Evangelism

12

Who Cares?

During my sophomore year, I (Steve) befriended a young pledge from Louisiana named Mike. He was a handsome, wealthy, fun-loving partier, like a number of my fraternity brothers. Mike and I spent many nights on the roof of our chapter house talking about our lives, our dreams...and his soul. He knew he wasn't a Christian, but he came to understand *exactly* what he must do to become one. He even promised me one night that when he did come to Christ, I would be the first to know. Never in my life had I been more burdened by God to intercede for someone's salvation. I would spend over an hour in prayer many late nights just crying out to God on Mike's behalf, so absolutely sure the Lord was going to redeem his life.

One afternoon there arose a great commotion in the fraternity house, including one guy running through the hallways and screaming at the top of his lungs. I opened my door as he sprinted past yelling, "Mike has been killed in a car wreck out by the lake!" Horrified, I bolted out of my room and grabbed the first guy I found to verify if it was really true. When he shook his head yes, I staggered to my knees and sobbed. I could not believe it. No way could this have really happened. The Lord had promised me! In total denial, I couldn't speak, eat, or concentrate on anything for days. Instead of sleeping, I wandered around the campus in a daze for three straight nights, hurling deep, heartfelt accusations at God.

At the end of my rope one morning, I heard a knock, and a fraternity brother who had never darkened my door walked in. With a bowed head and tear-filled eyes, he shared with me a side of the story no one else had heard. He and Mike had been at the lake and were about to smoke marijuana when a local youth minister walked up and engaged them in a spiritual conversation. Mike became so convicted of his empty life and sordid heart that he prayed to receive Christ right there on the beach. Once he made his decision, he got up, threw his bag of weed in the water, and turned, saying, "Let's get back to the house. I've got to tell Shad." As they were driving back up a steep mountain road, a speeding car rounded the curve in Mike's lane. He had to make an instantaneous decision between whether to hit the car head on and risk killing *everyone,* or sacrifice his own life by turning his vehicle to the right (and off the side of the cliff). He chose the latter and every other person in the accident walked away—except Mike, who was crushed by the weight of his car.

The moment I heard him repeat Mike's words, "I've got to tell Shad," I immediately envisioned my friend in heaven with the Lord with a huge smile splashed across his face. He was saved! Mike was with Jesus and waiting for me to join him for an eternity spent in praise of the Savior. God had kept His promise to me but waited three days to confirm it. From that point on, I determined *never* to give up on anyone, believing that God can answer our petitions.

→ THE BIG BAD "E" WORD

> "And He said to them, 'Go into all
> the world and proclaim the gospel
> to the whole creation.'"
>
> **—MARK 16:15, ESV**

The "E" word—evangelism—is a scary one for a lot of people, Christians and non-Christians alike. We'd much rather use a softer, less threatening word like "share." I have nothing against terms like this, unless we are using them to relieve us of our responsibility to win people to Christ. As scary as evangelism sounds, it is an essential beginning point for any person who wants to join God in His mission to bring worshippers from every nation to His throne. Reaching the world starts with introducing people who don't know about Christ to the good news and joining God as He rescues people from death to life in Him!

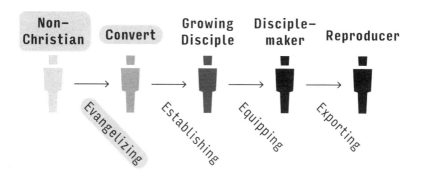

Webster's definition of *evangelize* is "to preach the gospel to; to convert to Christianity." Is it wrong to have your goal be to win others to Christ? I have had people accuse me, saying, "You don't really care about that guy. You're inviting him over for dinner and basketball *just* so you can lead him to Christ." My answer? "Exactly!" And for the charge of not caring, I beg to differ. If love is meeting other people's needs, and the essential need everyone has is to establish a personal relationship with their Maker and Savior, then the greatest act of love I could ever show anyone is to give them an opportunity to start that relationship. In fact, do I *really* love someone if I don't care about the condition and destination of their soul?

> "You have nothing to do but to save souls.
> Therefore spend and be spent in this work."
>
> **—JOHN WESLEY**

Some of you may remember someone initiating with you in the cafeteria or in your dorm room and asking you what your spiritual background was. They may have drawn a diagram on a napkin or asked you a question like, "How sure are you that you would go to heaven if you died?" Initially you may have been caught off guard, but aren't you thankful Christ pursued you through someone who cared enough to broach the subject and maybe risk the relationship? This is where evangelism begins. There must be caring people, moved by the Holy Spirit towards lost people who need Jesus. One simple but helpful way to describe the work of evangelism is this: sharing the truth of the gospel with a non-believer.

True evangelism always includes a clear presentation of the gospel (1 Corinthians 15:3-4; 2 Corinthians 5:21; Romans 3:19-26). We must explain that we have rebelled against our perfectly holy Creator and are deserving of only punishment, but instead of giving us what we deserve, He has provided a way of escape. He sent His Son to pay the penalty for our sin and has offered us Christ's perfect righteousness if we trust in His sacrifice on the cross and turn our lives over to Him in repentance. Sharing these basic truths with another person is evangelism. Real evangelism doesn't only happen when someone comes to Christ. We are not responsible for their response; our sovereign God is. Our task is to faithfully present the good news of the gospel with our lips and our lives, and leave the results to the Lord.

Wearing Christian T-shirts and bracelets or asking people how you can pray for them might be helpful in displaying the gospel, but they can't replace evangelism, nor are they necessary for evangelism. When Christians discuss evangelism, a popular quote often comes up: "Preach the gospel at all times. Use words if necessary." Doesn't that sound cool? The problem is that it's not biblical, or even logical. It's like saying, "Feed the hungry. If necessary, use food." Living a holy life will bring credibility to your words, but it is not a substitute for actually talking with someone about the gospel. The Bible says the gospel is a message to be *verbally* proclaimed and understood. Romans 10:14 is one of many examples of this: "How, then, can they call on the one they have not believed in? And how can they believe in the one of whom they have not heard? And how can they *hear* without someone *preaching* to them?" (NIV, emphasis added). The apostle Paul, Peter, and even Jesus Himself all used *words* to explain the good news. They boldly loved people with their deeds...and words!

→ CHRIST'S LOVE COMPELS US

"For Christ's love compels us, because we are convinced that one died for all, and therefore all died. And he died for all, that those who live should no longer live for themselves but for him who died for them and was raised again."

—2 CORINTHIANS 5:14-15

Any kind of gospel sharing needs to be gospel-motivated. We should be so astonished at the grace and forgiveness shown to us in Christ that the gratitude we feel spontaneously overflows in telling other people about it. We should want to share with people because we know that when the good news is shared, God is glorified. When we tell the story of what He has done to reconcile the world to Himself, His magnificent love and mercy are proclaimed, and more people come to worship Him.

> "Every saved person this side of heaven owes the gospel to every lost person this side of hell."
>
> —DAVID PLATT

The Great Commission should flow out of the Great Commandment, in which our love for others comes from our love for God. The other driving motive in evangelism that directs us towards the lost world (even when we don't want to go) is compassion. When we share the gospel, not only is God glorified but people who don't know Christ have the opportunity to cross from death to life by accepting the salvation Jesus offers. Delivering that message of hope is the greatest gift you can ever give someone.

> "For God so loved the world that he gave his one and only Son, that whoever believes in him shall not perish but have eternal life. For God did not send his Son into the world to condemn the world, but to save the world through him. Whoever believes in him is not condemned, but whoever does not believe stands condemned already because they have not believed in the name of God's one and only Son."
>
> —JOHN 3:16-18

God gave His only Son as a sacrifice so that He could offer life to people all over the world. When I read that second part of verse 18—"whoever does not believe stands condemned already because they have not believed in the name of God's one and only Son"—I can't help but think about my friends and family who don't have a relationship with Christ, as well as the people worldwide who don't even know someone who could tell them about Jesus. This passage and many others clearly teach that unless someone turns from sin and trusts in Jesus Christ, they will spend forever separated from God. Jesus clearly stated, "I am the way and the truth and the life. No one comes to the Father except through me" (John 14:6).

→ DOES IT BOTHER YOU?

Does it bother you enough to do something about it? It bothered Jesus enough to come down off His throne in heaven to become a man, live the perfect life, die on a cross, and take your sin and mine. Stop for a moment. This is a critical fork in the road. Do you really and truly believe Jesus is the *only* way to forgiveness and eternal life? You may say this is true, you may have read it in your Bible, and you may even answer correctly on a theology test, but do you *truly* believe this is real? If you do, then you know this truth *must* be shared with every person on the planet.

However, if you have bought into the culturally popular belief that there are many paths to God and everyone is free to choose the way that seems best to them, then I ask you to consider something. Why would Jesus, God's own Son, come to earth for 33 years, submit to a shameful, excruciating death, and then be resurrected...if there were *any* other way? God made the ultimate sacrifice because it was *required* to bridge the gap that sin creates between mankind and Himself. There was no other way. "Salvation is found in no one else, for there is no other name under heaven given to mankind by which we must be saved" (Acts 4:12). Let me be painfully honest, my friend: if you don't fully embrace this eternal and universal truth, there really is no need to continue reading this book.

Every ten seconds, 23 people die on our planet; 19 of them into a Christless eternity. Think about the thousands of students on your campus. If nothing changes, many of them are destined for a life of slavery to their sin and an eternity separated from God. No one cares more about those apart from Christ than the Father does. This is God's mission: to see people from every nation without Jesus come to know Him. When you align yourself with this mission to rescue people from their own sin and eternal destruction, you line yourself up with the very agenda of God. If we believe people apart from Christ are in need of rescue from sin and death, we need to *care* enough to *share*. Compassion must push us to overcome the potential awkwardness of talking about spiritual things because we care so much about our friends. Compassion must push us to cross cultural barriers, learn new languages, and go where the name of Jesus has never been spoken.

It is impossible to exaggerate the urgency of eternity. No effort we make to share Christ with lost people is overkill. Charles Spurgeon put it this way: "If there existed only one man or woman who did not love the Savior, and if that person lived among the wilds of Siberia, and if it were necessary that all the millions of believers on the face of the earth should journey there, and every one of them plead with him to come to Jesus before he could be converted, it would be well worth all the zeal, labor, and expense. If we had to preach to thousands year after year, and never rescued but one soul, that one soul would be full reward for all our labor, for a soul is of countless price."

→ "BUT WHAT IF...?"

What if they get offended?

We have to get to the place in our walk with God that our *love* for people trumps our *fear* of people. I admire the attitude the Apostle Paul had in evangelism and discipleship. In Acts 20:20 he says, "You know that I have not hesitated to preach anything that would be helpful to you but have taught you publicly and from house to house." If the truth could be helpful, Paul didn't hesitate to share it. His reason for being bold to share the truth was love. If love is your motive, people will sense that. I have found that most people are open to talking about spiritual things. Who do you know whose life could be helped by a relationship with the all-loving, all-powerful God? Just break the ice, lovingly steer the conversation towards spiritual things, and see what God wants to do. Yes, it may be awkward, but awkward conversations change lives. There are hundreds of people on your campus who are just one awkward conversation away from coming to Christ. Take the risk!

What if I share too soon and scare them off?

In Acts 4:20, Peter and John proclaim, "As for us, we cannot help speaking about what we have seen and heard." When you see a good movie, what do you do? You tell your friends about it. When you go on a date, you tell your friends about it. People talk about what's important to them. So if Jesus is really the most important thing to you, it should be natural to bring Him up. Even in the "getting to know you" phase of a friendship, sharing the story of how you came into a relationship with Christ and your commitment to walking with Him makes sense. Wouldn't it be more uncomfortable and even suspicious to avoid talking about the most important Person in your life for months and then springing it on your non-Christian friends later that Jesus is your everything?

What if they have already heard the gospel?

A lie you may believe is that most people around you have already heard the gospel. That's simply not true. You can go to almost any college campus in the world right now and find thousands of students who couldn't repeat the gospel to you to save their soul. That is literally what is at stake! People all around you have little to no true understanding of the gospel. I have shared with hundreds of students, and it's rare to find a college student, even a "Christian" student, who understands the gospel fully. Most people can't comprehend that salvation is a *free* gift from God and not something they can or must earn by being good. "For it is by grace you have been saved, through faith—and this is not from yourselves, it is the gift of God—not by works, so that no one can boast" (Ephesians 2:8-9).

One study shows the average person needs to hear the gospel seven times before they give their lives to Christ. You don't know if you are the first time or the seventh time someone has heard the good news, but you can play a part. Don't prejudge that someone is not interested in knowing Christ. The only way to find out if someone is interested is to ask them. No matter who I run into, my first step in helping them grow is to share how Jesus' death paid the price for their sins and that faith in Him is the way to abundant and eternal life. If they are breathing, they need Jesus. If they already have a relationship with Jesus, they won't be offended that I share the need for *everyone* to have that relationship. Hopefully, they will appreciate someone loving them enough to share truth with them and be challenged to be bold themselves.

→ BOLDNESS REQUIRED

Jesus promised when He gave us the Spirit that we would be His witnesses. "But you will receive power when the Holy Spirit comes on you; and you will be my witnesses in Jerusalem, and in all Judea and Samaria, and to the ends of the earth" (Acts 1:8). Boldness as His witnesses is a character quality rarely emphasised in churches today, but it was a high value to Jesus and the early church. When they were threatened with prison and death for sharing the gospel, they didn't even pray for protection, but for boldness. "Now, Lord, consider their threats and enable your servants to speak your Word with great boldness" (Acts 4:29). What if the greatest need in our generation is not new *methods* for sharing Christ, but new *boldness* to proclaim Christ?

A mark of every faithful follower of Christ should be a willingness to stand strong in their witness. It is actually the only logical response to the gospel message. "Therefore since we have such a hope, we are very bold" (2 Corinthians 3:12). What do you think would happen if students came together on your campus to confess their fears to one another and pray for boldness to share Christ? Does that sound like an army of laborers God would put to work bringing in His harvest? Remember, Jesus said the harvest is plentiful (Matthew 9:36-38). The problem is not the lack of spiritually interested people, but of laborers who will take the initiative to reach out to others with the gospel. The harvest is ready. God has prepared them. They are waiting for us to be bold enough to bring them the truth. Will you care enough to share?

→ EMILY'S STORY

"Before coming to the University of Idaho, I had only set foot in a church for my cousin's wedding. I was intrigued by God and wanted to go to church, but I wasn't about to walk into one on my own. All my life I didn't believe God even existed, so I couldn't fathom changing my mind. I didn't believe in an afterlife, so all I could hope for was to be good in this one."

"I came to college waiting. Waiting for someone to invite me to church so I could finally explore this thing that had been drawing me in for 18 years. It took only a week to get an invite, and I happily accepted. I found myself going every Sunday for the next few months, listening intently but asking zero questions. My know-it-all and people-pleasing tendencies worked against me, creating the illusion I understood everything that was being talked about. Eventually someone finally asked me if I had ever heard the gospel. I promptly replied, 'Well, I've heard the Word.' He explained to me that God created the world perfectly, but we messed it up; that's why He sent His only Son into the world to take the punishment we deserved. I looked him in the eye, pointed to the book we had been studying, and said, 'How can you believe that and still care anything about math? What we're doing here at college seems so unimportant compared to that.' I wasn't totally ready to accept Christ yet, but that night I admitted to myself that I 'possibly' believed in God."

"Later on, a girl I met at church named Taylor invited me for coffee and shared with me her story of believing in Jesus. As we sat in that coffee shop, I found myself once again waiting. Waiting this time, for someone to ask me if this was what I wanted—to give my life to Jesus and put Him in His rightful place as Lord and Savior of my life. Instead, sweet Taylor just asked me to think of any questions I had and to get coffee with her and another friend the next day. Just 24 hours later, I showed up to a new coffee shop and heard the gospel once again, this time from Cara. She was the one to *finally* ask me the question I had been waiting to hear all along: 'Is this what you want, Emily? Do you want to follow Jesus?' Those two questions were, at that point, the easiest questions I have ever had to answer."

"I accepted Jesus Christ into my life on the second floor of a downtown coffee shop and immediately went back to my dorm and told all my friends what had just happened. They were baffled, confused, yet supportive of me because of how excited they could tell I was. I shared the gospel with them for the very first time—within thirty minutes of making the decision to follow Jesus myself! It's all I'd ever known."

"I have now been a Christ-follower for five years. I work full time for that same church at the same university and will move with one of our church plants to another university town this summer. On the days when it doesn't seem worth it to go on campus again—to continually befriend new students, to share the gospel with them, to risk being rejected—I remind myself that there are others out there like me. Many students on our campuses are waiting, just waiting, to have their eternities changed."

R E F L E C T I O N   Q U E S T I O N S :

→ Of all the world's religions, do you believe there is only *one* way to God, heaven, and salvation and that is exclusively through Jesus Christ—and Him alone? Why or why not?

→ What is "the gospel" and how would you explain it to someone else in a clear and compelling way?

→ Have you ever presented the gospel to another person and gave them the opportunity to believe and receive Christ into their life? Share how that went.

→ Do you care enough about your family and friends to share the gospel with them? If so, who will you start with this week?

13

Open Doors Everywhere

When I (Paul) started to grasp the urgency of our need to share the gospel, I began attempting to share Christ, but only sporadically. I would read a book like this, get all fired up, and go share with a bunch of people. But eventually my zeal would fizzle out. I used to think evangelism was primarily something you "go do." I planned times of going out on campus to strike up gospel conversations with others, and even organized group events for the purpose of sharing Jesus with those who came. These are great activities, but what I discovered is that God wanted me to primarily share Christ "as I go." Evangelism is more of a lifestyle than an event.

We all have opportunities in our daily lives to present the gospel, but we must have discernment, courage, and discipline to take advantage of them. A lot of people think spiritual disciplines such as prayer and Bible reading should be daily habits you fight for but feel you should just "follow where the Spirit leads" when it comes to evangelism. Being guided by the Spirit and being intentional are not at odds with one another! Everything God calls us to do must be done intentionally. Often the Spirit is the one leading us to be disciplined and to make definite plans. Donald Whitney, in his excellent book *Spiritual Disciplines for the Christian Life,* says: "I am convinced the main reason many of us don't witness for Christ in ways that would be effective and relatively fear-free is simply because we don't discipline ourselves to do it."

→ THREE HABITS FOR EVERYDAY EVANGELISM

"Devote yourselves to prayer, being watchful
and thankful. And pray for us, too, that God
may open a door for our message, so that we
may proclaim the mystery of Christ, for which
I am in chains. Pray that I may proclaim it
clearly, as I should. Be wise in the way
you act toward outsiders; make the most of
every opportunity. Let your conversation be
always full of grace, seasoned with salt, so
that you may know how to answer everyone."

—COLOSSIANS 4:2-6

Your most fruitful efforts in sharing the gospel will probably be with those you already know, who are in your relational network and sphere of influence. Still, God wants to use you *wherever* you go with *whoever* you meet. These three habits for everyday evangelism, inspired by Colossians 4:2-6, will help prepare you. Discipline yourself to make these habits a part of your life, and watch the fires God will ignite all around you!

Habit #1: Pray Daily for Open Doors and Boldly Seize Opportunities

The first habit I see in this Colossians 4 passage is simple and life-changing—devote yourself to prayer, and ask God to open doors for the message. In his equipping guide *Operation Multiplication*, Billie Hanks Jr. says: "After extended observation, we have concluded that effective, lifestyle evangelism happens when a Christian specifically prays each morning, asking for opportunities to witness. Do you know why Christians aren't leading more people to the Savior? We aren't asking daily for opportunities to share our faith."

How would it change the way you go through your day if you were on the lookout for opportunities to share your testimony and the gospel? God may provide opportunities for you to "randomly" share with someone you just met, or He may open a door to a spiritual conversation with a friend. And really, there is nothing "random" about random evangelism. God is always at work in far more ways than we can imagine. In a way, evangelism is like a divine Easter egg hunt. God is already at work in people's lives, and we get the privilege of finding the "prepared ones" and helping them take their next step! "Sow your seed in the morning, and at evening let your hands not be idle, for you do not know which will succeed, whether this or that, or whether both will do equally well" (Ecclesiastes 11:6). You don't know which seed is going to sprout, but you can trust in the Lord to use your faithfulness to do what He wants in the lives of people.

Speaking of egg hunts, here's an example of God leading someone to evangelize in an unconventional way. A University of Georgia student named Garrett had recently come to understand Jesus' love for him and had a passion to share it with others. He took the opportunity at Easter to give out candy-filled eggs with a symbolic meaning to his class of several hundred students. It might seem cheesy to some, but this bold freshman then asked his professor if he could stand and share the meaning of the eggs with the class. He said yes! After he shared, a football player who was in the class approached Garrett with some questions, and they have started meeting together to explore the Bible.

If you are in the cafeteria, the weight room, or the library, sow the seeds of the gospel broadly and watch the Lord of the harvest work. As you go through each day, try to start casual conversations with people. It's easy to learn how to turn casual conversations into spiritual conversations. A tool to keep in mind is the "F.I.R.E." acrostic:

> **Find common ground:** Use anything you can use to break the ice and relate to the person.
>
> **Interests:** Try to discover what they are passionate about and ask lots of questions about those things.
>
> **Relationships:** Asking questions about their family background and relationships automatically takes the conversation to a deeper level.
>
> **Experience with spiritual things:** Say a quick prayer and ask a spiritual question. It's worth the risk!

Note: We have included a list of questions to make others spiritually hungry on TheFuelAndTheFlame.com. Check them out!

I have found that if I am comfortable bringing up spiritual things, the other person usually will be too. So pray, take a deep breath, and let God work. If you live out this bold lifestyle, you will find a lot more people are open to talking about God than you think. I have learned there is a direct correlation to how many students I share the gospel with and how many come to Christ. The more I share, the more decisions I see! In fact, there are people right now who would receive Christ into their life if we would only ask them to. Jesus addresses our fears and procrastination to witness in John 4:35: "Don't you have a saying, 'It's still four months until harvest'? I tell you, open your eyes and look at the fields! They are ripe for harvest." What Jesus is trying to show us is that there is low-hanging fruit everywhere if we would only ask God to open our eyes (and heart) to the spiritual hunger and receptiveness all around us.

In reality, most of us need to renew our faith that the gospel can actually do its job. The gospel is the *power* of God. Romans 1:16 says, "For I am not ashamed of the gospel, because it is the power of God that brings salvation to everyone who believes: first to the Jew, then to the Gentile."

How do you know if there's an open door? Bill Bright, founder of Cru, said this: "Whenever I am alone with a person for a few minutes, I assume that I am there by divine appointment to share the good news of God's love and forgiveness." Taking advantage of an opportunity doesn't have to be sharing the whole gospel every time. It can be learning someone's name in class, doing something fun with a non-Christian, letting someone know you believe in God, sharing a bit of your testimony, or inviting someone to church. You might even take the initiative to set up an appointment at a later date with a person you meet on campus or at a ministry event to allow for a designated time to fully explain the gospel message. Pray for opportunities and practice stretching yourself a little further than you would naturally go in initiating with people. Learn to "follow the Spirit... and do something."

Habit #2: Use the "Prayer, Care, Share" Strategy

To be a consistent witness to your friends and those around you, you can learn and appropriate a simple process we call "Prayer, Care, Share." Let's unpack it.

Prayer

Make an "Impact List" of 5-10 people to pray for every day. Ask God to draw them to Himself, provide opportunities for you to share with them, and soften their hearts to receive the gospel. Second Corinthians 10:4 says, "The weapons we fight with are not the weapons of the world. On the contrary, they have divine power to demolish strongholds." Praying is engaging in a spiritual battle for the hearts of people. The Bible teaches that non-Christians are dead, blind enemies of God (Ephesians 2; 2 Corinthians 4:3-4; Romans 5:10). This is who *we* were before Christ came in and gave us new life, took the blinders from our eyes, and reconciled us to Himself (2 Corinthians 5:17; 4:6-7; Romans 5:1).

If the Bible is accurate in these descriptions, then we must admit that although we may be gifted evangelists we are *not* the ones who ever save anyone. We couldn't even save ourselves, so how could we ever think we could save someone else? We say all this to strongly express our desperate need to beg God to draw people to Himself through our evangelism (John 6:44). Prayer warrior and missionary to China, Hudson Taylor, put it like this: "Learn to move man, through God, by prayer alone."

Care

The next thing to do is care for people. Colossians 4:6 says, "Let your conversation be always full of grace, seasoned with salt, so that you may know how to answer everyone." In 1 John 3:18 we are exhorted, "Dear children, let us not love with words or speech but with actions and in truth." Every person you meet is not in your life by coincidence but by a divine appointment ordained by God. You can really help people feel loved by simply initiating with them. Break the uncomfortable silence that happens when you walk past someone in the hallway. Take a genuine interest in your fellow students, remember their names, and look for opportunities to serve them. This means spending time with people, listening to their stories, and hearing about their lives.

If people sense you enjoy being with them, I can promise God will use that to open up their hearts to the message you have for them. You'll be surprised how your fellow students respond when you demonstrate Christlike love for them. Sadly, many of the people you spend time with every day have never experienced someone genuinely caring for them. It's such a beautiful and satisfying experience when you let Jesus love others through you.

Share

You have prayed for God to open their hearts and to give you an opportunity to speak the truth. You have drawn close to them to show them the love of Christ. Now it's time to take (or make) the opportunity to share the gospel with them. Don't be content to stop after the first two steps. While inviting them to church, starting a spiritual conversation, and sharing your testimony are all helpful, your goal is to individually present the gospel to each of the people on your Impact List this semester—and to give them an opportunity to respond. Ask the Lord for courage, and just go for it. I have never regretted being bold about sharing the gospel. God wants to move in people's lives, and He uses our prayers and simple efforts to show His love for them. I am always on the lookout for new people to add to my Impact List to pray for daily and pursue. The greatest joy in life is to watch God change lives right before your eyes. It's inconceivable, but He will use our weak and feeble efforts as a divine intervention to bring salvation and eternal life to your friend. And you get to be the tool in His hand to see it happen!

Josh used to do everything he could to avoid evangelism. Even when his college group from church went out to share together, he would leave conversations because he was so uncomfortable engaging people. He finally repented of his fear and started stepping out to reach others. Within a couple of weeks, he was sharing Christ weekly and inviting friends to his small group. One week he realized that every guest who was attending the group was someone he had met and invited to come!

God wants to use you to help people come to Christ. Most people start out fearful or skeptical of evangelism. If that describes you, ask God to help you walk toward your fears in the power of the Holy Spirit—and then ask someone with evangelism experience to help train you. I remember the first time I shared my faith. I was terrified before sharing, but the joy I felt afterwards was incredible. When we step out to share Christ, the Spirit inside us says, "Yes!" and gives us the help we need. Try it!

Habit #3: Plan Regular Times To Spend with Friends Who Need Jesus

Professor Howard Hendricks used humor and sarcasm in his teaching, like the time he said, "Sadly, it takes most new Christians about three years to eliminate all the non-Christians from their lives." It seems as if the longer that people are

Christians, the fewer non-believing friends they have. Christian students end up living with Christians, sitting with Christians in class, at meals, and at the library, and even praying for a job where their coworkers are all Christians. Their goal each day, after having a morning quiet time of course, is to attempt to scurry through the day, flying from one Christian friend and activity to the next, hoping to make it home that night *unscathed* by the world!

> "A ship in the harbor is safe, but that
> is not what ships are built for."
>
> **—JOHN A. SHEDD**

Jesus made a point to spend time with those who needed God's grace. Matthew 9:11-12 says: "When the Pharisees saw this, they asked his disciples, 'Why does your teacher eat with tax collectors and sinners?' On hearing this, Jesus said, 'It is not the healthy who need a doctor, but the sick.'" When Jesus was praying to the Father for His disciples before He departed, He said in John 17:15, "My prayer is not that you take them out of the world but that you protect them from the evil one." Jesus wanted His followers to engage the culture of *this* world, and one of the biggest felt needs of a college student is friends and a good peer group to belong to. So, what do you like to do for fun? Simply invite non-believers to do that with you. People are hungry for community and unknowingly starving for the gospel.

Let me challenge you to consider trying these three habits I've described for a month and see if God will lead you to more open doors to share your faith. Our student leaders at Chico State have a time each week when they discuss open doors they have and how they are taking advantage of them. They each have an Impact List of people they are praying for and sharing Jesus' love with. Almost every week I hear about one of their friends deciding to follow Christ. These habits are not theory. They're just biblical principles God's people have used all over the world to be more intentional in evangelism. What's stopping you from trying them out? Remember the last sentence of James 4:2: "You do not have because you do not ask God." God loves for us to ask Him (and others) and is waiting to answer our prayers. Start now to ask God to help you start sharing your faith and leading others to Christ. Start now to reach out and care enough about those around you to risk the relationship, in order to share the gospel—the power of God—with them.

REFLECTION QUESTIONS:

→ Do you perceive people around you to be generally open to spiritual things or closed? Read John 4:35 out loud and ask yourself if you really believe what Jesus says.

→ Evaluate your friend groups, daily activities, and your schedule. Are you mainly around Christians all day, every day...or non-Christians? In light of this chapter, what is the right mix for you?

→ Make an "Impact List" of the 5-10 people around you that you want to start praying for and looking for an opportunity to present the gospel to. Who's on it?

→ Who in your church or campus ministry could work with you individually to train you how to share the gospel and lead others to Christ? Will you contact them this week? hels

14

Just Do It

I (Steve) got a call one day from Terry, a younger college student whom I was discipling, who had just led a high school football teammate named Kirk to faith in Christ. Sometimes we try to help a new convert like Kirk break with old habits by taking him to his non-Christian friends to give his testimony. Terry had anticipated my challenge and had already set up a gospel appointment for Kirk to share his story with three former teammates.

I tagged along as a silent assistant so Terry and Kirk could take the lead. It was all Kirk, though, as he dove right into *his* version of the gospel Terry had shown him the day before. Cringing at how badly Kirk was butchering the presentation to these fragile young souls, I could barely contain myself. I resisted the temptation to jump in and save the day since Kirk was on a roll—I just wasn't sure where to! Finishing his sermonette and with incredible intensity, Kirk turned to the first guy and asked, "Well, Sam, what do you say? Would you like to receive Christ into your life?"

After a few awkward moments, Sam looked him right in the eye and said, "Yeah…I would."

Kirk then turned to the next fellow and said, "Lewis, do *you* want to take Christ as your Savior tonight?"

Another couple seconds of silence elapsed before Lewis shot back, "Yep. Me too."

Without missing a beat, Kirk trained his eye on teammate number three: "Tommy, you've heard these decisions, do *you* want to become a Christian also?"

Tommy nervously looked back and forth and finally said, "Sure."

Kirk then led them in a prayer of repentance and salvation, each of them repeating after him.

Bowing my head in prayer, I was in total disbelief. I was beholding the mother of all mess-ups, yet in spite of Kirk's assassination of the high and hallowed gospel message, these guys were giving their hearts to Christ! "How can this be?" I asked myself, only to be riveted right to my core by the Holy Spirit, through Paul's declaration: "When I came to you, brothers, I did not come with eloquence or human wisdom as I proclaimed to you the testimony about God. For I resolved to know nothing while I was with you except Jesus Christ and him crucified. I came to you in weakness with great fear and trembling. My message and my preaching were not with wise and persuasive words, but with a demonstration of the Spirit's power" (1 Corinthians 2:1b–4).

Even though I feel strongly about knowing and presenting the gospel in a clear and concise manner, I had forgotten it is the *power of God* at work, not fancy words or memorized illustrations. That day, I couldn't see the extraordinary boldness and initiative in Terry and Kirk because I was too busy critiquing their presentation. By the way, my cringing must not have discouraged them too much—they (and a number of *their* disciples) have been missionaries in a large, 1.4-billion-person communist country in East Asia for almost forty years now!

→ FILL YOUR TOOLBELT

One of the most common excuses people make for not sharing their faith is "I don't know how." My answer to that is simple—learn how! Sharing your faith is one of the reasons God didn't just "beam you up to heaven" right after you came to Christ. A Christian who says "I don't know how to share my faith" is like a carpenter who says "I don't know how to cut a board." Get help. Seek out training. There are great books, audio messages, and videos out there we recommend, and this book is filled with how-to's. However, the best way to learn to share Christ is what I call "Nike evangelism"—*just do it*! I have come to believe that as long as I am seeking to be obedient and sharing in love, God will use my efforts. Our Lord is way bigger than our imperfections, and His love for people is so massive that He will use us, often despite ourselves. So, let's have some fun and get started!

Would you believe me if I said praying for, meeting and loving people, and sharing the good news of Christ with them is the most enjoyable thing you'll ever do? Yes, it's a little shaky sometimes transitioning into a gospel presentation, but once you're embroiled in discussing the greatest person and message in all of history, you will not want to be *anywhere* else, talking about *anything* else! Learn and practice a gospel presentation, as well as a transition to introduce it. You might smile warmly, look your friend in the eye, and ask a question like:

"Preston, if you could know God in a personal way...would you want to?"

"Ali, how certain are you that you will go to heaven when you die? Would you like to know for sure?"

"Clark, I've got a short illustration here I'd love to show you that explains what the Bible says a Christian is. Mind if I take a few minutes and share it with you?"

"Stephanie, I'm trying to learn how to share my faith. I'm wondering if you would allow me to show you this illustration and get your response?"

"Anna, I'm so glad we are becoming friends. As we're getting to know each other, I want to make sure I tell you about the most important thing in my life. May I share my story with you?"

Isn't it amazing that in the same amount of time it takes you to study for a test, you could learn to use a tool to share the gospel with others for the rest of your life? Whether you read through a booklet, draw out a diagram, share from an app on your phone, or use only the Bible, pick a method that works for you to be able to share the gospel clearly and simply. The power is in the message. Not only do you want the person you are sharing with to understand that Jesus died to pay the penalty for their sins and that life with God comes through trusting in Jesus' sacrifice, but you also want them to feel able to easily pass this good news on to others. If you share the gospel with someone and they walk away with the thought, "That was so simple *even I* could share that with someone else"...congratulations! You just multiplied yourself.

→ TRUST POINTS

My friend Blake loves students. He lived with our family as an undergrad but went on to be the Student Mobilization campus director at Missouri

State. Starting from scratch, God used him to start and grow an amazing multiplying movement there involving hundreds of key students. Impressed with how many students were coming to Christ and getting involved, I started quizzing Blake. "How do you account for so many students making first-time decisions to follow Christ?"

"God does it, but He uses our 'trust points,'" he replied. Asking him to explain, he went on, "Trust is vital in any relationship. Remembering someone's name on campus is a small but important step to build trust. Sitting down with them in the cafeteria, joining them in a workout at the gym, or genuinely listening to them answer your questions about their school, family, and past are all things that add trust points. Them seeing the way you speak to and treat others certainly does as well."

Curious, I asked Blake, "So how many of these 'trust points' do you have to build up with someone before they would actually come to your bible study, or Christmas conference, or be willing to come over for dinner, or welcome you sharing the gospel with them?" He laughed and broke out into his big smile, saying, "Well, Shad, it's different for every student—and it's not like we actually keep a point tally! I just keep reaching out, loving, listening, inviting, and hoping their fears and questions and skepticism about me are answered. I can tell when their heart is softened and a warmth is there, and they become receptive to any invitation I might make to them."

> "We have to build the bridge of relationship
> to bear the weight of the truth."
>
> —PAUL STANLEY, THE NAVIGATORS

When I heard that, combined with the years and years of my observing Blake thoroughly enjoying the students around him, I finally understood. Gaining someone else's trust is a process that takes time, effort, and intentionality—but also a heart full of authentic love. God uses all our various contacts and gestures (i.e. trust points!) with others to open up and soften their minds and hearts, thus creating a beautiful pathway for the gospel right to the core of a person's soul. My story of coming to Christ reflects that very principle. Let me tell you about it.

→ MY PERSONAL TESTIMONY

I (Steve) actually became a Christian during my senior year of high school when Allen, an Athletes in Action staff member, took me out witnessing in an airport. As I read the *Four Spiritual Laws* tract to a teenage boy that Saturday morning, I realized I didn't really have Christ in my life. That afternoon, I bowed my head and, for the first time, transferred full control of my life to Jesus Christ.

Numerous times over the next several weeks, Allen set up appointments for me to meet with many of the other athletes in our high school. As I presented the gospel, just like it had been presented to me, a number of young men bowed their heads to receive Christ. (Despite my lack of follow-up, some are still walking with the Lord to this day!) A young football player named Scott was the first guy I shared with—actually the day after I received Christ. I went through the booklet with him, and when I asked him if he wanted to receive Christ into his life, he paused, looked up at me, and said, "But, I'm Jewish." I had not taken an apologetics course in seminary quite yet, so I shrugged my shoulders and replied, "That's okay." I was thrilled as he gave his life to the Lord! My point is this. Make sure the gospel tool you are using is so simple, so basic, and so transferable that the person you are sharing with could quickly and easily use it themselves; that's how the gospel gets multiplied over and over.

Below are a couple of simple methods for sharing the gospel message you can easily learn and pass on to others.

→ SHARE YOUR STORY

In Revelation 12:11 the aged apostle John shares with us how he and the other disciples were able to have victory over Satan: "They triumphed over him by the blood of the Lamb and by the word of their testimony." Two of the most potent weapons God gave us are the gospel (the blood of the Lamb) and our testimony. Being able to specifically explain to someone *how* the gospel has personally affected your life is the most practical tool we have in our "evangelism toolbelt." Our friends can question or oppose almost every one of our arguments, but they can't refute the fact that our lives have been changed by Jesus Christ!

Share the story of the difference your relationship with Christ has made in your life in three simple parts:

1. My Life Before Christ
Explain in a short but relevant way what your life looked like prior to coming to Christ. Mention a few areas in your life that may have been keeping you from the Lord.

2. How I Came to Christ
You'll want to spend the most time on this part of your story. Share what happened to make Christ a reality to you and what convinced you to follow Him. This is where you get the opportunity to explain the gospel. As our friend Mark Vance of Salt Network says, "Don't gloss over the crossover."

3. My Life After Christ
Lastly, give them a simple explanation of the ways your life has changed since coming to Christ. How has God replaced your old desires with new ones? How have you been growing in your faith?

Get started: Think through the details of how you began your relationship with Christ. Write out your testimony in a thorough way, breaking it down into these three categories. Then go back and shorten it to a smaller number of bullet points so you can share the essentials of your story in three minutes or less. Start rehearsing it with a friend. Ask friends, Christian and non-Christian, if they will let you "practice" your story with them. It can be very non-threatening, and who knows, you may lead someone to Christ!

→ TOOL TIME

There are a number of excellent methods of sharing the good news with others. If your church or campus ministry has a particular approach, learn and master that one. Here is a sampling of some great tools to get you started.

The Bridge Diagram
Whether you use the one-verse bridge (Romans 6:23) or a longer version, this tool (originally created by the Navigators) is usually drawn out for someone and graphically explains salvation through Jesus.

Knowing God Personally

Also known as the *Four Spiritual Laws*, this booklet from Cru highlights the Lordship of Christ and how to specifically pray to receive Christ.

God Tools App

A great resource that is available in multiple languages, and if it's on your phone, you always have it with you.

The Three Circles

A simple illustration introduced by Family Church in West Palm Beach, FL to equip their members to share God's truth with the people they talk with every day.

Big Story

This tool by InterVarsity speaks to a global awareness of the brokenness and sin in our world and points to the hope and redemption we all long for.

Gospel Appointments

An easily taught tool students can use for the rest of their lives, put together by Paul Worcester.

Whatever tool you use, make sure it includes the key elements of the gospel:

- We are all sinners, separated from a holy God.
- Christ died on the cross and rose from the dead to pay the penalty for our sins and make a way for us to have a relationship with God.
- Each of us need to put our personal faith and trust not in our good works but in Jesus Christ alone for our salvation.

Lastly—and I know this can be scary, but bear with me—the greatest thing you could ever do for someone is to actually give them an opportunity to pray and invite Christ into their life as their Lord and Savior. Let me explain.

→ ASK THE GOLDEN QUESTION

What is the most important question you could ever ask someone? Answer: the one that could change their eternal destiny. This "golden question" can be difficult to ask because our throat starts to constrict, our tongue gets dry, our eyes begin to dart, and our heart pounds faster. It takes courage to explain the gospel to someone, answer their questions, and then form these words with our mouth: "Wes, would you like to invite Jesus Christ into your life as your Savior and Lord...right now?" If there was ever a time to keep your eyes fixed on theirs, if there was ever a time to zip the lip and not try to rephrase or answer for them—now is that time!

Yes, there might be two or three seconds of awkward silence that may seem like an eternity, but never again during their lifetime will the Spirit of God have a better opportunity to bring them face-to-face with a holy and loving God who is asking them to make a decision. This is in no way intended to be an abrupt or confrontational question to "put them on the spot," but you need to pause long enough to give them some time to think and respond before you jump back in.

I believe one of the main reasons many of your friends have never received Christ into their life is because no one has ever *individually shared* the gospel with them, *asked* the "golden question," and then had enough love and courage to *wait* for a response. In fact, nine out of ten students that I ask, "If you could know God in a *personal* way...would you want to?" answer in the affirmative.

You don't need to be an extrovert or gifted in evangelism to be used by God to lead others to Christ. Sometimes introverts' quiet authenticity can actually be an advantage, disarming people and making them more receptive to the gospel. Mariana is a great example of this. One of the most shy people you will ever meet, she learned how to set up gospel appointments, how to ask the "golden question," and then stepped out in faith. Quietly walking up to and welcoming new girls at weekly ministry meetings, she talked to them, helped them feel comfortable, and set up a time to meet for coffee and further conversation. She thrived at these gospel "get togethers," knowing her purpose in that time was clear: to hear the other girl's story, share her own story, present God's story, and invite the girl to respond. Over the course of her time in college, this introverted but faithful sharer of the gospel led over 20 girls to Christ and discipled many personally. By the time she graduated from Chico State, she had a "downline" of girls she had led to Christ, who had led others to Christ, who had led others to Christ.

The Lord is not impressed with our ability, but our availability! Being someone God can use to help others cross from death to eternal life is not an issue of gifting or personality; it's an issue of obedience. Learn a method for communicating the gospel, pray for opportunities, and step out boldly to share the love Jesus offers with a world that desperately needs Him!

REFLECTION QUESTIONS:

→ What is the scariest or most challenging thing to you about sharing your testimony or the gospel with others?

→ Take some time to write out your personal testimony, and then start practicing with your family, friends, or small group. When will you do this and who is the first person you want to share with?

→ Does your church or ministry have a particular tool or method to share the gospel with others? What is it? Have you learned and practiced it?

→ When presenting the gospel, what is the "golden question"? Say it out loud to yourself, then practice looking in the eyes of a friend, asking the question and pausing to allow them to answer.

15

Your "Mission Trip" to Campus

When Thomas, a Kenyan college student, first heard about missions, he had only been a Christian for two months. He was keeping his salvation a secret, still living with his girlfriend, and at that point, he could see no difference in his life since becoming a believer. When a couple of guys who had come from America to Nairobi to mobilize Kenyan believers approached him on his campus talking about God's "desire for *all* peoples," Thomas actually listened.

These missionaries, part of the Campus Outreach (CO) ministry there, recruited him to go through *Xplore*, a study booklet from the Center for Mission Mobilization (CMM) that helps believers gain a heart for the nations. Desperate for a change in the way he was living, Thomas was excited to participate. There he heard about "unreached people groups" for the first time. He could hardly believe there were millions of people who currently have little to no chance of hearing the gospel, many living in and near Kenya. This knowledge weighed on him, and although he was already carrying a heavy load of responsibilities, he wanted to be part of the solution.

Before Thomas came to Kenyatta University, he worked hard to help his family. Growing up in a subsistence farming community outside of Nairobi, one of the only "ways out" of this mere survival existence for families was through saving up enough money for one of their children to further their education, secure a well-paying job, and support the family. But now his eyes had been opened to something greater than himself or even his family's needs. Thomas was unsure where he fit into God's big plan, but wondered if the Lord could use him in greater ways than just financially "saving" his family. Maybe God could use him to help *eternally* save his fellow Kenyans and East Africans who were out of reach of the gospel!

Now Thomas and a friend he recruited are halfway through a one-year missions program held in a Kenyan town where many unreached people reside. Living near those who are so close to him in culture yet so far from the truth of the gospel, Thomas is realizing how God has positioned him to play a role in reaching these people. Although he is grateful he listened to the message of the American mobilizers, he realizes his fellow Kenyans are much more receptive to him than they would be to an outsider bringing the same good news. Join us in praying that Thomas will continue to say yes to Jesus as he pursues God's heart for every tribe, tongue, and nation!

→ WHERE HAVE YOU BEEN SENT?

When you think of missions, do you imagine boarding a plane, crossing time zones, and trying to connect with people who live vastly different lives from you? There is certainly a huge need worldwide for Christians to leave what is safe and comfortable and take the gospel to areas where there is no one to proclaim the good news. But global missions strategists are also recognizing the power of mobilizing local believers like Thomas to reach his unreached neighbors. When missionaries are more like the people they are trying to reach, the gospel has fewer cultural barriers to cross. You should absolutely spend a spring break or summer on a cross-cultural mission trip, helping further the ministry of local believers. We hope many of you will even give years of your lives to taking the gospel to the unreached.

But what if, like Thomas, you also had a "mission field" of sorts that is closer than you think? Are there people who live where you live, eat where you eat, and spend their days doing the same things you do who might hear a message better from you—someone a lot like them—than they would from an outsider? Maybe your next "mission trip" isn't a trip at all, but would be just as radical as hopping on a plane to Nairobi. What if you were to get started by just walking across campus and being obedient to Jesus' call to make disciples of all nations…*right* where you are?

"As the Father has sent me, I am sending you" (John 20:21). Don't wait to be sent. You already have been! God sends His followers strategically into communities and relationships to share His message of love and forgiveness. If you considered yourself "sent" on a mission from God to the very place you are right now, would that change the way you spend your time?

One great thing about going on a mission trip is the intentionality you have to make an impact for Christ while you are there. What if you were on a "mission trip" every day? The college campus is one of the most strategic groups of non-believers on the planet. What if you approached every day on your campus with the same level of prayer, faith, and urgency that you approached a day on a mission trip?

→ YOUR "PEOPLE GROUP"

If you are praying for opportunities to share your faith each day, God will open all sorts of doors. But having a community you are aiming to reach with the love of Jesus will help you *most effectively* use the time you have in college to bring people to Christ. The best place to start is probably right where you are.

Think through the groups of people on campus you are naturally a part of or could easily connect with. Maybe it's your dorm floor, major, Greek chapter, sports team, club, apartment building, workplace, or even the group you came to college with from your high school. How could God use those existing networks of relationships to spread hope and love through you? Focusing your relational energy on caring and serving a *group* of people who are already in community with each other can create a multiplication effect, making it easier for you to reach more people (they are all together), foster community (they are already friends), and make disciples.

If you've ever built a campfire, you know that lighting random individual sticks around the campsite is not the way to build a roaring fire. But getting a spark to catch under sticks that are piled together allows the flames to grow and easily pass from one piece of wood to the next, creating the kind of fire that can warm a crowd. When the fire of the gospel breaks out in a group of students who are already relationally connected to each other, it creates the right conditions for a campus-wide wildfire!

→ PRAY LIKE CRAZY

Spiritual impact always begins with prayer. "Prayer is the real work of the ministry; service is just gathering in the results of prayer," nineteenth-century Christian leader and author S.D. Gordon profoundly asserts in his potent little piece, *Quiet Talks on Prayer.* Why is it then that I can spend two hours hanging out with a guy I'm reaching out to and enjoy the heck out of it, but if you ask me to spend just two *minutes* in prayer for him, it's agonizing? Here's how I might attempt to do it:

"Dear Lord, I, uh, pray for Matt right now, that you would, uh, bless him and, uh…" (I look at my watch and it's only been ten seconds), "…and Father, encourage him today and, uh, help him come to know you and, uh…" (I look again and only twenty seconds have passed)!

You get the picture. The enemy knows walls are broken down and hearts are penetrated by specific, constant intercession for the souls of people. I have seen so many conversions and life changes I know are a direct result of my petitions. What a fool I am, then, for neglecting—yes, even forsaking—the most important weapon you and I have: unleashing the power of God into someone's life through prayer! I have definitely observed a direct connection between how faithful I am to pray and how God works through my life and ministry. Wesley Duewel, in his excellent book *Touch The World Through Prayer,* challenges Christians to make prayer top priority: "You can influence more people for God and have a greater role in advancing Christ's cause by prayer than in any other way. It is not the only thing you must do, but it is the greatest thing you can do."

> "Prayer is never our last resort.
> It's our first line of offense."
>
> —CRAIG GROESCHEL

→ TEAM UP

"After this the Lord appointed seventy-two others and sent them two by two ahead of him to every town and place where he was about to go" (Luke 10:1). Jesus sent His disciples out to spread His message two by two. As the Lord directs your heart toward a specific affinity group or area of campus, there may be others He is leading to minister there as well. You might even grab a friend and together move into a dorm, rush a fraternity or sorority, or join a club that enables you to rub shoulders with more non-Christians. When possible, it is a game changer to team up with fellow laborers to pray together for your lost friends, serve the people in the group, and boldly and creatively share the gospel together. Some of my (Paul's) best friendships were developed as we teamed up to serve the Lord together in our dorm hall.

→ LIVE STRATEGICALLY

During their sophomore year, Jacob, Josh, and Kelton said no to all of the enticing offers to get a house off campus with their friends. Instead these three made a decision to move back into a dorm together at Chico State for the purpose of loving freshmen and sharing Christ. It was more expensive for these student missionaries to live on campus, but not as costly as moving overseas to share the gospel! They endured the cafeteria food, communal bathrooms, and the smell of weed in the hallways for the sake of being able to eat, sleep, and study in the same building as the guys they were trying to reach. Over the course of the year, God birthed a Bible study that had around 20 people from the dorm attending, and a dozen students ended up coming to Christ. The sacrifice these students made to live on mission during college paid eternal dividends.

The story of these three guys should prod you to ask yourself a very important question: *Why* do you live where you live? Was it a decision made from strategy or comfort? Many believers I know want to find a place where they can have their *own* bedroom, kitchen, TV, and...privacy. They don't want any interruptions, curfew, or rules. When I see this, I can't help but think about Proverbs 18:1, which says, "He who separates himself seeks his own desire" (NASB). The point is, if you and I really are Great Commission Christians, we're going to live in the *most* strategic place in order to impact others for Jesus Christ in the broadest and deepest way possible.

If I were trying to reach students in Austin, I wouldn't want to live in Denver, right? If I were trying to give my life and the gospel to a particular floor of guys in a dorm or a fraternity house, why would I stick myself in some apartment miles from campus? I promise you'll never again get a chance to live this close to such a large and receptive group of people. Take advantage of it! You'll be living in apartments and houses from here on out. If you can learn now how to walk with Christ and impact others for Him in the midst of a horde of other students, you will have the raw materials to do it anywhere, anyplace, for the rest of your life.

Living on mission with God and reaching the ends of the earth with the gospel requires us to choose to live in a strategic (rather than just comfortable) place for more than just your college years! So, have a "kingdom reason" for living where you live. Do whatever you can to do life with the group of people God has called you to reach. The supreme model is Jesus, who didn't just shout from heaven or visit us on weekends. God became a man and lived among us for thirty-three years.

→ SHARE BOLDLY

Salomon is a college football player who has a passion to share Christ with the guys on his team. When he joined the team he didn't know of any other followers of Christ, but he was open with his teammates about his relationship with Jesus from day one. I (Paul) challenged Salomon to see his team like a missionary sees an unreached people group. If he didn't share Christ with his teammates, who would? He was often made fun of for his beliefs, but he stood strong and boldly shared his faith. Salomon is an inviter, so he has been constantly recruiting his teammates to our college ministry large group. Fifteen of them have come, and six have made decisions to follow Jesus! Salomon and some of the teammates he led to Christ helped form the core for a brand new Fellowship of Christian Athletes ministry on campus.

It is such a joy to see these massive football players splash all the water out of our baptism pool at church on Sunday mornings as Salomon helps baptize them. One of the men he led to faith is Michael, who has grown tremendously and has now been used by God to help lead other guys on the team to faith. Salomon is a great example of a student who endured ongoing mockery for his faith but persevered. The result has been a squad of new believers who are helping spread the message of Christ to all of the athletes on campus.

As you are building friendships in the affinity group you are trying to reach, fly your "Jesus flag" early. Take opportunities to identify with Christ, initiate gospel conversations, and invite people to come with you to church or ministry activities. The gospel is best received when it comes from an "insider." Your friends are much more likely to hear the truth from you than from a campus minister or pastor. You may come to be known as the "spiritual guy/girl," but you will also likely become the person your fellow students come to when they need to talk about something real or unload a heavy weight they are carrying, giving you great access to shine the light of Christ on their situation.

→ SHOW LOVE

Faithful gospel ministry involves showing and telling. As you are broadly sharing the gospel within the group, look for simple ways to love and serve them as well. Being a person who shows love and speaks truth will open doors and invite trust. If it is a sports team, going to some of their games is essential. If it is a dorm hall, helping people move in or offering rides to Walmart may be a great way to serve. As you get into the lives of lost people, love can get messy. During college, I (Steve) can't tell you how many guys I bailed out of jail, or sobered up under a shower, or answered a late-night knock at my fraternity door for one of the men in trouble. I didn't mind at all. In fact, I was honored they would come to me in times of crisis and need. I felt like a real friend to them, and it opened up so many opportunities to share my source of hope and purpose with them. Ask God to open your eyes for creative (and even sacrificial) ways to show love in practical ways to the people He has called you to reach.

→ SEEK "PERSONS OF PEACE"

Cody shared the gospel with Noah. Noah put his trust in Christ on the spot and was so excited about his new life. Cody asked Noah if he had any friends who needed to hear this good news. The next day they set up a gospel appointment with Noah's friend Manny and led him to Jesus. Then Cody asked Noah and Manny if they knew of anyone else. They invited Ryan to a ministry event, and Ryan ended up coming to know Christ later that week. Now Ryan is helping launch a ministry reaching out to Greeks on campus. These students added links to their spiritual chains in an exciting, rapid succession. That can happen to you on your campus too!

The Lord may lead you to people like Noah who are "gatekeepers" within a group and can help open doors to more relationships. In Luke 10, Jesus sent out 72 of His disciples to go "ahead of Him to every town and place where He was about to go" (v. 1). In verses 5-7 He tells them to seek out a "person of peace" who will welcome them and serve as the home base for their ministry in the area. If this person lends their credibility to the missionary, it enables the gospel message to spread more rapidly within the group. Once you are "in" with the person of peace, you are in with their people as well. For centuries missionaries have taught us that if you "win the chief, you win the tribe." Why can't that principle work on a college campus too?

As you look at and pray for the various groups or networks of relationships you are part of (or close to), think through who the gatekeepers are, those "Noahs" who seem to know everyone. As you pray for and draw close to those potential "persons of peace," ask yourself some questions. Do you feel like you have some kind of initial friendship with this person? Are they open to hearing about Christ? They don't need to be a believer, just open. Are they willing to partner with you to recruit and host a Bible study for their friends? You could ask them like this: "Marian, I can tell so many girls on our dorm floor love you. Do you think that if you and I were to team up to start a weekly small group in your room on Biblical womanhood, some of your friends would want to join?"

As you build rapport with a gatekeeper, take time to hang out with them on their turf, getting to know their friends better. Join their intramural team. Find out where they do their study groups. Look for ways to connect in personal and non-threatening ways. As I have sought to influence my own affinity groups (and others around me) over the years, the Lord has opened up numerous doors for powerful evangelistic Bible studies. Starting a friendship builds trust. Trust builds openness. And openness is the essential heart attitude needed to receive Christ into their life as Savior...and Lord.

→ CONNECT NEW BELIEVERS

If you get to help someone become a follower of Jesus, praise the Lord! Now take them under your wing and teach them whatever you can about living for Christ. This person should become a VIP in your life. A warning: don't extract the new believer from their existing relational network. Yes, it's crucial to get them connected with other committed believers, but be careful not to monopolize all of their time. Teach them how to communicate the change Jesus is making in their life with their circle of friends, and go with them to share their story with people in the group. Do it with them, and keep equipping and encouraging them to share Jesus with as many people as possible without you. You may be surprised by how God can use a brand new believer to lead others to Christ.

Maybe, like our Kenyan friend Thomas, God has put you where you are for bigger reasons than you realize. Remember in John 4:35 how Jesus told His disciples to open their eyes to see the harvest all around them—people ready for the gospel, just waiting for a laborer to see the need and get to work. Your first mission field is right next door to you—and it is ripe for harvest. Ask the Lord of the harvest to open your eyes!

REFLECTION QUESTIONS:

→ Have you ever viewed your campus and the various affinity groups as a "mission field?" If you did, what would change about your perspective, relationships, activities, etc...?

→ Why do you live where you live? Is it for the sake of the gospel... or your own sake? In light of Proverbs 18:1, how could you live (now and in the future) more strategically?

→ Make a list of the various affinity groups or networks of relationships at your university. Which ones are you a part of? Which ones do you know someone in?

→ If you were to team up with an "insider" (a person of peace) in one or more of those groups to initiate a Bible study of some sort, which group would it be and which person would you approach?

16

Amber really wanted to overcome her fears and represent Christ in her dormitory. She had just returned from a summer-long ministry training program, and their "back to campus" emphasis helped give her the direction and boldness to plan her work and, hopefully, work her plan! She decided to try to meet every new freshman girl in her dorm as well as each student on her floor. Not only did she always keep her door open with a welcome sign on it, but she made it a point to introduce herself to anyone in the dorm she had not met. She arrived early to help girls move in, hosted a popcorn and movie night the first weekend, and took three carloads of girls to her church that first Sunday.

Even though most of the other juniors had moved out of the dorm into their own apartments, Amber chose to stay put and lay her life down for these young freshmen. It wasn't long until she was the ringleader of the entire dorm. Every girl liked and respected Amber, came to her with questions and problems, and wondered what it was that made her such a happy and sacrificial person. Amber started floating the idea of starting a Bible study on each of the dorm's three floors. Girl after girl responded enthusiastically, even though Amber did not know where many of them stood spiritually. She identified the two most influential girls on each floor and asked them to host the study in one of their rooms and to help recruit the girls from their floor. Feeling honored to be chosen by Amber the "dorm mama," they each went to work spreading the word and even started a fun competition to see who could recruit the most girls to their floor study!

By late September, Amber had three full-blown investigative Bible studies started. She recruited Sara, a Christian friend from off campus, to help her round up the girls a few minutes before nine each night, bring in a load of New Testaments to pass out, and then launch everyone into a fascinating discussion on a chapter of John. Each week's discussion focused on two questions: (1) Who is Jesus Christ? and (2) What does He want from me? Amber and Sara did not want to be viewed as the teachers or authorities but simply as discussion facilitators, working hard to to involve each girl in the conversations. At the studies and during the week, they poured out their love and attention on one and all. As she and Sara interceded for each girl every morning, it was obvious the Holy Spirit was penetrating the hearts of many of them and using a combination of three powerful tools: (1) the *truth* of the Word, (2) the *prayers* of Amber and Sara, and (3) the girls observing the unconditional *love* Amber and Sara had for them and each other.

→ GETTING PERSONAL

Several times a week, Amber and Sara would treat one of the girls from their Bible studies to a cup of coffee, spending some time getting to know them better and offering them a chance to hear and understand the gospel message. Over the course of the semester, the two leaders had promised each girl the chance to get a customized presentation of how to have a personal relationship with God, and miraculously, over thirty girls jumped at the opportunity. Amber had taken a step of faith, opened the funnel up very wide by meeting and serving over one hundred girls in her dorm. She asked almost forty of them to join small-group studies, shared the gospel with over thirty of them, and was now seeing girl after girl open up her heart to the Lord Jesus Christ. It was the most exciting, satisfying experience Amber and Sara had ever had in their entire lives. The Lord was on His way to transforming that campus because a shy college student decided to put her trust in a big God, walk toward her fears, pray expectantly, share the gospel, and love a bunch of young freshmen into the kingdom.

We can see from Amber's example two great ways we can "set the stage" for personal gospel conversations with people we are getting to know: evangelistic Bible studies and one-on-ones. Gathering a group together to investigate what the Bible says about Jesus or just inviting someone to sit down one-on-one to interact with the gospel can both be effective ways to introduce Christ to others. Let's start with the EBS:

→ **EVANGELISTIC BIBLE STUDY**

Amber and Sara had sown broadly and started building real friendships with the girls in the dorm. Their prayer and desire was to launch one or more evangelistic Bible studies. The goal? To move their friends toward a personal relationship with the Lord by getting them to interact with Scripture, talk openly about spiritual things, and warm up for a one-on-one discussion and opportunity to receive Christ. Call it an Investigative Group or Leadership Study or whatever...just name it something that won't frighten them away. I like to start "John Studies" and "Discovery Groups." I (Steve) have a weekly group of six fraternity guys right now we simply call a "Manhood Study." You get the picture.

Planning and Recruiting:

Think of the 4-10 people you definitely want to be a part of your evangelistic Bible study, and do all you can to make it happen. Pick a time that works best for your group and a meeting place that is easily accessible to the people you are inviting. You might ask one of the students you want there most if they will host the study and even help get everyone there on time.

I know it might sound a little exclusive, but I have always had two criteria for starting these evangelistic Bible studies. One, I need to feel like I have some level of rapport with each person, and secondly, I need to be pretty sure they are a non-Christian. And if the students I'm inviting already know each other or are part of the same affinity group, they naturally will want to come to be with their friends. So, normally, I don't open up these groups to everyone. In fact, I want each person to feel special and even privileged to be part of the investigative group. I might say, "Kurt, we're starting this Manhood Study next Thursday night at 9 pm with some of the guys you are close to on the intramural team, and we have six slots in the group. Four of them have already been taken, but I would love to give you one of these remaining two spots. It would mean coming and participating each week for six weeks. I think you would really enjoy it, but do you feel like that is something you would be interested in and want to commit to?" I also let them know there won't be any preaching, praying, singing, or any awkward religious stuff taking place—and they don't even need to bring a Bible. I will have one for everyone!

It's never too early in the semester or too late to start your evangelistic Bible study. Typically after the first 3 or 4 weeks of school is the ideal time, but don't be afraid to start sooner or later. Make the duration of the study 4 to 8 weeks, and like my dialogue with Kurt, let them know you'd like for them to commit to be there each week. Don't ask your friends to prepare for this study, but only to be faithful to come and contribute to the discussion.

Leading:

Atmosphere

You want the feeling of the room to be non-intimidating and loose. Typically, having food at a Bible study not only helps attendance but also helps the feel of the room. If you have a few sodas or even pizzas around, it helps people let their guard down and relax. As your time together progresses, hopefully it will begin to feel like a close community. Don't get too serious too quickly in these studies. Ask a lot of questions, get them talking about themselves, tell stories, start out each study with a funny YouTube video, whatever you can do to help this be a fun and relational atmosphere. Your friends want to attend a gathering with people they know, doing things together they enjoy. Make these small groups something they *want* to come to.

Ideally, the Bible study content itself shouldn't last longer than 30-40 minutes. You can have 10-15 minutes of relational time before and after, but making sure the study doesn't drag on will serve the people there and make them want to come back next week. Once you have reached your time limit, let everyone know they are free to go if they need to, but also can stay and hang if they would like. Or jump in the car and go out for some late-night tacos together!

Guided Discussion

One of the common mistakes of college students is assuming they can just show up and "wing" a Bible study. Take time throughout your week to prepare to lead your group's discussion. Ask your discipler or ministry leader to help you pick the content you ought to cover and familiarize yourself with it until you feel confident enough to be able to lead through it. Initially you might want to choose a topic that meets a *felt* need (i.e. relationships, time management, how to be successful) rather than some deep theological or controversial issue.

Remember, you are not the teacher but simply a discussion facilitator. And good discussion usually makes a good Bible study. You want to shoot for a dialogue (not a monologue!) where you are asking good open-ended questions, guiding the discussion, and doing a lot of listening and affirming. Don't spend as much time preparing what you will *say* as opposed to what you will *ask*. Work hard to bring questions that will really stimulate the group to open up and talk, as well as ways to apply the truth to their lives. Asking a closed-ended question, like "Did Jesus love His disciples?", will get a lot of blank, even embarrassed stares because people feel stupid responding to a question with such an obvious answer. But asking a more open-ended question, like "What are some ways you see Jesus show love to His disciples in this passage?" is always a much better conversation starter.

Even if a wrong answer is given, don't panic. Responding with something like, "That's interesting, Robert. What does someone else think?" allows the group to do the correcting, rather than setting yourself up as the authoritative "Answer Guy!" Good discussion will draw people into the group and help them feel a part of the action. Do all you can to be as inclusive as possible, especially trying to draw out the quiet ones in a sensitive way. Asking different people to read the verse each time or calling on certain people to answer can make everyone feel involved. Be careful not to be led astray by various "rabbit trails" that come up in the discussion. These can be tricky as you try to answer each one. Instead, graciously say something along the lines of, "I'd love to talk about that topic later, but let's deal with this one first and we'll come back to that if we have time."

Don't be embarrassed or scared to say you don't know an answer. Not faking it, but instead saying "I don't know" can be one of the most powerful things you can communicate in a small group. You might follow it up by saying, "I don't think I have a great answer for you right now, Callie. Why don't you and I connect this week and see if we can dig deeper and find an answer to report back to the group next week?" This lets everyone know they are not your humble students sitting at the feet of their all-knowing spiritual leader. No! It lets them know you are in process just like they are and that you *all* are taking this journey of discovery together.

→ **ONE-ON-ONE**

Just as Amber and Sara initiated coffee dates with the girls in their Bible studies, setting up a one-on-one time to get to know someone better and present the gospel is an effective, relational way for a friend to hear and receive the message of hope. This type of meeting gives you an opportunity to build trust and provides the perfect setting for you to hear more of their story, share your story, and then present God's story in a clear way. View this meeting as the beginning of an ongoing conversation about the gospel. Some will be ready to accept Christ and you'll continue to meet to follow up and disciple them. If they are not ready to make a decision, you can ask them if they want to keep exploring the gospel by studying God's Word—in a small group or one-on-one. Regardless of their response, they will never ever forget the time someone had enough courage and love for them to risk the relationship by sharing the gospel, asking them the "golden question," and letting them answer. They will forget 10,000 conversations during their lifetime—but not this one!

A few practical tips: Having a face-to-face meeting like this at a coffee shop or lunch spot minimizes the distractions that can often come when sharing Jesus in other settings. I can't tell you how many times I have been trying to share Christ at a party with the music bumping in the background or in a dorm room when the roommate walks in wearing a towel! Meeting at a set time with a clearly communicated reason for getting together also emphasizes the importance of what you are talking about. If your friend knows you are planning to talk about spiritual things when you get together, they will often begin to think about what they believe about God even before the meeting, and the Holy Spirit begins working on their heart.

You can set up a specific time to share the gospel with other students you are building friendships with...or with someone you just met. It's pretty simple to transition from a casual conversation about spiritual things to comparing calendars and establishing a when and where. Whether you are sensing an open door with the person who sits next to you in chemistry or wanting to make sure the freshman in your Bible study truly understands the gospel, establishing a time to share the good news individually is a great way to bring their focused attention to the truth of Christ. Most people are open to you initiating one-on-one time with them and are often honored that someone would take enough interest in them to set up such a time. Don't look at this meeting as a one-time event but a stepping stone to help cultivate an ongoing evangelistic friendship with a person.

Yes, the "E" word can be scary, but it can also be exhilarating. Taking the time to get to know someone, to pray for them, to share your life and testimony, and finally to take the awesome and powerful step to actually explain the gospel to them in a clear yet non-threatening way will be one of the greatest experiences of your life—and theirs too! You'll never know (on this side of heaven!) the eternal impact you will leave behind if you simply and consistently offer those around you a chance to respond to the claims of Christ. Many times over the years I have gotten phone calls from guys who start off by saying something along the lines of: "Shad, you might not remember me, but…" I instantly interrupt him, replying: "Of course I remember you, Terry. You're the football-playing, Corvette-driving, girl-chasing fraternity brother who would curse me out whenever I tried to share my faith with you!" After we have a good laugh together, he finishes his thought, "I'm sorry for the way I treated you back then, but I never forgot the questions you would pose to me. And I have been wanting to tell you for a while that I have committed my life to Christ."

Wow. That kind of call pours fuel into my flame for a whole month! Think about your time in college. What will you leave behind beyond a GPA or resume full of activities and awards? What if you were so in love with Jesus, so burdened for the students around you, and so willing to risk everything to present the life saving message of the cross to them…that it became one of the overriding passions and priorities for your time there on campus? If you and I really care for someone, we will take an interest in their soul, and getting them started in their brand new relationship with God is the just first step. Now comes the challenging part—saying no to your own agenda in order to say yes to your new converts and taking the time and effort to get them established in their walk with God and ministry to others. This next section is going to give you a path to walk on. To give you an idea of where we are going, here's a diagram that shows the overall process of moving someone from non-Christian to convert to disciple to disciple-maker. Our prayer for you is that these next several chapters will get you so fired up that you determine in your heart that *this* is the kind of world-changing legacy you want to leave behind on your campus!

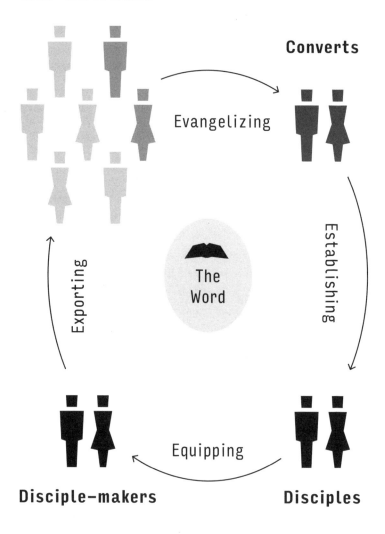

Modified from Mark Lewis, The Navigators. Used with permission.

REFLECTION   QUESTIONS:

→ What impressed you about Amber and Sara and the ministry they had with girls in their dorm? What could you take from their story and apply to your own life and ministry?

→ What group of students at your college do you think might be receptive to your invitation to a weekly evangelistic Bible study? When and how will you recruit them?

→ Have you ever led (or been part of) a purely discussion-oriented small group Bible study? How does it differ from a group where a teacher prepares and presents a lesson? Which do you prefer and why?

→ Take stock of your current priorities and activities in college. If you continue on this path, what will be the ultimate accomplishments and legacy you will leave behind? If you're not satisfied with that, what changes do you need to make now?

Build Your Chain:
Disciple-making Links

17

Jesus Is a Genius

I was mesmerized. A 104-year-old World War II veteran was wheeled to the front of the room in his heavily decorated Navy uniform. Then, one at a time, five other men walked up and stood in a row next to him.

A 75-year-old told the crowd how this war hero had discipled him, and the last thing the vet told him was, "Don't you be the last link in this chain."

Standing next to him, a 64-year-old man shared how the previous speaker had sacrificed his time and energy to train him as a Christian laborer. After pouring into his life for years, his discipler passed on the same exact message he had been given: "Don't you be the last link in this chain."

Next in line was a 50-year-old, then a 28-year-old, and finally a 21-year-old college student. Each of them told us the same story of a deep and lasting discipleship relationship with their beloved mentor standing next to them, and of course, the main message each had left their young disciple was—you guessed it—"Don't you be the last link in this chain!"

Reflect on the key people God has used in your life to get you to this point in your walk with Him and ministry to others. *You* are someone's link in the chain! Your spiritual leaders may or may not have done a good job of passing on to you all the whats, whys, and hows of being and making disciples. But regardless of your past, you now have the chance to start adding strong, lasting links to your discipleship chain. At the end of your life, won't it be cool to see how the Lord has used you to raise up mature and enduring disciples who have made disciples who have made disciples....and how the chain links go on and on? This is the key to multiplying laborers to reach the nations. And the time to start this world-changing endeavor?

Now!

→ THE MASTER'S PLAN

Jesus came to the earth to be a "light to the nations." He lived a sinless life and then died on a cross, taking the punishment for all of our sins. Then He rose from the dead, defeating sin and death. He made the ultimate sacrifice to free the world and reconcile us to God. As He left Earth to return to heaven, He entrusted a small group of His followers with spreading this message across the world. Making disciples of all nations is God's Plan A. In fact, there is no Plan B! Jesus' original followers were faithful to disciple others who discipled others who discipled others, etc...and now the baton is passed to you. We are following Christ today because Plan A works!

What did Jesus focus on during His three years of ministry on Earth? And what was He seeking to leave behind once He returned to heaven? As He launched out into His work, He obviously had a plan. He prayed all night, and by morning He knew exactly which twelve men He would choose to join Him in His world-changing endeavor (Luke 6:12-13). Robert Coleman, in his classic *The Master Plan of Evangelism*, puts it this way: "His concern was not with programs to reach the multitudes, but with men whom the multitudes would follow." Over the next months and years, Jesus modeled to them the very command He would give them in Matthew 28: to "make disciples." This was not a new concept to the disciples. From the "be fruitful and multiply" directive in Genesis, to the prophet Elijah training Elisha in Israel, to John the Baptist leading his disciples, the Twelve understood this essential mandate to pass on the faith they had received from their Teacher.

Now, as we have the entire Scriptures and look back on these examples, it's even more clear what Jesus wants us as His followers to focus on. Jesus is a genius, and our brilliant Master's plan can become the comprehensive, long-term strategy or "master plan" for our life too! We are to join Him, and His disciples, in this worldwide, history-long mission to "make disciples of all nations." The baton has been passed to us and we have the awesome privilege and responsibility to pass it on to others. It is surely an adventure of a lifetime that dramatically affects this life...and the next!

→ START HERE

As we embark on this idea of multiplying our life into others, start by look-ing *up* to the One who is graciously providing you this amazing opportunity. Don't worry if you feel like you don't have it all together. None of us do! We are all in process, continually asking God to keep changing us and growing us into the person He wants us to be. So as we begin talking about discipling others, don't be intimidated. Be excited! This is the God of the universe asking you to partner with Him in His eternal purposes here on earth. I promise you'll never receive a more profound or consequential invitation from anyone this side of heaven. Fixing our eyes on Jesus, looking to Him to fill us and empower us to walk toward our fears and doubts in the power of His Holy Spirit, will always be the day-to-day secret in influencing others for Christ.

The second place to look is *within*. Go back to The Wheel illustration we've described to periodically evaluate how you're doing in the basics of the Christian life. What areas do *you* need to stay focused on, in which you want to grow deeper and more consistent? Who is the person helping you to set goals in these areas, praying for your progress, and loving you enough to ask you the tough questions about how you're doing?

Your walk with God, your vision for your life, and your obedience to His mandate to make disciples—these are the critical components that make up the fuel. If the essential ingredients are there, our great God delights in igniting the flame to burn brightly for His glory. Our fuel and His flame provide the heat and light to make an eternal, enduring difference in this dark and broken world. If you're struggling with waking up each morning with a purpose to live for, you just found it! Letting the Lord Jesus Christ shine in you and through you each day to permanently impact the students around you and spread His name and fame to all nations is so much more fulfilling and lasting than any amount of popularity, good grades, or money to buy more things.

Observing and following someone who is willing and able to help you, then turning around and doing the same for another: this is really all disci-ple-making is. Whatever Jesus has given you or done in your life, that's what you can pass on to others. Don't wait until you become the perfect Christian or disciple—it will never happen! Start investing in others now. When you are having your quiet times, pull in a young believer to join you. If you are memorizing Scripture, recruit a friend to help you review your verses, and encourage them to knock out their "first five." If you have a witnessing tool you have learned, bring along another Christian as you take someone in your dorm through the gospel.

If you remember, in 2 Timothy 2:2 Paul exhorted his young disciple to look for faithful or "reliable" people to share his life with and who were "able to teach others also." The aged apostle was simply trying to help Timothy identify individuals who would be willing to take the Christian teaching and training he gave them and pass it on to others. Soak in everything you can from your discipler and immediately turn around to pour those things into your disciple. This is not a "sit down, let me instruct you" kind of teacher-student transaction we're describing here. No, it's a growing friendship marked by humility, servanthood, sacrifice, and teamwork, characterized by:

- A "we're in this together" attitude, where you're inviting another believer to walk alongside you through the ups and downs of life and ministry.
- A "let's learn from one another" approach, where God is working deeply in each of your hearts, and you want to listen and benefit from the lessons He is teaching *both* of you.
- An "iron sharpening iron" rapport, where you are teachable toward your disciple, willing to be challenged or even confronted by one another when needed.

One of my all-time favorite books is *Disciples Are Made Not Born* by Walt Henrichsen. Over the years, I have tried to take all my disciples through it in the early stages of their growth. It emphasizes that there isn't a gift of being or making disciples; we are *all* commanded to be a disciple and to make disciples. Each of us will do it according to the level of commitment we have, the amount of time we're willing to give, the kind of training we have received, and the flavor blend of specific spiritual gifts (and even personality!) God has given us.

But regardless of our capacity or approach, Jesus is commanding each and every one of us to "go and make disciples." As you are becoming a disciple as well as making disciples, major in knowing Christ, being like Christ, and doing what Christ did—laying His life down for the sake of others.

Truly, disciples are made not born, and if you want to be used by God to establish new converts and young believers as disciples of Jesus Christ, you too will have to lay down your life. Are you ready to do so? Are you prepared to learn and grow and change and obey in order to start adding links to your discipleship chain? Buckle up. Here we go!

→ DISCIPLE-MAKING 101

> "Him we proclaim, warning everyone and
> teaching everyone with all wisdom, that we
> may present everyone mature in Christ. For
> this I toil, struggling with all his energy
> that he powerfully works within me."
>
> —COLOSSIANS 1:28-29, ESV

Jesus is the focus. Teaching is the task. Maturity is our goal. God's Spirit is the life changer. We're here to help people make progress toward Christ and to multiply disciple-makers until everyone on earth has a chance to hear the good news. Understand that as you reach out to fellow students, everyone will be at a different place in their spiritual pilgrimage. So how do you discern where they are currently? How do you help move them along a path of maturity? What do you hope will be true of the person you are discipling a year from now? How about ten years from now? How about 40 years from now? Answering these questions should shape how you invest in others.

We've created some suggested markers for you to use that may help you know the next steps your fellow student needs to take in their Christian life and have outlined the process of guiding people from one growth marker to the next. These markers are not listed in any particular chapter of the Bible but are simply profiles created from some of the scriptural characteristics that should be present at each stage of a Christian's growth.

Note: By the way, before you start using these markers to evaluate students you are helping grow, you might start on yourself. Read and pray carefully over these profiles, and honestly determine where *you* are in this discipleship process, and what the next steps are—for you!

Disciple-making Profiles and Process

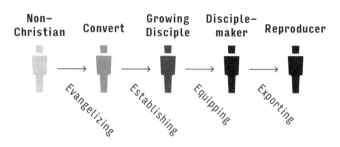

Non-Christian

We may not always know where someone is in their relationship with God, but Jesus gave us some startling indicators. In Matthew 7:13-14 He challenged His listeners: "Enter through the narrow gate. For wide is the gate and broad is the road that leads to destruction, and many enter through it. But small is the gate and narrow the road that leads to life, and only a few find it" (NIV). He's clearly communicating that the majority of people (by far!) are non-believers. Regardless of what part of the world you're in, this lopsided ratio of believers to non-believers applies to your campus too. So don't ever *assume* anyone around you has found that small gate and narrow road. A good rule of thumb is: "When in doubt, share the gospel." The Bible says we all are enemies of God unless we trust in Christ's sacrifice to restore the relationship our sin has broken. *Everyone,* regardless of how many years they've been in church, must *personally* respond to the gospel, repent of their sin, and make the decision to trust Jesus' sacrifice on their behalf in order to begin a relationship with the Father as a child of God.

Profile of a Non-Christian
- Trend of life is disobedient to God (Ephesians 2:1-3)
- Lack of spiritual fruit and hunger (Galatians 5:17-21)

Non-Christians are moved to **converts** through **evangelism**.

Convert

Someone may have prayed a prayer or raised their hand at a meeting indicating they received Christ, but how do you really know they have become a born-again follower of Jesus? There's no surefire way for you to be certain about your friend, but here are a few markers to help you discern if someone is a true convert:

Profile of a Convert

- Change of attitude toward Jesus Christ—now favorable (John 8:42)
- Change of attitude toward sin—now unfavorable (1 Corinthians 5:17)
- Understands salvation by grace through faith alone, not as a result of works (Eph 2:8-9)
- Desire to grow spiritually (1 Peter 2:2)
- Publicly professed commitment to Christ (Romans 10:9–10)

Converts become **growing disciples** by **establishing** them in the basics of following Christ.

Growing Disciple

A genuine salvation decision, combined with a track record of continued Christian growth, can begin to produce a strong foundation of faith. In this profile of a disciple are some suggested markers you can begin to pray (and then plan to build) into the life of your young Christian friend:

Profile of a Growing Disciple

- Meets the profile of a convert
- Consistent and growing in their love for God and others through regular time in the Word, prayer, fellowship, and evangelism. At least six months of growth demonstrates consistency. (Colossians 2:6–7)
- Demonstrates a heart for God, seeks out opportunities to grow spiritually, and is willing to make any sacrifice to prioritize their growth
- Observable changes in their attitudes and actions as a result of application of the Word and conviction of the Holy Spirit (John 14:21)
- Begins to grasp the worldwide mandate to be a witness locally *and* globally (Acts 1:8)

Growing disciples become **disciple-makers** by **equipping** them to pass on the training they have received.

Disciple-maker

One of the markers listed indicating this student is committed to the basics of the Christian life is that they are beginning to reach out to share their faith with others. Notice the characteristics of a disciple include having a heart for God and being willing to make sacrifices to *personally* grow. The additional characteristic of a disciple-maker is having a heart for people and being willing to make sacrifices to help *others* grow. In the Great Commission in Matthew 28, Jesus instructs His followers to "teach them to do all that I have commanded you." As you help your Christian friend build upon their foundation of *being* a disciple, you have the opportunity to show them how to obey the Lord by making disciples themselves. This profile can be a guide for you to do just that.

Profile of a Disciple-maker

- Is consistently growing as a disciple, increasing in their love for God and others (Matthew 22:36-40)
- Demonstrates a heart for people by investing in others relationally and spiritually (1 Thessalonians 2:8; Philippians 2:17)
- Willing to make any sacrifices to help others grow (1 Corinthians 9:19–23)
- Has been the major influence in taking a person from a convert to a disciple (Matthew 28:18–20)
- Has fully embraced the Great Commission with a personal plan to see it fulfilled
- Is becoming a "World Christian", seeing the nations through God's eyes and aligning their values, decisions, and lifestyle to fulfill God's worldwide purposes (Revelation 7:9)

Disciple-makers who are **exported** to make disciples of all nations and continue to repeat the process of multiplying laborers are called **reproducers.**

Reproducer

Bonus Material: If your friend has now actually made a disciple themselves, don't let them stop there! Your new disciple-maker needs to help their young disciple also "obey all the commands" Jesus gave us; one of which, of course, was to "make disciples." Continuing to add links to this discipleship chain is what spiritual multiplication is all about. There may be a few mature believers on your campus who will stay so committed and focused that they actually become what we call a "reproducer." Why can't that be you? Here's what's involved:

Profile of a Reproducer
- Is laboring as a disciple-maker
- Has been the major influence in helping at least one of their disciples become a disciple-maker, producing a third generation
- Has the knowledge, skills, character, and vision to *continue* over the long haul to make disciples who will make disciples with the goal of reaching all nations (Matthew 28:18–20; Acts 1:8)
- Has found their most strategic role(s) in the World Christian movement (goer, sender, welcomer, mobilizer) and is recruiting others to discover and engage theirs (Romans 10:13-15)

These basic distinctions can help you know what to pray for and build into the lives of the students around you. Again, these profiles don't include all aspects of Christian maturity and are not meant to define anyone's spiritual life; they are merely suggested "markers" as you aid and encourage other students along their journey. In discipling others, you need to know *where* you are taking them...and *how* to get there!

At this point you may feel overwhelmed or overconfident. Don't fall into either ditch, and know this: before you can make two disciples, you have to make one! So, pray diligently that the Lord would bless your efforts in sharing the gospel and give you a new convert who has made a genuine decision to follow Christ. As you become a spiritual parent, you will have the amazing opportunity (and responsibility) to help this baby Christian start to grow in their faith and become a sold-out disciple of Jesus. Don't stop there, but build as many strong, lasting links in that chain as possible. Not many Christian students truly reproduce themselves like this during their college years, but this is precisely what we are challenging and equipping you to do.

R E F L E C T I O N   Q U E S T I O N S :

→ If you lived during Jesus' time and had only three years to permanently impact the world, what would have been your approach? Jesus focused His time and energy on discipling 12 ordinary men. Why?

→ As you study the various profiles in this chapter, where would you place yourself right now? Why are you there?

→ Look again at the profiles. Where do you think God wants you? Why do you say that?

→ How will you get from where you are now to where you believe God wants you? And who will help you get there?

18

Brad was a strong, good-looking athlete who had been one of the most popular and charismatic leaders of the campus ministry he had plugged into, but that day he was reduced to tears as we huddled at a corner table in the back of the student center. He was about to graduate from college and wanted to confess something to me before he crossed the stage for his diploma.

"Shad," he whispered, "I have led over a hundred guys to Christ since I started here as a freshman."

"That's fantastic!" I responded.

"No, that's *not* fantastic," he shot back. Then gazing off in the distance like he was looking for something, he added, "You see, I don't know where a single one of them are."

"What do you mean?" I asked.

"I mean, I took them through the gospel, they prayed the prayer, I patted them on the back but never saw them again. I have no idea where they are or how they're doing. I feel like I have nothing to show for all my efforts the past four years."

As much as I tried to console my friend, reality was staring him in the face. He had been so desperate to start and develop a movement on the campus while he was there, but it was not to be. As he was nearing the end of his collegiate career, he was turning to see that there was no lasting legacy he was leaving behind. He was a great guy with great intentions, but he didn't really have the training, direction, or perspective he needed to make a *permanent* impact during his college years. Leaving that appointment, I took a slow, thoughtful walk back to my fraternity house, determined that during my college years, I would focus on building *quality* more than *quantity* into my personal life and ministry.

Rather than just trying to add up numbers of more and more people who have made professions of faith, we should focus on helping these new believers begin their walk with God and build a great foundation in their new Christian life. Don't be asking God for more converts until you've taken care of the ones He's already given you; in other words, don't love 'em and leave 'em!

→ THE DELIVERY ROOM

My wife and I (Steve) have five children; four were born in the same room of the same hospital, and our fifth we adopted from an orphanage in Ukraine. I remember the mixture of joy and relief we experienced when we brought our first child into the world. How thrilling it was to see Marietta, our baby girl, for the very first time.

What if, at that tender moment, I was to turn to my wife and the beaming medical staff standing there and exude, "Man, that was awesome! Good job, honey. Good job, everybody! Now, hop up, sweetheart. We have a lot to do and gotta go. Bye bye, sweet Marietta. Have a good life, little one! See ya"? What do you think the stunned doctor and nurses would say? "No, no, sir, this is *your* child. You can't leave her here. Giving birth is just the beginning. Now you take her home and nurture and care for her until she is an adult."

In the same way, the majority of Christian students I've known over the years were "birthed" in a one-on-one gospel presentation or group meeting during their growing-up years but were then left with no one to care for and nurture them to spiritual maturity. May I tell you why most Christians are spiritual orphans? It's because many who are willing to share the gospel want the glory and excitement of seeing a person come to faith, but they are not willing to pay the price to follow them up. Others may not understand there is even any work to be done after their friend accepts Christ. When someone takes Jesus Christ as their Savior, they become a child of God—born again, yes, but nevertheless a spiritual infant. Similar to parents of brand new babies, we have the responsibility as spiritual parents to care for these "newborns," helping them to adjust to the world and begin growing. Just as Jesus tells Peter to feed and care for the flock He will hand over to Peter, we also need to prepare ourselves to be able to nurture to maturity those whom God will entrust to us (John 21).

→ WET CEMENT

> "And now, just as you accepted Christ Jesus as
> your Lord, you must continue to follow him.
> Let your roots grow down into him, and let
> your lives be built on him. Then your faith
> will grow strong in the truth you were taught,
> and you will overflow with thankfulness."
>
> **—COLOSSIANS 2:6-7, NLT**

The process of a Christian's growth between a convert and a disciple is called "establishing," and whether you help birth a new Christian or meet a young believer who needs help growing, the first step in leading them to become a laborer is building the kind of foundation into their life that God and others have built into yours.

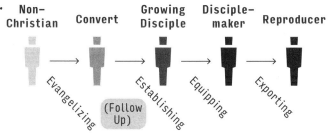

Non-Christian → Convert → Growing Disciple → Disciple-maker → Reproducer

Evangelizing (Follow Up) Establishing Equipping Exporting

Once a person makes the decision to embrace Christ as Lord and Savior, those first few hours, days, and weeks we spend ministering to that brand new believer is called "follow up." During this critical and vulnerable juncture, it means praying and working hard to provide this new or young believer with big doses of direction *and* affection. We not only need to help them understand the gospel and the plans God has for them (Ephesians 2:1-10), but we also need to love them in the same way Paul guided and cared for the Thessalonians: "Just as a nursing mother cares for her children, so we cared for you. Because we loved you so much, we were delighted to share with you not only the gospel of God but our lives as well" (1 Thessalonians 2:7-8, NIV). It might seem insignificant, but how you pray for them, what you help them believe, and what you do with them during this short "follow up" window of time will establish the long-term DNA of their entire Christian life.

New Christians are like wet cement. Most don't have an idea of what a real Christian is supposed to think, do, or be, and as a result, they take their cues from the believers around them. Whatever level of commitment and character they observe in the first three months is what they come to believe is the *normal* Christian life. That's why it is so important you take the lead in helping form and shape their values and convictions—*before* the cement hardens! If you emphasize daily quiet time, it will become a priority for them too. If evangelism is a way of life for you, they will adopt it also. If Scripture memory or servanthood is important to you, it will be to them too. You truly reproduce after your own kind during this oh-so-impressionable stage of a young Christian's life. And in my experience, that "wet cement" starts to harden around the six-month mark and it becomes part of their lifelong spiritual DNA. So regularly and deeply pouring yourself into this new believer will be a critical factor in determining the quality and quantity of their walk with Christ and ministry to others—for a lifetime. Here are some topics to discuss with them and things to do with them in the first days, weeks, and months after their conversion.

→ THE FIRST TWENTY-FOUR HOURS

Here are a few of the things I like to do with a new Christian as soon as I can after their salvation decision:

Present the Gospel and Rejoice with Them

"What?" you may ask. "I thought we had already done that." Correct! But, one of the best things you can do for a brand new Christian is to go back over—very slowly, point by point—the gospel message. Consider using a different illustration or tool this time. (For example, if you used The Bridge illustration the first time, use Knowing God Personally now to look at the gospel from a different angle.) Make sure the new convert *fully* understands what Christ has done for them and what their response to Him means. Here are some key verses to look up, discuss, and maybe memorize together:

"I have been crucified with Christ and I no longer live, but Christ lives in me. The life I now live in the body, I live by faith in the Son of God, who loved me and gave Himself for me." —Galatians 2:20

"God made Him who had no sin to be sin for us, so that in Him we might become the righteousness of God." —2 Corinthians 5:21

"Very truly I tell you, whoever hears My word and believes Him who sent Me has eternal life and will not be judged but has crossed over from death to life." —John 5:24

"For it is by grace you have been saved through faith, and this is not from yourselves, it is the gift of God, not as a result of works, so that no one can boast." —Ephesians 2:8-9

This new life Jesus has given them as a result of their faith in His work on the cross is something to celebrate. Rejoice with them! Ask them to pray out loud and verbally thank Jesus for forgiving and saving them. This will help reinforce their decision.

Memorize the Assurances

You might have your own materials, but I like to go over the Navigator booklet "Beginning with Christ" with new converts on the very first day of their Christian life. It addresses five lies Satan will *immediately* begin whispering in their ear but then provides a key Scripture to battle those lies with assurances of the truth:

1. Regarding **assurance of salvation:** "You don't think you are saved and your sins are forgiven just by believing and receiving Christ, do you? Surely that is not enough!"
   Memorize this battle verse: 1 John 5:11-12

2. Regarding **answered prayer:** "You don't think God is really personally interested in you? He's so far away and concerned about more important things. Surely you don't think He'll hear your prayers, much less answer them!"
   Memorize this battle verse: John 16:24

3. Regarding **victory over sin:** "You have life alright, but you are a weakling and will not be able to stand against temptation!"
   Memorize this battle verse: 1 Corinthians 10:13

4. Regarding **God's forgiveness:** "You've messed up again. Aren't you supposed to be a Christian? Christians don't do those things!"
   Memorize this battle verse: 1 John 1:9

5. Regarding **God's guidance:** "You don't really think God has a special plan for your life, do you? Why bother with Him? Make your own way!"
Memorize this battle verse: Proverbs 3:5-6

You can be sure the enemy (and even some of their non-Christian friends) will plant these kinds of questions and doubts in the fertile mind of a new convert. "Beginning with Christ" includes Scripture memory verse cards to battle each of Satan's lies. Whether you use this booklet or come up with your own verses, get your new brother or sister in Christ to start hiding God's Word in their heart. The devil will go running if they memorize and review verses on these key assurances.

Quiet Time

If possible, try to have a quiet time with the new convert the very next morning. If they don't have an easy-to-understand version of the Bible, get one for them. Help them download the Bible app and start on a daily reading plan. Show them how to read a chapter from the Bible, write down some thoughts, and make a daily application. Pray together for God to build a deep foundation for their new life in Christ. Help them make a prayer list, including praying for their roommate's salvation. Start from day one helping them have an outward focus.

→ THE FIRST WEEK

Help Them Identify with Christ

The two biggest hurdles a young believer faces are being able to tell their non-believing friends about their decision and breaking off the sinful activities they once engaged in. I'm not necessarily recommending this for everyone, but many times we have addressed this problem by asking a new Christian in front of their buddies, "Hey Brent, why don't you tell these guys what happened to you Wednesday night?" As cruel as it may seem, popping that question to an unsuspecting new Christian does them a huge favor. Once they take a big gulp, start talking, and fully identify with Christ in front of their friends, they are much less likely to keep joining them in old sinful habits—even if just out of sheer pride or embarrassment!

Invite Them to Make New Friends...but Keep the Old

Bring the new convert into the fellowship of your believing friends as soon as possible. They're at a very vulnerable stage, trying now to determine which group they are going to *primarily* identify with. Let them see they have a new set of folks they can hang with. Invite them to eat dinner with you, and bring them to your church and campus ministry meetings. Introduce them to other believers who can help them grow, but encourage them to stay connected, in a healthy way, with their current friends. The goal is for them to have solid Christian fellowship to nurture their walk with God while also living out their life change in front of their non-Christian friends. Strengthen them to stand strong against old temptations while shining the light of Christ into their existing relationships. Help them practice and become comfortable sharing their testimony of the difference the Lord has made in their life. Ultimately, though, if they are going to make it, they will have to choose as their very closest friends those who are running *towards* God, not away from Him.

Build a Growth Plan

When following up with a new believer, you should take ownership of getting them plugged into opportunities to grow in their new faith as soon as possible. Give them easy "on-ramps" to start building a foundation of walking with Christ. We have to remember that new believers are spiritual babies and require that level of care and intentionality. Continually invite and pursue them, even if they don't initially seem interested or don't show up. Keep taking active steps to make sure they get what they need. "Like newborn babies, crave pure spiritual milk, so that by it you may grow up in your salvation" (1 Peter 2:2).

Here are some other ways to help new believers grow:

- As much as you can, take them with you wherever you are going. Keep them close for the first few weeks, modeling life as a disciple of Christ and building a foundation for an ongoing discipleship relationship.
- Do the legwork of introducing them to other believers they share commonality with, building their network of Christian friends (e.g. "Have you met Kate? She lives on your floor and wanted to know if you would like to ride to church with her on Sunday.")

- Get them started on a simple, well-defined plan for reading the Bible, praying, and memorizing Scripture. Ask them frequently what they are learning.
- Help them find a small group to plug into, or start one for them and show them how to invite their friends.
- Set up a regular time to meet, and begin walking through discipleship lessons with them. Your ministry or church may have materials you will want to use. If you need some guidance in this area, we've developed something called "The Basics"—20 essential topics to go through with your new convert on the foundational truths of the Christian life, giving you the direction you need as you meet with them. Go to https://campusministry.org/tools/the-basics-discipleship-tools.

While all of these things are helpful, there are some core, "big picture" things you will want to work on with your new brother or sister in Christ.

Help Them Believe

About God: He is our loving and just Creator.

About self: We are hopeless sinners who have rebelled against a holy God.

About salvation: Our only hope for forgiveness and eternal life is Jesus taking the penalty for our guilt and giving us His perfect righteousness in return.

Romans 3:19-26, 5:6-11

→ THE FIRST MONTH

Think Evangelistically

Continue praying with your new disciple for their lost friends, helping them grow in compassion, and teaching them to look for ways to love and serve. Build relationships with the people *they* are close to, and take opportunities to share the gospel *together.* Starting your discipleship relationship with an outward focus will grow your new convert's heart for others and increase the likelihood they will make disciples themselves. Witnessing always helps connect the dots in their minds as to *why* they are praying, reading their Bible, living a holy life, etc.

Make Lordship Decisions

Begin helping your friend understand what it looks like when Jesus is King of someone's life. Teach them how to pursue victory in specific areas of sin they are struggling with. Share the practice of confessing sin and walking in forgiveness. Push them to start taking ownership of their own spiritual progress, faithfully committing to their growth plan. If they haven't yet, encourage them to join a solid local church, and show them what God's Word says about baptism. Help them understand the principle that love for God is not just about their feelings but should always lead to obedience. "Whoever has my commands and keeps them is the one who loves me. The one who loves me will be loved by my Father, and I too will love them and show myself to them" (John 14:21).

Below is Cru's diagram called the "Fact, Faith, Feeling Train," which sheds some light on the necessity of *believing* what God has to say about us rather than trusting our feelings as our source of truth. The engine represents the authority and promises of the Word of God and is supposed to pull the train. The middle car is the coal car, and every day we have a decision to make as to whether we are going to pour our faith into God and the promises from His Word or look to our feelings or emotions that day to dictate what we think or do. Our job is to chase hard after God rather than being led by certain feelings and to trust God to fill us with His peace, joy, and love as a result of consistent obedience to Him.

© Copyright Cru. Used with permission.

Help Them Believe

About God: He is sovereign and good.

About self: We are sons and daughters of God through our union with Christ.

About salvation: Our salvation wasn't based on our works, and neither is our remaining in Christ. We will make mistakes, but we are secure because our position with The Father is based on Christ's righteousness, not ours.

Psalm 115:3, 145:7; Galatians 3:1-6, 4:4-7

As the first step in establishing a new convert, "follow up" can often lead into an ongoing discipleship relationship. If you are able to continue to invest in your new Christian friend, you will help them grow into a disciple who is established in their walk with God and equipped to make disciples themselves.

Don't give up! It's so easy to lose patience with people when they are flaky or seem unmotivated. A specific example who comes to mind is a guy named Jon. When I (Paul) started meeting with Jon, I honestly didn't think he was going to make it. He had all kinds of wack theology and wasn't super teachable, but he was a new believer and was excited about meeting and getting connected to the ministry. I focused on helping him follow Christ and getting him engaged with the group. Over the course of a year, God did work, and Jon changed his heretical views just through his own study of the Bible and growing in faith naturally. He also developed more teachability. He grew to be a leader in our ministry, helping people come to Christ. Now as an alumni, he plays key roles serving Christ in a partner church of ours.

Just because someone is sending you mixed signals about how interested they are doesn't mean the Lord is not working in their life. Keep praying for them, loving them, and seeking to get them connected. I am so glad I didn't give up on Jon. There were times I wanted to, but God did his thing! Disciple-making really isn't about us. Our part is being persistent and showing up. God does all the heavy lifting! Let's ask Him to give us faith that He can radically change people's lives.

REFLECTION QUESTIONS:

→ Remember back to when you initially came to Christ. Was there someone there the first few days, weeks, or months to get you growing and going? If so, what did they do? If not, what difference do you think it would have made in your life?

→ After reading this chapter, what would be the first five things you would do with your new convert to get them started growing spiritually? Craft your own plan.

→ Why is memorizing key verses so critical for the new believer? Have you memorized the five assurances included in this chapter? If not, when could you do that?

→ Why is it so important for the new believer to develop a second set of friends made up of committed Christians? What difference will that make?

19

Handcrafted

As we stand in line outside the new restaurant, peering longingly through the window, our mouths water. Watching as someone behind the glass uses a recipe passed down through generations to lovingly create and cook the pasta we are about to order, we are filled with confidence that the hour-long wait will be worth it. In a world that runs on mass production, anything labeled "artisanal" or handmade stands out from the crowd and may become highly sought after. From coffee shops and bakeries to shoes and even luxury cars, the labels "small-batch" or "handcrafted" connote exceptional care and quality. Handcrafted often costs more to buy because it costs more to make; intentional investment, attention to detail, and the love and care of the artist are poured into each masterpiece.

Likewise, laborers are never mass-produced. Although there are certain truths and training *all* disciples should receive, they are handcrafted (by God and you!) through the process of establishing and equipping. Taking the qualities, convictions, and disciplines that have become the foundation of your life and passing them on to others is a time-consuming labor of love.

Helping a convert build a solid "undergirding" based on following Jesus is called establishing. While establishing focuses on strengthening their relationship with Jesus, equipping is training them to add more links to the discipleship chain—i.e. teaching them to reproduce what you are doing with them with another person. Equipping is passing on the knowledge, skills, character, and vision of disciple-making. The art of knowing when and how to successfully build the life of Christ into your disciples requires an investment of love and intentional time.

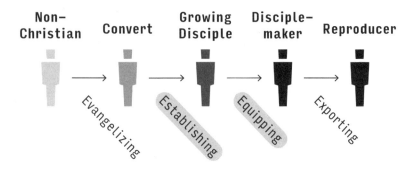

→ HANG-OUT-OLOGY

If you search the gospels and observe the way Jesus made disciples, you will find a life that is being imparted to others. Jesus "appointed the twelve that they might be with Him" in His everyday life (Mark 3:14). He wasn't asking them to meet together for a once-a-week discipleship group but to "follow Him" as He made them into "fishers of men" (Matthew 4:19). Jesus and His disciples traveled together on long trips, camped and ate together, talked about all kinds of subjects and difficult issues, visited crowded cities together, sailed and fished together, prayed together, climbed mountains and traveled through deserts together, worshipped in synagogues together, and were even persecuted together. We typically only focus on Jesus' teaching, but look at His amazing "all-inclusive" model here for life-on-life disciple-making. Quite the three-year "small group adventure!"

Drawing from Jesus' example, we see two principles emerging: association and demonstration. Jesus is associating with, or being *with*, His disciples while He is living out the kind of life He is calling them to. We might call this concept of association "hang-out-ology." Yes, He had an incredibly clear and intentional purpose for being here on earth, but He didn't let that take Him away from spending extensive time with His disciples. This gave Him a chance to consistently demonstrate in front of them the kind of life He was calling them to live. We see Him teaching about prayer and then praying in front of His disciples, proclaiming God's Word to others and then modeling application of key verses, and teaching about servanthood and then washing their feet. He wasn't just explaining how to live the Christian life but was also giving them a real-time example to follow: the most powerful, world-changing "show and tell" demonstration history has ever seen!

Let's learn from the Master, knowing that in the context of an ongoing relationship, we have the opportunity to transfer massive amounts of truth to another believer. If we only view our discipleship relationship with someone as a once-a-week training session, we will be shortchanging them. A simple saying to memorize is that we will have *no impact without contact.* We must be around our disciples a lot if we hope to watch them grow into sold-out followers of Jesus and lifelong disciple-makers. Now you may have a lot of Bible knowledge or even have the spiritual gift of teaching, but what your young friend primarily needs is demonstration more than just explanation. Living out our lives in front of them will bring credibility to our words. Robert Coleman, author of *Master Plan of Evangelism*, says, "One living sermon is worth one hundred explanations."

So what will it take to get good time with your disciples? If we are truly going to give our lives away to others, it will take unselfishness, sacrifice, servanthood, and legitimate friendship. Disciple-making may cost you a nap, a favorite TV show, or an activity you love. The Lord may ask you to put your early mornings, late nights, and even weekends in His hands—to use for His purposes. Are you willing to do whatever it takes to multiply your life? Get ready for a challenge as you get your eyes off of yourself and onto your disciples.

→ DIRECTION AND AFFECTION

I (Steve) had two different men disciple me in college. One took me through ministry materials each week during the "required" one-on-one meeting we'd agreed upon. At the end of my freshman year, he graduated, we shook hands, and I've never heard from him since. Later in college, God gave me a second man to disciple me, Vic Underwood, who loved me in spite of myself. I'd never met someone who cared, served, prayed, and invested in my life like Vic did. He didn't do it to impress others or even just out of obedience to God; he did it primarily because he *enjoyed* being with me, the highest compliment you can pay anyone. Even though I was like a wild bucking bronco when it came to respecting or submitting to his spiritual leadership, he never gave up on me.

Vic and I lived together my senior year, and I witnessed his servant's heart in the way he constantly made my bed and fixed the meals. I repaid his kindnesses by begrudgingly sitting in his early morning Bible study with a blanket wrapped around my head to protest the ungodly hour. Once during a prayer walk we took together, in the middle of his very sincere petition, I glared at his bowed head and scoffed, "You're the biggest phony I've ever met!" If there was ever a time I deserved for someone to call me a slimy imbecile and whack me, it was then. Instead, he patiently smiled, put his hand on my shoulder, looked right into my eyes, and quietly uttered four unbelievable words: "I love you, Steve."

To be honest, I don't remember any pithy statements or deep doctrine that Vic gave me back in those days—only his unconditional love offered to an arrogant, rebellious college student. He saw potential in me and stayed in the saddle no matter how much I tried to buck him off. The investment he made has reaped eternal dividends, and over forty years later, he still cares for, prays for, and supports me!

If you want to see your campus ablaze for Christ and build disciples who will launch out as laborers into the world, purpose-driven, love-filled relationships will have to permeate your life and ministry. Why? Because disciple-making is a powerful combination of direction *and* affection. My first discipler gave me all direction (going through materials) and almost no affection (building a friendship with me). Vic took us through some good stuff, yes, but the core of his discipleship was him pouring his life into me—almost on a daily basis for two years. Your fellow students aren't crying out for more impressive discipleship lessons but for someone to love them enough to form a lasting bond—a deep and meaningful relationship built on the person and purposes of Jesus Christ.

→ KNOWLEDGE, SKILLS, CHARACTER AND VISION

Once they know that you care, they'll care what you know. So how can you take the key resources and truths you have in your disciple-making tool belt and share them with those you are seeking to raise up? Discipleship training definitely includes knowledge but also involves skills, character, and vision.

Skills, character, and vision are the application of knowledge. Knowledge and skills can be *taught*, but character and vision must be primarily *caught* from a person close to you.

Once your friend has been established as a disciple, it will be time to expand their vision and outward focus to see the world and life through *God's* eyes. This is the move from establishing to equipping, and it requires even more modeling and teaching from you. In preparation for your time with your disciples, don't just "wing it"; you will need to come prepared. We have included a helpful One-to-One Planning Guide in Chapter 21. As you pray, think, and plan for your disciple each week, here are some "basics" you will want to include:

Biblical Knowledge
Get Them in God's Word
You are helping your disciple know God intimately, and He has taught us what we need to know about Himself in Scripture. The Bible also shows us God's plan of redeeming all mankind. As you think through a plan to train and equip your disciple, the Word of God should always be the centerpiece. It paints the picture of the One we worship and the mission we are on with our Savior. Paul exhorted Timothy to do the same with the men he was working with: "All Scripture is God-breathed and is useful for teaching, rebuking, correcting and training in righteousness, so that the man of God may be thoroughly equipped for every good work" (2 Timothy 3:16-17).

Rather than just trying to pass on to our disciples bits of wisdom that we have picked up in our Bible reading and study, teach them how to get into God's Word for *themselves*. You've probably heard the old adage: "Give a man a fish, feed him for a day. Teach a man to fish, feed him for a lifetime." If we apply this to our use of the Scriptures in our relationship with our disciple, we see that if we only tell them what we know, we will be feeding them for a short time. But if we emphasize early on *how* to study God's Word in a thorough and accurate way, we will actually be setting them up to walk with God and continue growing in their knowledge of Him for a lifetime. From day one, each Christian needs to begin nourishing themselves with the Scriptures: reading, studying, memorizing, and meditating on its commands, promises and principles.

Read Good Books with Them

> "It's not what you can teach them. It's
> what you can get them to learn."
>
> **—MAX BARNETT**

Although God's Word is the primary source of knowledge, we ought to also encourage our disciples to read or listen to books and podcasts by Bible teachers. Don't feel like you have to have all of the answers.

Seek out truth together. Working through a basic theology book with your disciple is a great way to grow both in your knowledge of God and of His Word. You will also want to point your growing believers towards great resources about other world religions, cults, church history, apologetics, and the current state of missions. Reading an occasional biography together about Christian leaders from previous generations can be incredibly motivating.

Practical Skills

If knowledge provides the what and the why, learning the skills is the how.

For example:

- How to study the Bible
- How to have a quiet time
- How to trust God
- How to meet people and build relationships
- How to present a personal testimony and the gospel
- How to follow up a new Christian
- How to recruit and lead a small group
- How to set goals and priorities and manage time
- How to make a disciple

To truly transfer a skill to someone, you must first *tell* them how to do it, then *show* them how to do it, *observe* them as they do it, *give feedback* on how they did it, turn them loose to do it, and then *stay close* so you can encourage them to *keep* doing it! You'll move from teacher, to partner, to observer in each skill area. Each time you begin working on an area, whether it is personal or ministry-related, you must think and pray through a simple, practical, and transferable plan to help them learn and use the skill.

It's critical that you not only teach but also model these skills to your disciple. Timothy spent seventeen years watching Paul, and at the very end, the aged apostle could confidently say to his partner in ministry, "You, however, know all about my teaching, my way of life, my purpose, faith, patience, love, [and] endurance" (2 Timothy 3:10). Yet as essential as living this "way of life" in front of them is, it is not enough. You must *explain* the biblical basis for the steps of faith you are taking. This will help them grasp for a lifetime the what, why, and how behind the Christian life.

> "It may be true that some things are better
> caught than taught, but other things must
> be taught before they can be caught."
> — CHRISTOPHER ADSIT, *PERSONAL DISCIPLEMAKING*

Disciple-making must involve both authentic relationships and systematic biblical training. If you take a shortcut in either area, you will struggle to produce fruitful disciples who will make disciples.

One of my favorite "Timothys" was a student named Trey. I (Steve) met Trey during his senior football season at the University of Arkansas. As he and I built a relationship, I invited him to stay after graduation to get more training; we would spend time together every day studying the Word, praying over the campus, going to meet students, and sharing the gospel. I have never met someone who was as much a "man of application" as Trey was.

He would watch me launch and lead a Bible study and then immediately duplicate it with a group of swimmers he had recruited. He watched how I shared the gospel and led guys to Christ, and the next day—he was doing it. He saw how I planned for a one-on-one discipling appointment with a student and could instantly do it himself. He wasn't satisfied with just knowing; it was the *doing* that wound his clock, so he would constantly observe, learn, and apply all in one seamless step. He continues to be a man of application, who not only has mastered a myriad of personal and ministry skills but has been passing them on to hundreds of others over the years.

Godly Character

Different areas of knowledge and skill can be *taught* over a shorter period of time. However, for a person's character to be permanently changed from the inside out, it has to be *caught*—usually over a period of years. This is such a foundational area, because if a disciple does not have basic Christlike qualities such as holiness, faithfulness, humility, and a strong work ethic, then no amount of knowledge, skills, or vision can make them a laborer in God's kingdom.

Spend as much time as you can (in all kinds of different situations) with your disciple to see what areas of character they are strong in and which areas need work. Pray godly qualities into their life, model it for them, memorize passages with them, and create projects designed to help them develop particular character areas. It takes time. In other words, don't expect someone who has been a "taker" all of their life to suddenly become a "giver" after a twenty-minute Bible study on servanthood!

This won't be your favorite thing to do, but to help someone grow in character you must practice the principle of biblical correction. "Whoever rebukes a person will in the end gain favor rather than one who has a flattering tongue" (Proverbs 28:23). You want to create a culture in your discipleship relationships that allows you to speak into their lives and give correction in a gentle manner. If you love those you disciple, you will tell them the truth. "Then we will no longer be infants, tossed about by the waves and carried around by every wind of teaching and by the clever cunning of men in their deceitful scheming. Instead, speaking the truth in love, we will in all things grow up into Christ Himself, who is the head" (Ephesians 4:14-15, BSB). We must speak the truth *in love* to those in whom we invest. They will never grow to be who they need to be without it. Shoot straight with people, being mindful to communicate with kindness. If they are teachable and if they are truly becoming a disciple—they will always love you for it.

Vision and skills will never be able to outrun character. As we grow in Christlikeness, it actually helps all other aspects of training. It is the soil in which knowledge, vision, and skills can grow.

Eternal Vision

Vision is the engine that pulls the train of our lives. It's our "why." Each believer needs to understand that all of life is about glorifying God by co-laboring with Him to bring worshippers from every nation to His heavenly throne. Having a clear-cut vision for your life and ministry helps bring meaning to all the efforts spent on gaining knowledge, skills, and character. If you want people you are discipling to have a God-sized vision for *their* lives and ministries, then it's going to have to be pumping through *your* veins as well. It can't just be a talk you give or a quote you read; it has to be authentic in your life if it's truly going to be transferred to your disciples.

Eternal perspective must ooze out of your every pore if you are going to pass it on. Those you are investing in should see you weep over the lost in prayer and observe you making sacrifices to advance God's kingdom. As Professor Howard Hedricks once said, "If you want them to bleed, you have to hemorrhage." Seek to give them an outward focus by praying *for* them and *with* them over the campus and the world. Always be asking them the "why" questions about their personal goals, use of time and money, ministry strategy, and future plans. Consistently expose them to visionaries who can keep painting the broad strokes of bringing *all* of our hopes and dreams under the lordship of Christ and His plan of making disciples of all nations.

It will take time to plan and prepare to infuse other students with knowledge, skills, character, and vision, but if you will persevere in equipping your disciples in these critical areas, it will produce an incredible multiplying effect! Here are some sample areas for you to think and pray over as you work with your disciples:

KNOWLEDGE

- Attributes of God
- Substitutionary death of Jesus Christ
- Baptism, indwelling, and sealing of the Holy Spirit
- Doctrine of the Trinity and roles of Father, Son and Holy Spirit
- How the Bible was put together and views of the authority of Scripture
- Hermeneutics (basics of Bible interpretation)
- Spiritual warfare
- The creation and fall of man
- Storyline of the Bible
- Sin, justification, sanctification, glorification
- Judgments and eternal rewards
- Eternal security of the believer
- The kingdom of God
- Purpose and role of the local church

- Sabbath, baptism, and the Lord's Supper
- Return of Jesus Christ and views of the end times
- God's view of sexuality
- Understanding the major religions
- Understanding the major cults
- Answering common objections to Christianity
- Overview of the Old and New Testaments
- History of the Christian church
- God's heart for the nations
- What happens to those who never hear the gospel?
- History of missions
- State of the world and missions

SKILLS

- Having a daily quiet time
- Memorizing and meditating on Scripture
- Praying using different methods
- Being filled with the Holy Spirit
- Social skills, meeting people, and starting relationships
- Sharing the gospel using various tools including personal testimony
- Following up with a new Christian

- Starting and leading an evangelistic Bible study
- Preparing for and leading a small group discussion
- Studying a book of the Bible using the inductive method
- Recruiting to and leading a discipleship group
- Forming and leading a ministry team
- Preparing for and delivering a message or workshop
- Recruiting someone to a conference or training project
- Presenting The Wheel illustration
- Presenting The Hand illustration
- Sharing the vision of fulfilling the Great Commission
- Determining biblical priorities, setting goals, and managing time
- Giving counsel to someone with a need/problem
- Discovering and developing spiritual gifts
- Developing world vision and building it into others
- Godly decision-making
- Centering dating relationships on Christ
- Recognizing and battling in spiritual warfare
- Stewardship of time and money

CHARACTER

- Abiding in Christ
- Compassion
- Contentment
- Controlling our thoughts and attitudes
- Courage in the midst of fears
- Discipline
- Excellence
- Faithfulness
- Fear of the Lord
- Following leadership
- Generosity
- Giving and receiving scriptural correction
- Gratitude
- Guarding against or overcoming bitterness
- Handling stress
- Healthy relationships
- Honesty
- Honoring parents
- Hospitality
- Humility
- Integrity
- Joyfulness
- Obedience to Christ
- Patience
- Perseverance
- Personal holiness and self-control
- Reconciling relationships
- Servanthood and privilege mentality
- Sexual purity
- Submission to authority
- Teachability
- The tongue
- Trust in the Lord
- Work ethic

VISION

- Heart for God
- Heart for people
- Heart for the Word
- Heart for the world
- Eternal perspective
- A lifetime of walking with Christ
- A lifetime of multiplying disciples
- A strategy to fulfill role in the Great Commission
- Living the World Christian habits (praying, going, sending, welcoming, mobilizing)
- Continuing growth and discipleship training
- Personal ministry target strategy
- How to invest their post-college years well
- Preparing for marriage, family, and career
- A game plan for lifelong generous giving

REFLECTION   QUESTIONS :

→ After learning all that it will require of you to help another person become a disciple, does that frighten or intimidate you... or excite you and make you anxious to get started?

→ Explain what it means to provide direction and affection for a student you are discipling. Give some practical examples of both.

→ As you look at the four lists of possible training topics to work on with your disciple, list two areas you yourself feel like you need to work on in each of the four main training categories (knowledge, skills, character, and vision).

→ What sacrifices do you think you will have to make in order to disciple someone the way Jesus did and the way we describe in this chapter? Who can help guide and encourage you?

20.

Choosing Wisely

When Campus Outreach first launched a team at Sam Houston State University, staff noticed the usual stereotypes that can mark sororities and fraternities. Students were engulfed in drugs, extensive drinking, casual sex, and disunity among the different organizations. "We have seen the culture of Greek life change over the past five years," said Melissa, the women's area coordinator. "Particularly, God raised up generations of laborers in one particular sorority at Sam Houston: Alpha Delta Pi. He used the lives of several women to start a movement of believers that still thrives today."

It all started with Jenny. She shared her faith with Leah. After Leah came to Christ, both Leah and Jenny discipled and influenced a second group of women who began to labor on campus. Three other believers joined Jenny and Leah, and through their efforts, four more women from ADPi sorority surrendered their lives to Jesus. Those four shared their faith, and two more came to Christ the next year. The links on their chains were growing!

As each year began, a new generation of ADPi believers enthusiastically shared their faith with the lost women in their sorority. The Lord has allowed more and more ADPis to start new lives in Christ each semester through the labor of a faithful few. In fact, Taylor, one of the women who came to Christ from this group, is now laboring as a full-time campus worker with Campus Outreach. She is focusing on ADPi, as well as another sorority, Alpha Chi Omega, with the hope that God will continue to move and multiply in the Greek system at Sam Houston State. "By God's grace, the trend continues," explained Melissa. "It's a beautiful picture of multiplication."

Remember our addition versus multiplication chart? Even winning 10,000 people a day to Christ can't keep up with the exponential power of multiplication! Yes, adding thousands per day to the kingdom is an impressive number in the early stages (on left), but if a disciple-maker stays faithful to raise up one more disciple-maker each year (and no one is the "last link"), the multiplication strategy (on right) has the amazing potential of winning the whole world to Christ. Check out the numbers!

	Evangelist	Disciple-Maker
Year 1:	365,000	2
Year 2:	730,000	4
Year 10:	3,650,000	512
Year 20:	7,300,000	210,994
Year 30:	10,950,000	190,406,656
Year 38:	13,870,000	8,124,017,323

However the magic of multiplication doesn't happen by accident. It requires diligence and faithfulness by each disciple. The key to reaching these numbers is an *unbroken* chain. If God's big goal is reaching all nations with the saving power of the gospel, making disciples who will make disciples is the way He has modeled for us to get there. Keeping the big picture in focus will help you make critical decisions about where and how to spend your disciple-making time and energy.

"He appointed twelve that they might be with him and that he might send them out to preach" (Mark 3:14, NIV). While He was on earth, Jesus loved everyone but purposely proportioned different amounts of time with different people. He had the masses who followed Him, the seventy whom He taught, the twelve whom He discipled, the three whom He brought into His inner circle, but then just one whom He passed off the key leadership role to. We would be wise to model our ministry strategies off of Jesus.

→ FOCUS ON THE FAITHFUL

"I have a lot of friends that need Jesus, and I want to learn to share the gospel with them like you did with me," Michael told Andrew, the campus ministry staff member who led him to Christ. Just six weeks after beginning his relationship with Jesus right outside the campus union at Florida State University, Michael asked Andrew to teach him how to share The Bridge gospel illustration. For the rest of the semester, they spent time learning how to share their faith and then going on campus to present the good news.

A few months later, Michael asked, "Andrew, do you think it would be a good idea for me to disciple a freshman guy next year like you did with me?" Absolutely amazed at what God had done over the past school year, Andrew replied, "Michael, I think that's a great idea!"

In just a few short months, God took a non-believing student and grew him into a disciple who is not only laboring in college but wants to continue to make disciples for the rest of his life. Why can't this be your story too?

"The things which you have heard from
me in the presence of many witnesses,
entrust these to faithful men who will
be able to teach others also."

—2 TIMOTHY 2:2, NASB

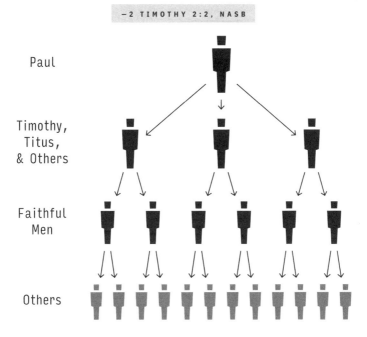

Our goal in making disciples is to keep the chain growing, multiplying laborers to reach the world. This means loving broadly but investing strategically. "All people are equally valuable, but not all people are equally strategic" is what Bill Bright, founder of Cru, taught. Because our goal is multiplication, find those who are the most responsive to your input and help them as much as possible. It's obvious from the verse above that one of Paul's last instructions to Timothy was to be very picky about who he chose to invest himself in. So don't select a student too quickly—let them show themselves "faithful" and "able to teach others also" before you dedicate a lot of your time and focus to them. To give you some guidance on what type of people to pray for and commit yourself to, consider those who demonstrate F.A.I.T.H. (Faithfulness, Availability, Initiative, Teachability, Heart for God and People). Those people are *most* likely to take what you teach them and pass it on—keeping the chain growing! You will know you've found a FAITHful person when you see these qualities:

Faithfulness

You're looking for someone who will meet you when they say they will, and show up for Bible study prepared (even if they have a big test the next day). You want a friend who you'd share a personal struggle with and trust they wouldn't dare pass it on to someone else. Reliable and dependable, they simply *do* what they *say* they will do. Without faithfulness or loyalty to God, to you as the discipler, and to their own word, it is really hard to start taking anyone anywhere! The faithfulness of a potential disciple is a great way to gauge their level of seriousness about growth. If they are good at saying a lot of impressive words but aren't ready to back them up with reliable and consistent actions, they probably aren't ready to be discipled.

Availability

College students are notorious for frantically filling up their schedules and then complaining about how busy they are! Jesus told some fishermen to follow Him in Matthew 4:19-20, and they "*immediately* left their nets and followed Him" (ESV). That's availability. Look for others who are willing to be flexible, change their schedules, and even give up things in order to meet with you or take advantage of spiritual growth or ministry opportunities. They can have all the potential in the world, but if they're not prepared to carve out the time to become who God wants to make them, you'll be beating your head against the wall. Let's face it, when someone says, "I don't have the time," what they're really saying is "I don't want to." We all make time for the things we really *want* to do, right?

Initiative

It's hard to steer a parked car, and that's exactly what some people are like. As much as you pray for them, challenge them, and bring them along as you do ministry, nothing seems to motivate them to take action in their own personal life or ministry. If you pour your life into someone who doesn't want to take what you've given them and pass it on, your efforts will reach a "dead end." You want to direct your time, energy, and training toward someone who isn't lazy or apathetic but a person of application. So, if you find yourself always having to initiate in order to meet with them, or it's like pulling teeth to get them to come to Bible study, you may be working with the wrong student. Pray that God will give you a key student or two who will aggressively take what you give them and be willing and able to pass it on to others.

Teachability

Does this person *want* to spend time with you, even seek you out? Do they ask you questions, seeking your guidance in their Christian life and personal ministry? Are they thirsty for knowledge and a seeker of truth? Are they quick to repent? Are they open to you and others pointing out areas they need to work on? Proverbs 9:8 is a huge indicator: "Do not reprove a scoffer, or he will hate you; reprove a wise man, and he will love you." Care and correction are a necessary part of the discipling process. If someone is resistant to your input into their life or character, you may not be able to help them grow.

Heart for God and People

We can't really know the motives of others, can we? Some believers are caught up in trying to please or impress others by engaging in the right activities and attending the right meetings. Be praying and looking for individuals who have a *genuine* hunger to intimately know the Lord. They are willing to "seek first the kingdom of God and His righteousness," making sacrifices like Matthew 6:33 teaches. That heart for God should also produce an interest in reaching out to others with compassion and concern for their lives and souls. If they seem to be entitled or self-absorbed instead of serving and sharing their faith with others, they may not be willing or able to pass on what you give them. When the Lord gives you a student who loves

God, likes and enjoys others, has a network of friends, and is willing to push aside other priorities to help people grow, I would encourage you to put a priority on pouring yourself into them!

As you consider these qualities in those you are hoping to disciple, think about your own life. Which of these areas do *you* need to grow in most to become a person of F.A.I.T.H.? None of us have ever arrived, but the time to start working on these blocks in your *own* foundation...is now. You can't reproduce something that is not in your life.

→ NO DEAD-END DISCIPLESHIP

Let me plead with you not to be guilty of "dead-end discipleship." This is pure busyness without any real strategy, and it happens when Christians meet with Christians to make them more Christian but never break out of their "holy huddle" to engage lost people. When water flows into a pond but no water flows out, it's just a matter of time before the smell becomes unbearable. God made us to be conduits with water flowing in *and* out at the same time. Brian Zunigha at California Baptist University says, "Discipleship without evangelism is not discipleship. It's actually just recycle-ship." Too often, what passes as spiritual multiplication is nothing more than reorganizing Christians. There are no shortcuts to experiencing true spiritual multiplication. We need to raise up disciples who have the faith, courage, and spiritual maturity to "labor" among lost people until God saves someone.

Jesus was clear in Matthew 4:19: "Follow me, and I will make you fishers of men." The goal was not just to have an audience for His good works but to train them to fish by watching Him fish. Jesus called His disciples to be *with Him* as He traveled from town to town, crowd to crowd, teaching and ministering. Yes, occasionally He drew them away for some debriefing, prayer, or rest together, but for the most part He was on the go, preaching and reaching the masses. His goal was to provide His followers with a real, live, walking, talking, twenty-four-hours-a-day classroom, full of object lessons for life and ministry. He was influencing many, and in the process, training a few, thus providing dynamic discipleship to His followers—in the context of *ongoing evangelism*.

Just to help me remember, I call this DICE—Discipling In the Context of Evangelism. Jesus modeled this (especially evident in the book of Mark) where He was constantly on the go reaching out to others but would use every scenario, every opportunity, every pit stop to pour truth and life lessons into the 12. Here are some practical ways to help steer your disciple-making clear of dead ends:

- At the beginning of every discipling relationship, start praying together for the conversion of their lost friends and family. Keep expanding this prayer list.
- Encourage disciples to choose a "pocket of people" (i.e. an affinity group) on campus with whom to live or build relationships, and begin broadly sharing the gospel with them in that group as opportunities arise.
- Take them with you when you have gospel appointments. If someone comes to Christ, you could have your disciple do the follow up with the new believer. It's important that they gain experience in practical ministry.
- Make sure all you teach and do with them is transferable and simple enough that they could easily see themselves able to quickly share the same things with their friends and contacts.
- As you train them in a discipline or discipleship concept, plant seeds of vision and spiritual reproduction. I slip subtle phrases into our discussion like: "When *you* lead another student to Christ, this is a tool you can use to follow them up." It's fun to see their eyes light up as they sense you believe in them!
- Pray daily and specifically for God to grow your disciples into laborers and for Him to provide them with someone to lead to Christ and disciple soon. Pray together for this *during* your meetings.
- Provide coaching and training once they start discipling someone. Spend time each meeting discussing how it is going with their disciple, helping them pray, plan, and act to help move their disciple along the continuum from convert to disciple to disciple-maker.

Jordyn was a residential leader in her dorm at Tarleton State University and was looking forward to investing in the girls in her hall. During move-in week, she prayerfully met all of her freshmen residents and sought to find out where each of them was spiritually. Only one girl in her hall, a believer named Ashley, seemed willing to talk with her about Jesus. Because of her role in the hall, Jordyn's residents didn't initially trust her, which made sharing her faith really difficult. So Jordyn began investing in Ashley and invited her to jump into the awesome community she had found with the Baptist Student Ministry on campus. Ashley was excited to learn how to present her testimony and the gospel, and she and Jordyn spent time praying for their hallmates.

By the middle of fall semester, Ashley's roommate Kaylee came to Christ. Ashley took the initiative to start discipling Kaylee, just like Jordyn had discipled her, and together they began to pray for and share with their hallmates. They started a Bible study in their dorm room, and by spring semester had so many girls coming they had to move it to the common area on the floor. By the end of the year, fifteen freshmen girls had begun a relationship with Christ. Jordyn poured her life into Ashley, a freshman full of F.A.I.T.H., who invested in Kaylee—and between them the entire hall was impacted by the gospel!

To be the best stewards of the gospel, we want to invest in people who will truly absorb and utilize the training we give them, being obedient to evangelize and make disciples themselves. God's amazing love spreading through the awesome power of multiplication can move like wildfire from your campus to those who have never heard! The Lord can use you to be the spark that ignites a fire that spreads across your campus—and to the world!

REFLECTION QUESTIONS:

→ Jesus specifically chose just 12 men—and didn't choose
others—to disciple. Today, though, choosing a certain student
to disciple over others feels unfair or too exclusive to some.
How can you avoid letting the culture dictate your ministry and
instead follow the example of Jesus?

→ Which of the five characteristics (FAITH) do you personally
feel strongest in right now? Why? Which of the five do you feel
weakest in right now? Why that one? What can you do this week
to start growing in that area?

→ As you are making a decision about which student(s) to begin
discipling, put in your own words what characteristics they
should have.

→ As you disciple someone, why is it not enough just to teach
them how to share the gospel? Why do you need to actually
immerse your disciple in regular, ongoing evangelism?

21

Plugged In

Zach had no spiritual background when he started as a freshman at the University of Northern Colorado, but when some fellow pledges invited him to an evangelistic Bible study in his fraternity, he went. The first time he said yes to their invitation was just because his friends were going, but Zach continued to show up to Bible study, week after week, learning more each time about Jesus being his Maker and Savior. After the fall, he committed to going to a Campus Outreach winter conference and even recruited nine of his friends to come with him to help them learn the things he was learning!

At the conference, he heard about a summer project and committed to go to investigate what it would look like to really follow Christ. He recruited several of his fraternity brothers to join him for the summer as well. At the project, Zach realized his huge need for Jesus and surrendered his whole life to Christ. In the fall, he started a fraternity-wide evangelistic Bible study, as well as a growth group with three freshmen who were new Christians. Guess what? Zach is going back to the summer project this year as a group leader and is excited about the opportunity to influence the guys he recruited and will lead this summer!

The essential knowledge, skills, character, and vision your disciples need in order to reproduce will happen in the context of relationships. Your one-on-one input, along with their friendships with other students who are also becoming laborers for Christ, is the fertile soil in which your disciple will grow into a world changer. Getting students you are leading plugged in with other believers will provide fellowship and accountability beyond what you alone can give them. If you are helping someone grow into a laborer, spend time thinking through the groups you will encourage them to connect with, as well as the intentional time you will spend training them.

→ GROWING IN GROUPS

Helping someone develop into a laborer without connecting them to a community of fellow disciples will be slow, challenging, and incomplete. Having peers alongside them who are equal in maturity will push them to grow together. As you seek to help establish young believers, try to get them coming to a regular large group meeting of other students, a small group Bible study, conferences, and retreats.

Large Groups

Encourage students you disciple to get connected with a good local church. Introduce them to the leadership, find out what the process is for joining and getting publicly baptized, and perhsps even find a place you can serve together. If you are a part of a campus ministry with weekly meetings, go to these, and bring your disciples with you. Large group meetings are not to be a substitute for small group and one-on-one discipling but rather a supplement that reinforces what they're learning in their small groups.

Small Groups

Small groups are the backbone of your ministry. If your goal is ultimately to raise up disciples who make disciples, then a small group is the place where you can more specifically challenge the people you are leading and observe their FAITHfulness. Much of Jesus' discipleship took place in the context of a small group. Whether you call it a growth group, vision group, discipleship group, action group, or just plain 'ol Bible study, it needs to have a few essential characteristics:

Clear Purpose, Plan, and Commitment

As the discipler and facilitator of your group, you will need to come into each semester and into each weekly group meeting with a plan. This small group is your chance to influence multiple disciples at once—and don't underestimate the power of them motivating and sharpening one another. Come each week with a prayed-up, thought-out plan so you won't waste this awesome opportunity. Don't think you have to be on staff with a church or have a seminary degree to lead a small group. The essential ingredients are a love for those students and a love for the Word. However, your end goal is not just to have Bible studies but to be moving them along the growth process toward becoming a fruitful laborer themselves.

Determine which students have been FAITHful and get them in groups together. If possible, start small groups among people who know and like each other and have things in common (e.g. they live in the same dorm, are part of the same team, are all freshmen or international students, all live off campus, are all education majors, etc.) If you are starting evangelistic Bible studies in affinity groups with relational connections, these can grow into discipleship groups as members come to Christ and commit to grow.

I would suggest setting clear commitments so everyone knows exactly what they are joining. Being too free-spirited and loose on the front end may result in a lack of follow-through. At the same time don't set the bar so high that it's unrealistic, or your small group will get discouraged and give up. Evaluate each participant's spiritual hunger and faithfulness, and design a growth group with challenging but reachable standards.

Examples of three different levels of standards for your group:

1. Just come every week for an hour with no preparation.
2. Prepare in advance and memorize a verse.
3. Significant preparation, memorize two verses, and meet for two hours.

It won't take long to see who is going to be faithful to come, prepare, participate, and apply what they are learning in the group. Progressively setting higher standards at each level not only challenges the participants but gives you an objective way to help you determine who you should invest in—always based on who is *most* FAITHful. Investing deeply to train those who are investing themselves is strategic if you want to make disciples who will go on to make disciples. As this study winds down, be thinking about what kind of group you want to invite the faithful ones to consider next. Give it a different name, choose higher standards, and expect an always growing commitment to an outward focus of taking personal responsibility for the Great Commission.

Good Discussion

Another essential component of a good small group is that everyone is involved in the open dialogue. Sharing is usually the best format for growth rather than teaching. Discipleship happens most effectively when you can help your disciples discover truth on their own rather than you "educating" them. A big chunk of the preparation you will do for your small group is thinking through and crafting just the right questions. Each question you ask should move your group closer to the objective you have picked for your time together. Self-discovery is the goal of a good question. Never tell anyone something they could discover on their own!

So, don't view yourself as a teacher but more as a discussion leader and, most of all, a friend and fellow learner. Whether you choose relevant topics, fill-in-the-blank Bible study materials, or just take on a chapter a week from a book of the Bible, make sure your time is centered around the study and *discussion* of the Word. You can practice your preaching somewhere else. Instead come prepared with awesome questions you open up one at a time, like beautifully wrapped presents; then watch with excitement as they devour each question like a kid on Christmas morning!

I've been training students to prepare and ask questions in small groups for centuries. (Well, not quite!) If you choose to create your own questions, always start by prayerfully thinking through what your small group objective is for the week. What one powerful principle or conviction do you want the participants to walk away with from that study? Once you've discerned that, you can start to craft the three basic types of questions you will ask in the group time: discovery questions, understanding questions, and application questions. You can remember these by thinking of the sequence: what, why, and how.

- The **Discovery** Question—An open-ended, well-worded question that introduces a topic. It's a "what" question that looks for facts and content.
- The **Understanding** Question—A more narrow, well-worded follow-up question that forces everyone to wrestle with the meaning of what was uncovered from the discovery question. It's a "why" question that looks for purpose and provokes thought.
- The **Application** Question—A direct, well-worded final question that challenges participants to make these relevant truths a reality in their lives. It's a "how" question that looks for ways to specifically apply this to their lives.

Each time you ask a question, you will want to go through three phases: first, you *launch* the question, then you *guide* the discussion, and finally you *summarize* all the input.

- **Launch** the question: In a conversational tone, begin the dialogue on the given topic with that well-crafted, open-ended question. After you ask it, be quiet and wait for an answer. Don't try to reword the question.
- **Guide** the discussion: Affirm your group's answers and ask a few of the others to elaborate. You are simply the facilitator. Picture yourself trying to keep a beach ball up in the air and passing the discussion around, making sure everyone is contributing. Keep your main objective in mind as you seek to guide them toward it.
- **Summarize** the input: Wrap up each set of questions with some conclusions and a summary statement. This is not a time to teach but a time to affirm them by briefly restating what was shared.

So, start with your main objective, and then pray and think through your three types of questions to help guide the group toward that objective. Each time you ask, keep the launch, guide, and summarize phases in mind:

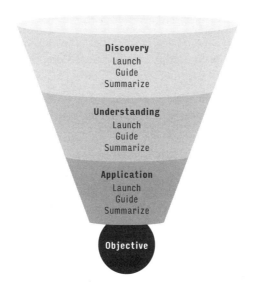

→ ONE AT A TIME

As we mentioned before, the large group and small group meetings are simply supplemental to the one-on-one discipleship you can give someone. This individualized input is the most effective way to meet each disciple where they are and help them take their next step toward becoming a laborer. The primary way to learn where your disciples are is to spend a lot of time with them. As you hang out and observe them interact with others, you will get a clear idea of the areas they need to work on. So rather than just sharing whatever you're currently learning, think about what will be best for them to learn based on where you perceive them to be. Take a little time each week to pray, think, and plan how to best serve the friend you are discipling. Asking these questions will help: What is the current status of their spiritual life and ministry? What can I work on with them this week to move them toward the next step of maturity?

Below is a suggested outline for preparing for a one-on-one with your disciple. As you use this approach or one of your own, remember that even if you create the perfect next step, you still need to fervently ask God to grow them. "Unless the LORD builds the house, those who build it labor in vain" (Psalm 127:1). To spend this much time praying and thinking deeply how to grow your disciple each week may seem overwhelming to you. I understand. That's why Jesus said, "The harvest is plentiful, but the laborers [or workers] are few." It does take hard work, week in and week out, to guide a young believer along the path of growth and fruitfulness. I venture to say, you will be the *only* person in that young believer's *whole* life who will *ever* take weekly time to specifically pray and plan for their spiritual maturity. Truly a once-in-a-lifetime opportunity for you—and them.

One-On-One Weekly Planning Guide

Disciple's Name:

Date:

Where are they in their personal and spiritual growth?

- What is their greatest need right now?
- What is the next step to meet their greatest need?
- Based on my observations, what area of knowledge, skill, character, or vision do I need to focus on this week?

- How can I help them grow in this area? (Circle one or more):
  - Do it in front of them
  - Tell them why
  - Show them how
  - Do it with them
  - Connect them with another person
  - Keep them going
  - Help them reproduce it
  - Share a tool

Where are they in their personal ministry?
- What is their greatest need right now?
- What is the next step to meet their greatest need?
- Based on my observations, what area of knowledge, skills, character, or vision do I need to focus on this week?
- How can I help them grow in this area? (Circle one or more):
  - Do it in front of them
  - Tell them why
  - Show them how
  - Do it with them
  - Connect them with another person
  - Keep them going
  - Help them reproduce it
  - Share a tool

Is there something I could do this week to give them some affection or direction?
- What do I need to pray for them about?
- What encouragement can I share with them?
- Is there a challenge, responsibility, or assignment I need to give them?
- Is there something fun we could do together that would deepen our friendship?

We are firm believers in having a list of basic biblical principles and training objectives we want every disciple in our ministry to walk through as they build their life on a solid foundation. Notice we said "training objectives" instead of lessons. Yes, lessons are an essential part of the process, but the goal is that these concepts will be integrated into the disciple's life. We don't "move on" beyond the basics until we are convinced of true progress in the bottom-line essentials of what it takes to have a vibrant walk with Jesus Christ. LeRoy Eims, author of *The Lost Art of Disciple Making*, says, "In helping a young Christian grow, you need a step-by-step building program in mind. You can develop certain objectives you want him to attain before he undertakes others. You want to see him go from taking in spiritual milk to partaking of spiritual meat."

May I tell you about one young college student who really put this into practice? At a Division I University, Ted was a scholarship football player as well as a pre-med student when he was led to Christ by a teammate involved in our ministry. Ted started growing, sharing his faith, and influencing other athletes almost immediately. He got a taste of leading other guys to Christ and discipling them to disciple others...and was hooked. Each week he worked hard to complete his workouts and study sessions in order to maximize his time in building his own displemaking chains. The Lord answered his prayers for stronger discipline, time management, and work ethic to get it all done. In fact, he became so committed to his Great Commission calling on that campus that he scheduled *everything* out, even the weekly outing (Thursday nights from 7-9 pm) he would have with his very beautiful girlfriend—now wife!

There were students all around Ted who were spending *all* their time with girlfriends, or working out to look like a Greek god, or being fanatical about studies and grades. But Ted didn't care. He put blinders on and knew exactly what God wanted him to major (and minor!) in while in college. It wasn't long until Ted became, in my humble estimation, the "most thorough discipler" I've ever known. In the midst of all the demands on him, and now all the various groups and men he was leading, he would hide out each Sunday afternoon to do nothing but specifically pray and customize a plan for each of his men for the upcoming week.

He would spend 1-2 hours working through a planning sheet like the one we just explained in order to be able to provide the kind of direction *and* affection each man needed. And when one of his key men led a guy to Christ, now Ted was thinking how to help his guy...help his guy. And when that third generation guy started to grow and lead others to Christ, sure enough, Ted was allotting his Sunday afternoon to pray and think through *each* link in the chain—i.e. how he could equip his key man to disciple his key man to train his new convert how to share his faith. Can you tell now why I call him the "most *thorough* discipler" ever? I fall short of Ted's standard in my own ministry prayer and planning, but I strive towards it. You can too! As you pray, think, plan, and build into the lives of your disciples and their disciples in such a deep and impactful way, these 5 Cs may help.

→ THE 5 C'S

If we want to reproduce disciples who are grounded in their faith, we must learn how to impart the basics. A concept that has helped me build a strong foundation in people I disciple is the "5 Cs."

Christlikeness: Do it in front of them

If I want to see my disciples live out the life of a Great Commission Christian, I must live it out in front of them. I cannot hope to see the people I am leading practice these spiritual disciplines if they don't ever see me doing them. The classic discipleship principle always rings true: more is caught than taught. My example and model cannot be overstated.

Confidence: Do it with them

I need to have purposeful involvement in the life of my disciples. This means not only sharing my faith in front of them but also alongside them. I need to let them see me study the Word but also study the Word with them. Shared experiences and feedback ought to be a regular part of discipleship.

Conviction: Teach them why

As important as the previous two principles are, if we do not combine them with conviction from God's Word then we will create modern-day Pharisees. Yes, we spread a world map out in front of us to pray over various nations together, but *why* do we do that? Our disciples must be convinced from God's Word why a life centered on Jesus Christ and His purposes is something they ought to pursue with all of their heart, soul, mind, and strength. Thus, gradually weaning them off *our* convictions to make sure they are forming their *own* is critical.

Competence: Show them how

The Christian life doesn't come naturally. We must come alongside new Christians and show them *how* to pray, how to meet people and build relationships, how to resolve conflict, how to recruit a disciple, etc.... Skills and tools for personal growth and ministry are much needed for new believers, and we as disciple-makers are the people to patiently and practically teach them—in an excellent and thorough way.

Consistency: Keep them going

Give constant encouragement and provide regular accountability to those you are leading. Walk beside them, and keep them going! We want our disciples to continue living out the basics of the Christian life as well as reproduce them in others. The point is always to try to move them from extrinsic motivation to intrinsic—from the "ought to" to the "want to." Spend time together as long as it is possible. When one of you moves on, stay in communication and encourage them to get connected with new groups and leaders who can help them continue to grow.

So, keep your disciples plugged into large groups of other believers who are headed in the same direction, small group Bible studies to challenge and encourage them, individual training times focused on personalized growth, and—most importantly—the true power source. Just watch as the Father of lights shines His beacon from your campus to the whole world!

REFLECTION QUESTIONS:

→ Do you have a large group meeting you attend that is full of committed believers you would want to bring a young convert to? Describe it.

→ Have you ever been part of a small group where the leader did not teach but mainly asked questions? What kind of an experience was it for you and the others?

→ What would an ideal discipling relationship look like to you? Is there someone who would be responsive (and faithful) to your invitation to disciple them?

→ As you read over Ted's story of how thorough he was in his praying and planning for each of his men, did you feel overwhelmed? Or were you motivated to be used by God in such an impactful way in the life of another believer?

22

Two Are Better Than One

"Two are better than one, because they have a good return for their labor"
—Ecclesiastes 4:9 (NIV)

God wants to raise up other students who will stand alongside you to impact your school and the world for Christ. To reproduce a laborer who has the same conviction, perspective, and "know how" you do is a monumental achievement that—apart from the power and blessing of God—is absolutely impossible! There may be things in this chapter you feel like you could never accomplish. Don't feel like the Lone Ranger. Here's a prayer I often pray, especially when I feel inadequate and powerless:

> "Lord, I can't...but then you
> never said I could.
>
> Lord, You can...but then You
> always said You would."

So hang on as we challenge you to not only trust God for big things but to aspire to spiritual impact. One of my heroes of the faith was William Carey, the first missionary from the West to go to Asia in 1792. After 40 years of ministry, he proclaimed: "Expect great things *from* God. Attempt great things *for* God." Are you up for it? Let's do this!

→ REPRODUCE YOURSELF

You cannot produce disciples or disciple-makers in bulk. Let's say that in a particular group or sphere of influence, you were able to meet 15 students and get to know each of them a bit. You prayed for them and loved them, and you were able to individually invite 10 to participate in a small group. Eight say yes, and six show up. Through a series of increasingly challenging small groups and one-on-one interactions, there emerge three students whom you would describe as faithful. As you spend time with each of these three, you realize one or two are not just faithful, but people of F.A.I.T.H. as we've described. These one or two students will be who you deposit your life into over the next months and years.

> "Why do something others can or will do, when
> you could do something others can't or won't?"
>
> —DAWSON TROTMAN

The apostle Paul had a ministry team consisting of Sopater, Aristarchus, Secundus, Gaius, Timothy, Tychicus, and Trophimus (Acts 20:4). Titus would certainly have to be included also, but as far as we can tell, Timothy (whom he spent seventeen years discipling) was the primary person he invested in. The final letter we have from Paul is the tear-stained second letter to his protégé in which, knowing the end was near, he expressed his desire to see him one last time: "I thank God, whom I serve with a clear conscience the way my forefathers did, as I constantly remember you in my prayers night and day, longing to see you, even as I recall your tears, so that I may be filled with joy" (2 Timothy 1:3–4, NASB).

Like parents who have great joy when their children grow up to embrace their values, Paul could depart this earth knowing he was leaving a legacy— someone to carry on his work the way he would. It is unlikely Timothy made it to Rome before Paul was martyred, and yet the apostle could die a satisfied man, knowing Timothy would perpetuate the message to "faithful men" who would "teach others also." The chain would not be broken.

If God blesses you with a faithful person to pour yourself into, every moment is precious as you seek to pray, love, serve, and build into them the essential knowledge, skills, character, and vision needed to be a lifelong laborer for Jesus Christ. Now that you have a full-fledged partner in ministry, the equipping process continues as you lay out a game plan to empower this key student to be a laborer and leader who will do exactly what you do.

→ THE SYNERGY OF MINISTRY TEAMS

It may take you a year or two of challenging, persevering grassroots minis-try to get this far, and many people never do. But the formation of a ministry team can have an explosive effect in reaching your campus and raising up laborers to fulfill the Great Commission. The funnel continues to narrow as you take students through the investigative group stage, select the most responsive ones to form a discipleship group, and finally, invite the students who want to link arms and labor alongside you to form a ministry team. You are inviting them to really step up and stand shoulder-to-shoulder with you as you reach the campus and the world for Christ. You are asking them to become partners, and the shift has taken place—they are no longer part of *your* ministry, you are now part of *theirs!*

Regardless of the names you give your small groups, these are the three basic stages:

Investigative Group—(or evangelistic Bible study) strictly inward-fo-cused, trying to help each student make Jesus Savior and Lord

Discipleship Group—combination of inwardly and outwardly focused, establishing each student's foundation in Christ as well as starting to equip them to begin laboring for Him

Ministry Team—primarily outwardly focused, equipping each student to develop their own personal evangelism and disciple-making ministry

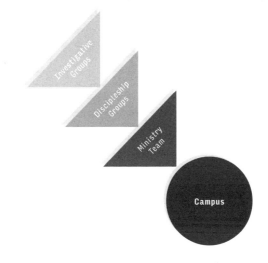

→ MY FIRST MINISTRY TEAM

God granted me (Steve) the privilege of putting together my first ministry team the year I graduated from college. I decided to stick around for a
couple of years after I finished my bachelor's to get more training from my
discipler and to finish up the work I had started with these six men: John,
Dennis, Ted, Lewis, Dave, and Terry. To finally "whittle down" to these six
guys took two years and a gazillion hours of prayer, relationship building,
evangelism, one-on-one establishing appointments, Bible studies, conferences, and who knows what else! The initial funnels had included many
groups and myriads of men, but most of them took various "exit ramps" as
the months wore on and the commitment level rose. I still loved all of them,
and they knew it; but I had literally poured myself out for these six, because
they had endured and emptied themselves out in return. Now, as the "lone
survivors," we were banding together to impact the campus for Christ. The
best word I could find to describe our ministry team was:

> **synergy:** the interaction of individuals such that the
> total effect is greater than the sum of the individual
> effects

I will never forget the first time we gathered in my upstairs one-room
apartment near the campus to pray and make battle plans. As the hours
rolled by that night, and with only a small lamp for light, we huddled in a
circle, all leaning forward and listening. You could feel the power and sense
of destiny in that tiny room, as each man knew the incredible price he had
paid to be sitting there. I had led four of the men to Christ through investigative Bible studies and one-on-one evangelism appointments. The other
two I "adopted" because of their faithfulness to a challenging, yearlong 5:30
a.m. Bible study I started—and their passion to share the gospel with others.

Think Big, Start Small, Go Deep
All six had a dorm or campus "people group" they were praying for, where
they were building relationships, sharing the gospel, inviting to small
groups, and relying on God to move. My job was to pray for them, encourage them, gather them weekly for inductive Bible study, strategize with each

one individually, and spend time in *their* sphere, helping equip them to establish *their* ministry. I was teaching each man how to start from scratch, and as Campus Outreach staff teach their student laborers, to "think big, start small, and go deep."

When Dave, John, or Terry met guys in the group they were laboring in and built a friendship, we would say they had a "toehold" in that group. If one of those friendships blossomed into a discipling relationship, we would say they had a "foothold" in their sphere. If one of the ministry team guys was able to equip a student who was now evangelizing and discipling in their own affinity group, we would then tally it up as a "stronghold." Here's the progression:

Toehold–You have a friend in your ministry sphere.
Foothold–You are discipling someone in your sphere.
Stronghold–You are equipping someone in your sphere who is now taking responsibility to reach others in that group. You can start over in another sphere if you choose.

As we prayed and strategized together, our goal was to develop a stronghold in every affinity group on campus. By the time I left for seminary two years later, we had not reached our goal. But we did have a depth chart made up of 268 students who were all plugged into small groups and either discipling or being discipled by someone involved in our ministry. Our banding together radically impacted each of our lives, and the sum total of our joint efforts created a campus-wide movement of laborers being trained and placed in a myriad of new affinity groups on campus. A small, grassroots "ministry team" had multiplied into a full-blown movement that was about to start touching the world for Christ. God was at work and we were hanging on for dear life!

→ FROM THE CAMPUS TO THE WORLD

Even more important than just reaching our campus for Christ, the experiences these ministry team members had laboring in college gave them the preparation and passion they would need to launch from the campus to impact the world. Since college, two of the men have spent their lives ministering in China, one in Germany, and two are lay leaders in their state-side churches. One did not persevere.

The final step in the discipleship process is exporting disciples into the world. I know this sounds like I'm shipping big wooden crates to overseas markets rather than helping fellow students find their most strategic role in God's mission. But in order to come full circle and reproduce ourselves into others who will go and do likewise, we need to send out (i.e. export) Christian laborers into this lost and dying world. Joining God by raising up workers for His harvest is called mobilization. Here's one definition:

> **mobilization:** deploying an army of laborers whose lives are shaped around the Great Commission to the front lines in order to reach the world for Christ

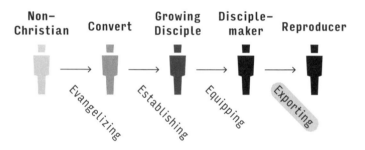

→ HOW MANY WORLD CHANGERS ARE ON YOUR CAMPUS?

Let's speculate together. At this very moment, how many groups or individuals at your school do you think are planning or carrying out a campus-wide, world-changing strategy of evangelism, establishing, equipping, and exporting laborers to fulfill the Great Commission? I would *like* to say you're one of many staying up late tonight plotting and praying to take over your campus for Christ, but we would be very naïve to think so.

Some would say the following estimates are generous, but if you are on a campus of ten thousand, depending upon what part of the world you're in, there may be up to five thousand students who are members of a church or attended as a child. Out of these "churched ones," there might be 1,000 who have *truly* received Christ into their lives as Lord and Savior. Of the

1,000 genuine born-again believers, possibly 250 are actively growing in their faith, and even fewer—maybe 50—could be called "growing disciples" according to our profiles. Out of those 50 sold-out disciples, how many have *personally* led another student to Christ? Hopefully, 25 have. How many of the 25 have intentionally followed up their new convert and begun to disciple them? Ten would be a liberal figure.

And finally, how many of those ten students could say they continued in obedience to the Great Commission and have actually made a disciple? I would be amazed if there were five students on your campus right now who have taken another student through the whole discipleship process Jesus laid out for us in the Scriptures. And, taking off my sandals in fear of treading on holy ground, I dare not even speak of the possibility of a student on your campus becoming a reproducer (i.e. equipping a disciple to become a disciple-maker, truly multiplying their impact). Here's the estimated breakdown:

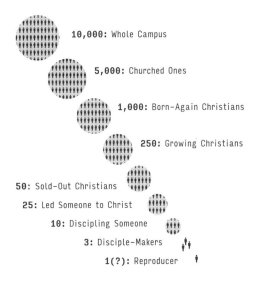

10,000: Whole Campus

5,000: Churched Ones

1,000: Born-Again Christians

250: Growing Christians

50: Sold-Out Christians

25: Led Someone to Christ

10: Discipling Someone

3: Disciple-Makers

1(?): Reproducer

Whether you think my estimates are too high or too low, we can probably agree that winning others to Christ and helping them become disciples and disciple-makers is definitely a tall order. It is certainly a God thing, but He wants to use you to pull it off! And when you provide the fuel, God can produce a flame that burns bright enough to reach from your campus to the

ends of the earth. That's what Bill Bright, founder of Cru, believed about
the awesome potential of winning, building, and sending college students
to take the gospel to the nations. One of his famous statements—"Reach
the campus today. Reach the world tomorrow."—has always been a huge
motivator for me, knowing that every college or university has the potential
to be an incredible launching pad and sending base to thrust laborers out
across the planet. Would you like to see the Lord use your life and ministry to touch other nations with the gospel? You can and we're about to tell
you how!

REFLECTION QUESTIONS:

→ Could you picture yourself leading or being part of a 4- to
6-person ministry team someday, each one equipped and then
pulled together to impact your *whole* campus for Christ? What
excites you about that possibility?

→ Think of the different living groups, affinity groups, or relational
networks you are part of or know of on your campus. Which
ones do you already have a "toehold" in? How could you move
that to the "foothold" stage?

→ Think about your own campus. Are those numbers listed on the
"How Many World Changers on Your Campus?" graphic too high
or too low for your school? Why do you say that?

→ We are about to move into the final section of the book
that highlights mobilization. We define mobilization here
as "deploying laborers whose lives are shaped around the
Great Commission" to reach the world for Christ. What would
it mean for you to for *your* life to be "shaped around the
Great Commission?"

Go Global:

You Are a Missions Mobilizer

23

Miranda came from a middle-class family near St. Louis that loved her, took her to church, and did their best to instill good values in her. However, she was never quite satisfied with her station in life, always comparing herself with others and wishing she could have nicer clothes, a cooler car, and a charge card to do with as she pleased. When she got to college, she turned her back on God and on her parents' upbringing and instead chose to run with the fast crowd. This group of hedonists were into seeking thrills, obtaining material possessions, and arrogantly flaunting their "It just doesn't get any better than this!" attitude to others. Miranda spent two years chasing this dream and trying to fill the emptiness in her soul, only to come to a dead end one day when, after receiving a notice that her $20,000 credit card limit had reached its max, she purposely got drunk and ran her convertible into a tree.

Now laid up in intensive care, Miranda had plenty of time to reflect on her life and the choices she had made. When she was released from the hospital, she went back to her campus apartment, got down on her knees, and determined to return to God and start searching for real meaning in her life. A high school friend had been bugging Miranda to come to a campus ministry event with him, and she decided now was the time to quit making excuses. The program that evening consisted of a visiting band of missions mobilizers called The Traveling Team that went from campus to campus sharing the story of God's heart for the nations.

Miranda had grown up in church, been a leader in Fellowship of Christian Athletes, and even tried to keep up with what was going on in the world, but she had never heard passages or stories like the ones the speaker was unfolding that night. She sat mesmerized, learning that God had given her all these different blessings in life (health, education, finances, technology, salvation, the Bible, etc.) not to horde for herself but to give away to others. Realizing she had basically always been a "taker" rather than a "giver," she became resolute about making a real difference in the world she was hearing about. She set up an appointment to meet with one of The Traveling Team reps the next morning, and as they chatted, Miranda started to see her whole life flash before her. This confident, self-sufficient girl broke down crying, repenting of her selfishness, her ego, and her inward-focused Christianity.

The Traveling Team rep plotted out a timeline for spiritual growth and mission involvement for Miranda and then connected her with that campus ministry's staff woman. Together, they started meeting for quiet times, Bible study, and working through the *Xplore* study the Traveling Team rep had given her. A year later, Miranda finally got the chance to go with a summer missions team to Kiev, Ukraine, where she spent two months getting to know students, sharing her faith, and leading them to the Savior. By the fifth week, she was hooked. This was *exactly* what God had created her to do. She no longer cared about what others possessed and what she didn't. Instead, she became eternally grateful for all that God had blessed her with and purposed to spend her life giving it away to the desperate and those separated from Christ.

Now a changed woman, Miranda came back to campus serving and sharing the Lord with every international student she could and immersing herself in giving rather than taking. Miranda is now about to graduate and has been offered a high-paying position with a large advertising firm, but instead she is trying to figure out a way to become a university English teacher in a closed country. The difference in her is a real, lasting peace and fulfillment in her heart. She's found an endless source of joy that only comes when we say no to ourselves and yes to God.

Looking back, Miranda remembers the things in The Traveling Team presentation about God and His world that lit a fire in her heart and moved her to reframe and refocus her life in light of God's passion to reach all people. We want to share some of those same powerful truths. This chapter is divided into three sections to give you a clearer vision of God's Word, God's world and God's work. Our prayer is that this knowledge will add fuel to your mission flame, enabling it to grow into an all-consuming fire. Let the facts inflame you!

→ **GOD'S WORD**

God's heart for the nations shines through in every book of the Bible, and it is His passion that drives our own. From the beginning, God blesses His people to be a blessing to all nations. "Now the Lord said to Abram, 'Go from your country and your kindred and your father's house to the land that I will show you. And I will make of you a great nation, and I will bless you and make your name great, so that you will be a blessing. I will bless those who bless you, and him who dishonors you I will curse, and in you all the families of the earth shall be blessed'" (Genesis 12:1-3, ESV). God makes a promise to Abraham to make him into a great nation as innumerable as the stars in the sky and the sand on the seashore. God's purpose was that through this family, He would bless all the families of the earth. Jesus, the greatest blessing to all nations *and* a descendant of Abraham, is the fulfillment of this amazing promise!

God's desire to be exalted by all peoples *will be* fulfilled. "Be still, and know that I am God. I will be exalted among the nations, I will be exalted in the earth!" Psalm 46:10 proclaims loud and clear. In this psalm, King David encourages us to quiet ourselves and meditate on the awesomeness of God. As we contemplate the attributes of His character and the power of His actions, we begin to see that His glory is such that the only appropriate response is that everyone everywhere would worship Him. This is where all of history is headed; God our Creator, our Father, and our Savior will be worshiped by *all* nations. The revelation to John and to us is a vision of this desire becoming a reality: "And they sang a new song, saying, 'Worthy are you to take the scroll and to open its seals, for you were slain, and by your blood you ransomed people for God from every tribe and language and people and nation'" (Revelation 5:9).

Author and pastor Dr. John Piper illuminates this ultimate objective in an excerpt from his book *Let the Nations Be Glad*: "Missions is not the ultimate goal of the Church. The glory of God is the ultimate goal of the Church because it is the ultimate goal of God. The final goal of all things is that God might be worshipped with white hot affection by a redeemed company of countless persons from every tribe and tongue and nation. Missions exists because worship doesn't. When the Kingdom finally comes in glory, missions will cease. Missions is penultimate (the next most important thing);

worship is ultimate. If we forget this and reverse their roles, the passion and the power for both diminish." Please read that again, nice and slowly, to let it really sink in.

A global thread purposely and supernaturally runs from Genesis clear through Revelation, calling us to forget the pitiful, transient allurements of this world and turn our eyes toward bringing glory and honor to this magnificent Lord and His worldwide objective of recruiting the nations to be His "white hot" worshippers!

→ GOD'S WORLD

Our family has started doing new 1,000-piece puzzles together when we get together for the holidays. Everyone is excited at first, quickly finding and putting together all the edge pieces and the obvious, uniquely colored ones. (Yes, we *always* start with the easy pieces.) But as the hours roll by and all that is left is a couple hundred tiny pieces of dark forest that all look alike—that is when it gets tough. Most everyone gradually disappears from the table, and only one or two have the vision and tenacity to see it through to the end. The more I think about it, puzzles and reaching the world for Christ have a lot in common. The main similarity? We always focus on the easy parts first and leave the hardest ones until the end. Here's an example. There are hundreds of churches in my cozy little college town, with many more being planted each year, all feeling called by God. In contrast, there are tens of thousands of other cities and towns around the world, many much larger than ours, that have absolutely no churches.

> "We talk of the Second Coming; half the world has never heard of the first."
>
> **—OSWALD J. SMITH**

Why the disparity? Either God has a distribution problem or we have an obedience problem. I guess it's human nature to tackle the enjoyable and painless tasks before we do the difficult and complex ones. But this is no fun holiday puzzle. Eternity is hanging in the balance for billions of lost souls, and we have the unbelievable opportunity to "stay at the table," joining Him in completing His history-long, worldwide puzzle of getting the gospel to every corner of the planet—especially the hard places. We call it "the final frontier" and the urgency of this dilemma begs the questions:

<u>If not now, when? If not you, who?</u>

The world is definitely like a mysterious and perplexing gigantic puzzle. Our God and Creator decided to divide us up into thousands of distinct "people groups." A people group is not a country but a *nation* (translated *ethne* in the Greek language). When Jesus said to "make disciples of all nations" in Matthew 28, He could not have meant countries; those boundaries and names have changed hundreds of times since then. He meant "*ethne*," or ethnic groups: bands of people who share the same unique language, customs, appearance, and religion. Although there are about 225 countries, there are approximately 17,000 of these unique *ethne* around the world, ranging from 2,500 to 25 million people. Almost two-thirds of these groups are "reached" (i.e. they have a church led by their own people reaching out to its own people), while one-third are "unreached" (i.e. they are still waiting for a laborer to come and plant the message of Christ and have a church established in their people group). There are lost people all over the planet and excellent mission efforts being carried out on each continent, but most of these "unreached people groups" we're describing lie within a certain area of the world called the 10/40 Window.

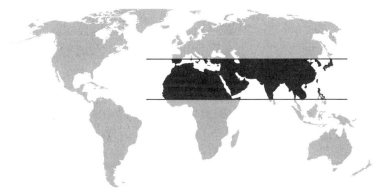

Named for its location—between 10-degrees latitude and 40-degrees latitude above the equator, stretching from North Africa across the Middle East and including just about all of Asia—this is truly the final frontier. Estimates are that well over half of the world's population lives in this box, with over one billion Muslims, one billion Hindus, and one billion Buddhists, secularists, tribals and animists combined. It's not only the least evangelized, most illiterate, and most economically disadvantaged part of the world with hundreds of millions starving, but it's also where, each year, the majority of Christian martyrs worldwide are killed for their faith.

Satan has a stronghold on this portion of the world like none other, intimidating the Christian church to such an extent that less than 10% of the world's missionaries dare go there to live and minister. The real obstacle to finishing the job of reaching these unreached people is not just a lack of money, knowledge, materials, or even opportunity. It is, and always will be, a lack of workers willing to go to one of these people groups and lay their lives down to bring the message of salvation and see it take root. Why, after 2,000 years of having the command to preach the gospel to every person, are there still so many people who have never once heard the name of Jesus?

> "86% of all Muslims, Hindus, and Buddhists
> in the world will live and die and
> never even meet a Christ-follower."
>
> —CENTER FOR GLOBAL CHRISTIANITY

In his book *Counter Culture*, David Platt pleads with believers to take the plight of unreached people seriously: "When will the concept of unreached people become intolerable to the Church? What will it take to stir our hearts and lives for men and women whose souls are plunging into damnation without ever hearing of salvation? This cannot be conceivable for those who confess the gospel. For if this gospel is true, and if our God is worthy of praise from all people, then we must spend our lives and mobilize our churches for the spread of Christ's love to unreached people groups all around the world. Jesus has not given us a commission to consider, but a command to obey."

Praying for Laborers

You can tell a lot about a person by who their heroes are. For most, it's a star athlete, famous celebrity, politician, or billionaire entrepreneur. I'd like to challenge you to reconsider who you are lifting up and wanting to emulate. Why not move from the temporal to the eternal, from the worldly to the world changers? Since coming to Christ, Christian leaders (especially missionaries) have been the men and women I (Steve) have admired and respected the most. My wife and I have read numerous mission biographies together over the years. Doesn't sound too romantic, you say? You'd be surprised!

One of our missions heroes, 20-year-old Englishmen Hudson Taylor, had this experience when God called him to spend his whole life sharing the gospel in China:

"On Sunday, June 25, 1865, unable to bear the sight of a congregation of a thousand or more Christian people rejoicing in their own salvation, while millions in China were perishing for lack of knowledge, I wandered out on the sands alone, in great spiritual agony; and there the Lord conquered my unbelief, and I surrendered myself to God for this service. I told Him that all the responsibility as to issues and consequences must rest with Him; that as His servant, it was mine to obey and to follow Him — His, to direct, to care for, and to guide me and those who might labor with me. Need I say that peace at once flowed into my burdened heart? There and then I asked Him for 24 fellow workers, two for each of the 11 Chinese inland provinces which were without a missionary, and two for Mongolia; and writing the petition on the margin of my Bible. I returned home with a heart enjoying rest such as it had been a stranger to for months."

Next time we gather with other believers at church or on our campus, let's ask God to open our eyes to a moment like this. Seeing many worshipping *here,* may we be burdened for all of the places *there* where worship cannot happen until someone acts.

→ GOD'S WORK

A number of years ago, someone asked Dawson Trotman, founder of the Navigators, "What is the need of the hour? Some say it's larger staff teams or facilities, better communication, transportation, or literature. Some say if we just had more money, then we'd get the job done. What is the answer, Daws?"

With a burning heart Trotman responded, "What is the need of the hour, you ask? God is the God of the universe, and He will supply every need we have to pull it off. The need of the hour is an army of soldiers dedicated to Jesus Christ, who believe that He is God and that He can fulfill every promise He ever made, and that nothing is too hard for Him. The need of the hour is people who want what Jesus Christ wants, who believe He wants to give them the power to do what He has asked. Nothing in the world can stop these people."

How about you? Are you willing to rise up in this hour of need as a dedicated soldier of Christ who wants *only* what He wants? Trotman believed this kind of laborer would not (and could not) be stopped until the job was done and the Great Commission fulfilled. Although Trotman never got past one semester of college, supported himself as a gas station attendant, and weighed only 125 pounds ringing wet, he had a contagious passion for the world that couldn't be contained. He would zero in on the men he was discipling, slam his fist into his hand, and with a booming voice proclaim, "The world for Christ!" They knew he believed it with every fiber of his being. After Trotman drowned in 1956 while saving the life of a young girl at a lake, Billy Graham preached at his funeral and declared that he had never known anyone who had touched more lives for Christ than Dawson Trotman.

Does the world burn on your heart? If it does, then this powerful, uncontrollable fire will multiply, passing from you to those you disciple and ultimately to the world. How can you grow your heart for the world and how does God want to use you? That's where we're going in this next chapter.

REFLECTION QUESTIONS:

→ Why do you think so few people, even Christians, really care that there are billions of people on the planet totally cut off from the gospel and even knowing about Jesus?

→ What fact or statistic in this chapter most impacted you? Why? What do you think is the solution to this worldwide dilemma?

→ Study and describe the characteristics of the 10/40 Window in your own words. Almost half of the world's population lives in that box, but the church has not yet penetrated huge portions of it. What is it going to take to get the gospel to every people group in that window?

→ In light of this chapter, what are some specific and practical things you could start doing to grow your concern and love for the lost in other nations? Will you start this week?

$$24$$

Your Most Strategic Role

Our all-knowing and all-loving God has decreed before time that you and I, as His precious children, would have the distinct privilege of co-laboring with our Heavenly Father at this juncture in history to help complete what He has started. What began in Genesis ends in Revelation where His Son, the Lamb of God, sits on the throne and receives the reward for His suffering from believers from every nation, tongue, tribe, and people (Revelation 7:9). If you are a believer, you are going to be there and part of that magnificent eternal tapestry. You will look or speak differently than most there. You might have a different worship style than those around you.

No worries. It will be a glorious day for all of us—a beautiful symphony of praise to our Lord, singing "Amazing Grace" in 7,000+ languages. If that is our final destination, what are we to do with our time and life between now and then? How can you and I be a strategic and faithful tool in the hands of God to make sure that everyone is present and accounted for on that Revelation 7:9 day? Let's try to come up with some practical ideas.

→ WHAT IS A WORLD CHRISTIAN?

The Lord yearns for us not to be worldly Christians (we have plenty of those!), but to be "World Christians": those who not only view the world and life from God's perspective but share His heart for all people, doing what we can to see the nations reached.

The very last thing Jesus uttered before He finally departed this earth and ascended into heaven is found in Acts 1:8: "But you will receive power when the Holy Spirit has come upon you; and you shall be My witnesses both in Jerusalem, and in all Judea and Samaria, and even to the remotest part of the earth." His final words could have been so many different things: "Get along with each other," "Love your mother," "Don't cuss," etc, etc...What would *you* have said?

Buy *why* did He say this, and what does it mean? To truly understand what Jesus was communicating here, we need to put on our tri-focal eye-glasses. We are all commanded to be simultaneously giving of our time, talent, and treasure to reach all three geographic areas: our Jerusalem, *and* Judea-Samaria, *and* the remotest parts. Like the bumper sticker that says "THINK GLOBALLY, ACT LOCALLY," wherever we are and whatever we're doing, we are to be carrying out a world vision. Reaching every people group on earth is a team sport in which every member of the body of Christ plays a vital role. Let's look at five habits a World Christian should adopt as they seek to live a life on mission with God.

→ GOING

Jesus gave us the command to "*go* and make disciples of all nations," yet most of the church chooses to *stay* far away from the areas of greatest need. There are about 600 million active Christians in the world today. The estimate is that we only need 100,000 of them to be long-term, cross-cultural mission-aries to finish reaching every unreached people group. That means if 1 out of every 6,000 Christian disciples would go, the light of the gospel could penetrate the remaining darkness. With 600 Bible-believing local churches for every one unreached people group in the world, you would think we could together recruit enough qualified goers to complete this task. Let's pray Matthew 9:36-38, asking the Holy Spirit to raise up and launch out workers to fill this quota!

College students have these amazing seasons called summers where they can spend 6-8 weeks "abroad," taking advantage of numerous opportunities to do cultural exchange programs on college campuses among unreached people groups. Picture yourself this summer on the other side of the world, sharing the gospel with a student who has never heard the story of Jesus. The mission trip I (Paul) took the summer of my sophomore year was one of the most life-changing experiences ever. God can use an adventure like this to stretch your faith, shape your character, and grow your heart for the nations. He may even give you a vision to go long-term to the unreached!

What would keep you from investing at least one of your summers in college in a strategic mission experience? How can you start preparing to go?

We love short-term missions, and if we have convinced you to go on a summer mission trip, we will be doing backflips out the window. However, we are also asking God to spark something in many of your hearts to make longer term commitments. Let's be honest—the Great Commission will not be fulfilled through short-term missions. The need of the hour is for people to move to an unreached people group, learn the language and culture, and invest their lives in bringing the gospel to people who won't otherwise hear about Jesus. This can't be done in six weeks.

What's more, many people might be *willing* to go but are *planning* on staying. Or they, like most, are waiting for a voice from heaven or emotional calling from on high telling them to be a missionary. Interestingly, this is one of the only areas of life we apply this "lightning bolt calling" concept to. We need folks who are *planning* on going, but are *willing* to stay if that is most strategic for the kingdom! Hudson Taylor, missionary to China, pierces our hearts with plain truth: "With these facts before you and with the command of the Lord Jesus to go and preach the gospel to every creature, the burden of proof will lie on you to show by what circumstances you were meant to stay out of the foreign mission field."

→ PRAYING

> "Prayer needs no passport, visa or work
> permit. There is no such thing as a 'closed
> country' as far as prayer is concerned...
> Much of the history of missions could
> be written in terms of God moving in
> response to persistent prayer."
>
> —STEPHAN GAUKROGER, BRITISH
> PHILOSOPHER AND HISTORIAN

If we will be faithful to intercede for the nations, our prayers will break down strongholds of sin, soften the hearts of leaders, open the doors for missionaries, and pave the way for nationals trying to win their neighbors. Dick Eastman, author of *The Hour That Changes the World*, claims prayer is the most powerful and effective weapon we have to bring about real, lasting change in people and nations. As Eastman says, "To pray for world evangelization is to serve on a 'Great Commission Fulfillment Committee' that meets daily in the courts of heaven." Gotta' love it!

> "For My house will be called a house
> of prayer for all nations."
>
> —ISAIAH 56:7

Do we really believe our prayers can make a difference for the unreached around the world? If we did, we would devote ourselves to passionate and persistent prayer for the nations! When I pray, I often have to remind myself that it is not just an intellectual exercise but a dynamic moment of spiritual impact. Sometimes I have to ask God to give me faith that my prayers will make a difference. "And without faith it is impossible to please God, because anyone who comes to him must believe that he exists and that he rewards those who earnestly seek him" (Hebrews 11:6, NIV).

A common barrier to interceding for the world is not knowing where to start. It's rare for God to give us a burden to pray for something we don't know anything about. We must feed our minds with "prayer fuel" so we can pray intelligently and strategically. One tool that has been a game changer for me is *Operation World*. It is a book as well as an app with statistics and prayer requests for every country. If you follow their daily prayer guide, you can pray for every nation on earth over the course of a year. Another great tool is the Joshua Project app. Each day they feature an unreached people group to pray for. There is something powerful about believers all over the world coming together to pray for the salvation of the same souls on the same day. On the Prayercast website, you can watch brief video prayers for many nations around the world, interceding as you look into the lives of the people you are praying for.

Adding one of these tools to your daily devotional life will be a great start to developing a habit of praying for the nations. Get newsletters from missionaries you know personally and pray for their ministries. Joining with others to pray can also be a great way to grow your faith and focus in prayer. If there is not a group of people praying for the world on your campus, start one. God is calling many of you reading this book to stretch yourselves, open your eyes and hearts to what is happening in the world, and make an earth-shattering difference among the nations from right where you are!

→ SENDING

Christians around the world are some of the wealthiest in all of history, with a total net worth of tens of trillions of dollars. Yet the estimate is that we give only one-tenth of one percent (000.1%) of our income to reaching the unreached. I've seen studies that show we spend more on cosmetics, on pet food, even on Halloween costumes for pets than we do on reaching the world for Christ! However, a huge part of being a sender is sacrificial giving.

Through giving, anyone can make an eternal difference among the unreached. When you invest in missions, you enable missionaries to have the money it takes to physically go to the nations. "How, then, can they call on the one they have not believed in? And how can they believe in the one of whom they have not heard? And how can they hear without someone preaching to them? And how can anyone preach unless they are sent? As it is written: 'How beautiful are the feet of those who bring good news!'" (Romans 10:14-15).

I love the simplicity of the Apostle Paul's logic. Only those who hear the gospel can be saved. The only way to hear the gospel is for someone to preach it. For someone to preach the gospel, it takes people to send them. If there is no sending there is no preaching. If there is no preaching there is no salvation. The act of sending creates a chain reaction that leads to the salvation of unreached people.

Out of the 100,000 students who volunteered for missions from 1886 to 1930 with the Student Volunteer Movement, about 20,000 actually went and 80,000 stayed at home to help fund them. Imagine applying that ratio today, having four people team up and each provide one-fourth of a missionary's support. This kind of sacrifice would allow us to make tremendous strides in getting funds to the front lines. I don't know specific giving stats for other countries, but 96% of all money given by Americans to Christian causes stays in the U.S.! I estimate the worldwide church has roughly 3,000 times the financial resources and 9,000 times the manpower needed to finish the Great Commission.

You may be reading this as a broke college student and thinking, "Someday I hope to have money to give to missions." But guess what? You don't have to wait for a big bank account to be a generous giver/sender. In God's economy, generosity is not measured by the greatness of the gift but by the greatness of the sacrifice. "As Jesus looked up, he saw the rich putting their gifts into the temple treasury. He also saw a poor widow put in two very small copper coins. 'Truly I tell you,' he said, 'this poor widow has put in more than all the others. All these people gave their gifts out of their wealth; but she out of her poverty put in all she had to live on'" (Luke 21:1-4).

To be a financial sender you will have to take a radical look at your lifestyle in order to scale it back and give more to God's kingdom work around the world. Being a strategic sender should be no less sacrificial than going to the nations as a missionary. Every Christian has the same responsibility for fulfilling the Great Commission. The only difference is the role that we each play. Joining God's mission through giving means denying some of your *wants* to contribute to the *needs* of reaching the unreached. Giving in such a way that you feel the sacrifice will deeply connect your heart with the mission. Is there an activity or item you regularly indulge in (pizza, coffee, nails, gaming) that you could deny yourself in order to *send* the money instead of *spending* it? We have also seen students creatively raise money for missions, organizing events such as a "Ramen Party" where they get together to eat ramen noodles for lunch and pool the $10 they would have spent at Chipotle to give. Build the habit of giving now, and start making investments that will make you rich for eternity!

→ WELCOMING

The United States, along with numerous other countries, host huge numbers of international students. Well over five million people are studying outside their home country, and over one million of those in the States. In addition to our opportunity to welcome students, there are professionals, immigrants, and refugees from other countries too. How are we to view these people and how are we to treat them? God had some strong words for the Israelites as to how they were to relate to foreigners: "The foreigner residing among you must be treated as your native-born. Love them as yourself, for you were foreigners in Egypt. I am the LORD your God" (Leviticus 19:34).

Many of these people come from "closed" countries where it is very difficult for missionaries to go.

It's almost like the Lord told us to go to the world and gave us all these resources to do so, but we instead chose to stay and enjoy the comforts of home. "Well," God says, "if you won't go to them, I'll just bring them to you—right to your campus and doorstep. Is this close enough now?" Loving them, winning them to Christ, and sending them back to their home countries to share the message of Jesus might be the most strategic ministry of all.

In his excellent book *Live Life on Purpose,* Claude Hickman shares a challenging story. "At one of the larger universities we visited, my wife Rebecca met with a girl to talk about world missions. As they talked, the girl obviously had a heart for China, and believed strongly she was called to be a missionary there. She wanted to learn Chinese, and it was all that she could do to not quit school right then and go to China. Finally Rebecca asked her, "Well, are there any Chinese students here at your campus?" The girl looked back at her, kind of confused, then responded, "Well, yeah, but they cluster together and they all live in one dorm." Rebecca asks, "Well, have you ever visited that dorm?" "No," she replied, "It's all the way on the other side of campus. And they just stay to themselves!" Finally Rebecca pointed out the obvious, "Tonya, what makes you think you're going to cross an ocean and reach Chinese people, if you won't even cross the campus to reach out to them?"

Many of today's international students will be tomorrow's world leaders. But if you're like me, you have ignored or neglected them far too often. And sadly, statistics show almost 80% of international students will study in the U.S. four to six years and never even enter an American home. They want to, of course, but are not invited. We can change all that if we believers choose to embrace a "World Christian" perspective and lifestyle. God can use us to touch the world right in our own backyards because the nations send their best and brightest to our universities. It's sobering to know that if the international students from closed countries at your school don't hear the gospel during their time there, they probably never will. I pray that gives all of us a renewed sense of urgency.

So do you have room in your life for one more friend? What if that friend was an international student? The ministry of International Students

Incorporated (ISI) encourages us to try it and see what God will do. Pray for them. Love on them. Give them rides to the airport, take them shopping, and invite them to visit church with you (many will accept just out of cultural curiosity). Let them see what your life and your faith are all about. You might just end up sending them back with a vision to reach their own country for Christ. That's definitely the most strategic (and cheapest!) way to infiltrate the nations with missionaries. You never know when your simple act of reaching out and initiating a friendship might change eternity for a person—or even a nation.

A friend of mine named John who was involved in reaching international students at the University of Texas at Arlington befriended a Japanese student, Kaz, and over the course of two years led him to Christ. Before he left for Japan, Kaz wrote this letter in broken English to John and his other friends in the ministry.

Dear My Friends,

Well, it's time to say goodbye to all of you. Before to say that, let me tell you something. It has passed two years since I came to Texas. I still remember the first day. I was so excited about the UTA life, studying, research and experiencing different culture and meeting new people. There was one thing I never imagined that I was to become a follower of Christ. My life has been changed a lot after I became a Christian. I have been greatly blessed by God. He has given me a purpose of life, joy to live with Him and He set me free. I realize that I am a sinner and weak, but I don't worry about my future because God is always with me. I would like to thank all of you guys from the bottom of my heart. You helped me make this decision. When I was reading Bible three weeks ago, God gave me a word that clearly tells me why I am going back to Japan. "Then Jesus came to them and said, 'All authority in heaven and on earth has been given to me. Therefore go and make disciples of all nations, baptizing them in the name of the Father and of the Son and of the Holy Spirit, and teaching them to obey everything I have commanded you. And surely I am with you always, to the very end of the age'" (Matthew 28:18-20). Now I can clearly see why God has placed for me in Japan. I want to live for Him who saved me and changed my life. I am going back to Japan where it is a dark place where Christian is just 1% of population. I am sure Satan will attack me in many ways, but I am ready to protect myself, and even I don't worry about that because I put all my faith in God. Keep praying for me that God will give me the church where I can grow and more other Christian and possibly start ministry. I also pray for people of Japan who have never heard about gospel. Again thank you for everything you have done for me. I am so blessed to know you. I am so proud of all of you, and I will miss you. Enjoy your life in UTA and God bless you. Love you all.

Your Brother in Christ,

Kaz

→ MOBILIZING

A World Christian is someone who is practicing the habits of going, praying, sending, welcoming, and *mobilizing*. A mobilizer has been awakened to God's heart for the nations, and as they are sprinting toward the goal of fulfilling the Great Commission, they take the time to turn around and help others see the urgent need for missions. At the end of the day, mobilization is discipleship. It is helping other believers see a more complete picture of what it means to be a follower of Christ and their role in God's grand story of redemption. Todd Ahrend, founder of The Traveling Team, says, "Very few students have been introduced to the fact that 3 billion souls are without Christ. Even fewer students realize their lives can be used to impact the eternal destiny of these people. We need to motivate students by sounding the trumpet that life is about more than just themselves."

Dr. Ralph Winter, founder of the Perspectives on the World Christian Movement course, believed, "The number one priority is for more mission mobilizers." Standing before a crowd of college students, Dr. Winter challenged them, saying, "Suppose I had a thousand college seniors in front of me who asked me where they ought to go to make a maximum contribution to Christ's global cause. What would I tell them? I would tell them to mobilize. All of them." Why would a former missionary and now missions leader seek to talk people *out of* becoming missionaries? Because the need to sound the alarm is so great.

Imagine a fire broke out on the roof of your dorm or apartment right now. You would have some choices to make. One option would be to scream, run outside to turn on the garden hose, and begin to squirt the blaze. Your efforts alone would surely not be enough to save your building. But what if instead, at the smell of smoke, you called the fire department to wake up the station full of 100 sleeping firemen to come put out the blaze? Yes, it'd take five or six minutes for the firefighters to get up, drive over, hook their huge hoses up, and begin spraying, but they would definitely be more likely to put out the fire and save your building. You and your tiny stream of water don't compare to rallying a team to come and pour thousands of gallons of water on the fire.

The person living for God's global purpose knows the task is bigger than one person. They need to mobilize as many committed World Christians to going, sending, praying, and welcoming as they can. The untapped resources of the Church are unbelievable. The mobilizer is trying to redirect the money, energy, and hearts of the church for the cause of the Great Commission. You don't have to be a great public speaker or writer to become a mobilzer; you just need to be a disciple-maker. The first step is living out the World Christian habits described in this chapter and encouraging those you disciple to do the same. Challenge them to go on a summer mission trip with you. "Come with me" is much more powerful than "You should go."

What if you started your Bible study or discipleship meeting by watching one of the short Prayercast videos together and asking God to move in the hearts of people across the world as He moves in yours? Take someone you are discipling (or a whole discipleship group) through the *Xplore* study, or take the Perspectives course together. Your passion for God's glory will be contagious as others see you making sacrifices to give generously, pray fervently, and possibly even go yourself. Some of the greatest mobilizers in history have been students who were preparing to go long-term, but before leaving spent some time challenging other students to join them. If you can mobilize even one person to join you on mission for God's purposes, then the impact of your life in the world has been doubled! What can you do to help mobilize those you influence?

→ FRONTIER MOBILIZING

Would you be surprised to learn 8 out of 10 Bible-believing Christians live in Africa, Asia, and Latin America? That's news to many Western Christians. For the past two hundred years these places have been considered mission fields, but now they are home to the vast majority of the world's Christ-followers.

Praise be to God who has planted a light in many parts of the earth where there once was only darkness! His Spirit is working mightily in and through these believers who live within the same region, the same nation, and often in the same city as the unreached. Yet this 80% of the Church (who are most strategically suited to reach their unreached neighbors) currently only send about 20% of the world's missionaries. If the three billion people who are least reached with the gospel are going to hear about Jesus, this traditional mission *field* must be transformed into a radical new mission *force*!

Whereas frontier missions focuses on sending missionaries to the least reached peoples around the world, frontier mobilization efforts partner with and equip the global church to send missionaries to the least reached peoples in their own regions, nations, and cities. These believers don't need to cross an ocean to encounter those who have never heard of Jesus; in fact, sometimes they merely have to cross the street! Like no other time in history, Jesus' church is larger, in more places, and more ethnically diverse than ever before. Because of this, different parts of the body of Christ are geographically and culturally close to most of the least reached peoples of the world.

Consider a few countries where the church is right next to the unreached:

India has 26 million believers and regional access to 1.6 billion unreached people.

China has 80 million believers and regional access to 340 million unreached people.

Indonesia has 14 million believers and regional access to 330 million unreached people.

Kenya has 20 million believers and regional access to 76 million unreached people.

Nigeria has 50 million believers and regional access to 160 million unreached people.

In addition to geographic proximity, many in the global church are only a few cultural steps away from certain least reached peoples. Brazil and other nations in Latin America are not geographically close to unreached peoples, but they have access because of their kindred culture and increasing favor in the Arab world. The Latins and Arabs have similar appearance and customs. They like and receive each other. Imagine if the over 50,000,000 believers in

Brazil created a missionary sending pipeline right to the heart of the Arab world. In fact, it is already starting to happen!

The disciples of Jesus never considered reaching out to their geographic neighbors, the Samaritans, until Jesus started mobilizing them, taking them to nearby Samaria and telling them to "open [their] eyes and look at the fields [right in front of them]. They are ripe for harvest" (John 4:35). When they finally did go to their neighbors in Acts 8, many Samaritans believed and were baptized.

Jesus was a mobilizer, and so are you. Fulfill this divine calling by spending your life pointing everyone you can toward the person and (worldwide) purposes of Jesus Christ. If this particular role of mobilizing God's people to reach all nations is especially fascinating to you, pray about going as a frontier mobilizer. Consider living alongside and empowering the global church, aiding them in advancing the Great Commission by sending their *own* missionaries to the unreached.

REFLECTION QUESTIONS:

→ Describe a "World Christian" in your own words. Why would God want you to aspire to be this kind of believer?

→ List the five World Christian habits/roles listed in this chapter. How could you start to engage and grow in each of these five areas?

→ Even though Jesus commands us to go to the nations, leaving our home country and becoming a "goer" seems to be the scariest prospect for many Christians. Why is that? Are there any doubts, questions, or obstacles you have that would prohibit you from being a goer?

→ Think about your family, church, campus ministry, circles of friends, and contacts. What specific and practical ways could you start to "mobilize" them toward embracing and living out this World Christian perspective and lifestyle?

25

Not for College Days Alone

To show you what a fossil I (Steve) really am, I was part of the Greek system during a time when guys (yes, guys!) would gather around the piano after dinner and sing fraternity songs. I would sing a terrible backup baritone to everyone's sentimental favorite, "Not for College Days Alone." But looking back, the significance of my fraternity rituals *did* fade over the years, and so the vision and passion we gain in college can slip away as well.

In the midst of those college years, I went to a conference to hear Walt Henrichsen (former pastor, Navigator staff leader, author, discipler, and maker of audacious statements) speak. He stood before about a hundred of us "sold out" student laborers at a leadership summit and proclaimed, "Twenty years from now, only five of you will be walking with Christ and impacting others for Him with the same intensity you are today." I was stunned. "What?" I silently protested. "Who do you think you are? Only five out of a hundred are going to keep pressing on like we are now? Absurd!"

→ THREE POTENTIAL PITFALLS

At the time I thought maybe he was using reverse psychology on us, yet I now realize he was simply sharing a shocking truth. I haven't kept up with those 100 student leaders, but I have done informal surveys of many of the committed Christians I've known while in college. The dropout rate, especially the first three years after graduation, is horrendous. Many take vows of lifelong dedication to Christ and the Great Commission, but as the trials and temptations of this world come along, many—most, really—bail out. Here are three choices (among many) that graduating laborers make that have the potential to knock them off course:

Job

I have talked to so many students over the years who are accepting positions with companies based upon salary and climate. "Yeah," they might say, "I think I'm going to take the job with Dell Computers because they're offering $5,000 more a year, and I like the warmer weather of Austin." Money and temperature are fine, but there are much bigger, more eternal factors to consider.

I like to train our graduating students to make decisions like this with two questions in mind:

- Where can I go to continue to get the best *training* to keep growing in my walk with Christ and personal ministry?
- Where can I go to make the greatest *impact* for the kingdom of God?

I appreciate a little extra cash and a warm day, but if it means you have to sell your soul to a company or be cut off from people in some backroom computer lab or, even worse, have no idea how you're going to keep getting personal and ministry growth and training opportunities, you simply have to tell that company recruiter, "Thanks, but no thanks!"

Mate

I give talks and seminars all over the world for college students and churches and, regardless of the topic, I am compelled to always fit this sobering thought into my message: "Who you marry will make you or break you." Simple to say and hard to apply, especially when so many are pushing the senior panic button, realizing they might graduate without finding a spouse. Here's another obvious profundity: "You will marry someone you date." If this is true (and in America, it is), then only date someone who has the qualities you are looking for in a lifelong partner. Make sure they have the same goals, values, passions, and vision as yourself. Getting married is the scariest, most risky decision someone ever makes, so give that guy or gal of yours some time to develop a track record; the only way you can be sure of what they *will* give themselves to in the future is looking at what they *have given* themselves to in the past. Make sure you and your prospective date or spouse are running the bases of life in this order:

- 1st base: Master (Jesus Christ)
- 2nd base: Mission (Great Commission)
- 3rd base: Mate (a partner who has also taken the time to run the bases properly)

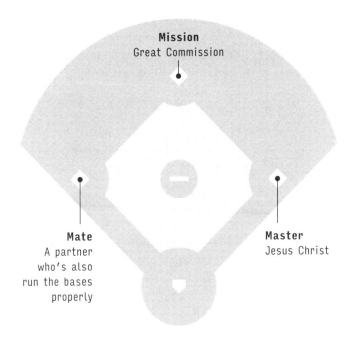

Lifestyle

I was 28 years old and very impressed with my 26-year-old "friend," Carol (my wife-to-be), to whom I was afraid to even mention the "M-word" for fear of saying something I couldn't follow through with. So, as we walked along one night, I asked, "If we were to 'solidify' our commitment someday, do you think you could live on $10,000 a year?" She said yes, so I pressed on. "Do you think we could live on $8,000 a year?" (Remember, these are 1982 figures!) She shook her head in the affirmative, so I added, "How about $6,000?" Finally, when I got her down to $4,000 a year, she blurted out, "It doesn't matter how much you make, I would not be marrying you for your money!" Well, I breathed a huge sigh of relief because I had always been fearful I would marry someone who claimed to love God and wanted to reach the world for Christ, but five to ten years into the marriage would be more interested in houses, cars, clothes, and vacations.

I'm not saying you have to live at the poverty level to please God. But, according to Roberta Winter (co-founder of the U.S. Center for World Mission), every believer is to live a "wartime lifestyle," seeking to evaluate every expenditure in light of the worldwide spiritual battle we're engaged in. If you choose a mate with different values, if you decide to go into big-time debt, if you subtly gravitate toward accumulating things rather than giving your life away to others—it's just a matter of time until the fruitfulness in your life will be choked out.

> "God doesn't bless us to increase our
> standard of living, but to increase
> our standard of giving."
>
> **— RANDY ALCORN**

In his excellent book *Spiritual Multiplication in The Real World*, Dr. Bob McNabb did a research thesis on graduates from disciple-making college ministries and their effectiveness at making disciples in the "real world" after college. He was trying to get to the bottom of why so many who are fruitful disciple-makers in college end up *not* making disciples after college. His conclusion was that the most important factor for someone multiplying after college was whether or not they were a part of a disciple-making *team*. In light of this, we challenge you to be strategic about where you spend your first few years after college.

Instead of making job, mate, and lifestyle decisions like the world does, why not team up with some of your closest co-laborers, move to a city with a great church and missional community, and then work on finding good, flexible jobs where you get to be around people? It would be better to get a position that pays less money and be a part of a spiritual environment that is going to help you thrive than to get the best job in the world and be isolated from fellow laborers who are engaged in significant training and ministry opportunities. Carrying your passion for making disciples beyond college and into the real world is not easy, but it is possible! Like I shared, following Christ as *Master* will always be first base for every believer. Committing yourself to fulfilling His *mission* is the essential second base. Then and only then will you really be ready to allow God to bring along His perfect *mate* to run the bases right beside you for a lifetime.

→ HAVE YOU BEEN "CALLED"?

So, if you choose to put your mission above your profession, does that mean you should "go into full-time ministry"? If you are considering ministry as a profession, is that something you have to be "called" to? The concept of calling is a hard one that can raise a lot of questions among Christians. The Greek word *kaleo* means to call, summon, or invite. All of us are *called* to become like Christ, to abide in Him, and to bring glory to Him through our lives and personal ministries, regardless of what our vocation happens to be. But God has made us all different, and our personality and gifting will each be suited to a unique role or calling.

One of my first experiences with this idea of "calling" was during my first day of seminary, which turned out to be a get-to-know-you day as each instructor posed the same request at the beginning of class: "Tell us your name and how you were *called* into ministry." As I sat and listened to story after story of running from God and finally surrendering, walking the aisle after breaking down in tears, and a vision one student received in the middle of the night, I wasn't sure what to say when my turn came. I was tempted to say "pass," but instead confessed, "Well, I became a Christian in high school and found out the Bible commands us to share our faith and make disciples, so I went to college and started winning some of my fraternity brothers to Christ and discipling them. I enjoyed it so much I thought maybe I'd like to witness and disciple *all* the time and just thought maybe taking some of these seminary courses might make me more effective in my ministry." Being the only one the prof did not affirm with nods and "amens" made me a *little* uncomfortable, but the loud and impassioned follow-up question was the real stinger: "Yes, brother, but how were you *called* into the ministry?" It was obvious that my first response did not satisfy him, but I had no other answer, no dramatic story, no tears, surrender, or vision to tell me (or persuade him) that I had really and truly been called!

Later reflecting on that day and the way some of my professors and classmates reacted to me made me a little frustrated. If God calls all of us to follow Him and embrace the Great Commission, why would I need some kind of additional emotional experience to "confirm" this calling? To me it was a clear command from Scripture, right there in black and white for all of us to see and obey. Was I somehow being pressured to place my experience as a higher authority than the Scriptures? I'm not saying emotional experiences are bad or that God will not use them in our lives, but the Lord is looking for obedience more than goosebumps, and the heart *and* the mind need to work together to discern His will for our lives.

Many Christian laborers in college wrestle with the question of whether they should go into full-time ministry, into the secular work force, or go on for more education. I usually encourage these graduating-senior followers of Christ to apply the traditional means of praying, reading Scripture, getting counsel, and making "pros and cons" lists, but I also include one question that has tremendous bearing on this issue of discovering God's will. With enthusiasm and anticipation in my voice, I ask, "If you could do *anything* in the world with your life, what would it be?" I give them a blank piece of paper and ask them to dream and then write down what they could get *most* excited about doing with their life. Not what their parents or girlfriend or academic advisor wants them to do, but what is deep within *their* heart. When they finally start jotting something down, I read it and 9.9 times out of 10 pass the paper back to them and say, "Go do this!"

I'll admit I probably have a little more "wide open" view of helping a person discover God's direction for their life, but I believe this exercise strikes at the core of understanding what we were designed to do. Psalm 37:4 says, "Delight yourself in the Lord, and he will give you the desires of your heart." If you are truly seeking to please God in all of your ways, then the desire of your heart will certainly line up with what's on God's heart. If you possess a love for God, a love for people, and the vision and training to build upon and carry out those two loves, you will find a way to bring glory to God through fulfilling the Great Commission—wherever you go and whatever you do. You'll be exporting the flame that burns on your campus to a world in desperate need of the light that only Jesus Christ can provide.

→ **"GIVE US TWO YEARS, AND WE'LL CHANGE THE WORLD"**

The Summit Church, led by J.D. Grear, challenges graduating college seniors to let ministry be the determining factor in where they pursue their careers:

"You have to get a job somewhere. Why not get one in a place where you can be part of a strategic work of God? Give us two years, and we'll change the world." Let us challenge you to seriously consider giving your first two years after graduation to make a strategic investment for advancing God's kingdom. There is another movement of churches and college ministries adopting this strategy and challenging graduates to "give a year and pray about a lifetime." Most mission agencies have programs where you can go serve among the unreached for one or two years after graduation. I have never met someone who invested these impactful years in missions and regretted it. You have your whole life to play it safe. Going for a year or two is a perfect way to make a significant eternal difference and explore long-term missions.

If your church or campus ministry has a one- or two-year staff internship program, that could also be a great option to consider after graduation. Here's why we think a post-graduation ministry experience like this should be on your list:

1. **It's an incredible opportunity to pour back into your campus ministry or church.**
   If you are already having a fruitful ministry, you will be able to continue multiplying disciples on campus full-time with no classes to worry about. This is often when you get to watch spiritual multiplication really take off!

2. **It's the perfect way to continue your training as a laborer and grow into a leader.**
   The staff who have been investing in you already know you and can take your training to the next level as you gain more hands-on experience in leadership and disciple-making. Pastor Harold Bullock says, "Your 20s are for training," and time spent working alongside wise leaders who can offer development and feedback is an investment in your foundation as a lifelong laborer.

3. **It's an ideal choice to explore longer-term vocational ministry or missions.**
   Raising support, reaching out to various ministry spheres on campus, discipling multiple students, and leading groups will be a great test drive for what a lifetime of missions or vocational ministry could look like. The skills you develop as a staff member can help launch you into a lifetime of ministry, whatever God calls you to do long term.

→ **PERSEVERE OVER THE LONG HAUL**

Spencer, one of my (Steve's) best friends, used to be a top collegiate marathon runner who went to school in a different state. I'd promised him for years that I would run a marathon with him someday. So, to keep my promise, a thousand of us "runners" descended on Fort Worth, Texas, on a cold and rainy Saturday in late February. Even though I had made the commitment to run with Spencer months earlier, I had failed to include one minor detail in my schedule—training! I had not run a single day in seven months, but hey, no problem. I perceived myself as an indestructible, 24-year-old warrior who could climb any mountain, swim any ocean, and certainly wasn't going to break a sweat over a puny 26.2-mile marathon! With my "vast" knowledge of long-distance running, I figured it best to keep a light stomach, so I just had a donut and coffee before the race.

Even though there was a torrential downpour, I was fine until the 22-mile mark, when I hit the proverbial "wall." I know this because during the final four miles of the race, three different medics who were bicycling against the flow (looking for runners in dire need) stopped, got off their bikes, grabbed me by the shoulders, and asked if I was okay. Exhaustion and thirst were attacking me, but the real killer was my own body—it was screaming out for food! I hadn't "carbed up" like real runners do, and my muscles had used every ounce of protein they'd ever possessed.

Early in the marathon, I'd foolishly sprinted out, fantasizing that I was going to be one of the top finishers. I didn't last ten minutes before reality set in, and I began to pace myself, finally admitting it was going to be a long haul. Spencer, the true athlete among us, only had two hours and thirty-seven minutes to contemplate his life that day. To say the least, I had much, much more time to mull over the similarities between walking with Christ and running a marathon!

The main insight I took away? Running the race with Christ is like running a marathon, in that the measure of a laborer is what it takes to stop you. Is it a discouraging semester, a broken relationship, financial loss, an addiction, or just the busyness and pressures of life swallowing up your passion and love for Jesus? If you terminate your all-out pursuit to fulfill the Great Commission because of one of these reasons (or a thousand others), you have sold out really cheaply. The enemy will provide many easy, even attractive, exit ramps for you throughout your lifetime. Instead, hang on for dear life to your first love and this divine purpose He has given you on earth. As we join God on His mission, we need to remember this isn't a hundred-yard dash, it's a marathon!

> "I have fought the good fight, I have finished the race, I have kept the faith." —the Apostle Paul to his disciple, Timothy, at the end of his life
>
> **(2 TIMOTHY 4:7)**

As you graduate from college ministry, one of the first exit ramps you will have to steer clear of is graduating from *ministry* when you graduate from *college*. How can you continue to live as a laborer, investing in others out in the "real world"?

→ COMMIT TO A CHURCH

We have emphasized the importance of continuing to connect with other believers who are on mission together to fulfill the Great Commission after college. This is such a huge factor in your continued growth and longevity as a laborer that we have even suggested you place more weight on the church you will plug into than the job you will take when deciding where to move after graduation. Whether you are able to jump into a passionate community of mission-minded believers or find yourself struggling with a church experience that pales in comparison with your college ministry, you can continue to multiply disciples. Your after-college church experience will largely depend upon your willingness to *commit* and *engage*.

No matter how many you visit, you will not find a perfect church. You also won't find a church community that feels just like your college community did. Rather than trying to recreate what you had in the past, focus on the future. Find a solid Bible-believing church whose values and mission you can partner with and help advance. Make the best church choice you can, and then be the best church member you can be: join a small group, find a place to serve, give, and be fully a part of the body. When you see things that need to be better in *your* church (which you will), do what you can to make them better. Yes, you are young and still have a lot to learn about walking with God, but you will also soon realize that the training you have received in college has equipped you to serve your church in significant ways. Investing deeply invites the wisdom and accountability of other believers into your life and will sustain you through the transitions and seasons to come. Trust that God will continue to grow you as you share the passion and vision He has given you with your local body of believers.

→ KEEP FUELING THE FLAME

Have you ever heard the saying, "vision leaks"? This means if you get pumped full of vision in college and then go out and do life without replenishing that vision, your life will probably end up looking different than you hoped it would. If you want to labor for a lifetime, you are going to have to be intentional about refueling the flame in your heart for God's mission. Consider using our suggested resources, books, podcasts, conferences, etc. to continually refill your vision tank.

> "Do not say that God allowed the flame to wane. Have you fed the fire? Information is the fuel. If the fire has died for lack of fuel, it is your own fault."
>
> —ROBERT WILDER, STUDENT VOLUNTEER MOVEMENT LEADER

What is your life about? Answer that question, and keep your mission right in front of you, making every decision in light of your overarching vision. A lifetime of walking with God is made one faithful choice at a time. Most people don't make a dramatic left turn to stop following Jesus or laboring with Him; they just slowly drift, allowing the momentum of life to pull them off course. You never graduate from the basics of building your foundation on Christ. Keep showing up every day for your time alone with the Lord. Keep pouring the Word of God into your mind and heart. Keep talking to other people about Jesus and helping others learn to walk with Him. The best way to maintain your passion for making disciples is to keep making disciples. Nothing can fuel your flame for God's kingdom like a front row seat to watch Him work in someone's life!

→ LEARN WHAT YOU DON'T KNOW

If you haven't figured it out yet, you soon will: college doesn't teach you everything you need to know about life. Making disciples as a student certainly has its challenges, but one of the exit ramps that derails many graduates is not being able to figure out how to do "real life" and ministry at the same time. There's a lot to learn about a lot of things, so don't be afraid to humbly ask for help in this season. Invite mentors and wise counselors to share their experience with you. Ask questions rather than pretending to have the answers.

Take training courses like Financial Peace University, or read books to learn how to budget, give, invest, pay off student loans, and make wise financial decisions. Get experience balancing hard work and healthy rhythms in life. Learn about your design and gifting. Pursue emotional health; work to resolve past hurts and grow in your communication and relational proficiencies. Understand how to really honor your mother and father, as well as your whole family. Strengthening foundational life skills will help keep issues in these areas from becoming distractions down the road and keep you on the path to laboring for a lifetime.

R E F L E C T I O N   Q U E S T I O N S :

→ Knowing that many college grads don't stay true to the commitments and convictions they gained in college, what can you
do now to help insure you're still growing in Christ and making
disciples five years after graduation?

→ Reflect on your ideas for your future job, mate, and lifestyle
after college. What can you start doing now to help insure you
will make wise and godly decisions in these critical areas in
your post-grad years?

→ How close to graduation are you, and would you seriously consider investing at least 1-2 years to pursue full-time kingdom
work on your campus or another country? Why or why not?

→ How important is the local church in your life right now, and
why will it be even more essential when you finish college?
After graduation, when and how will you go about finding the
very best church for you? How can you really plug in?

26

Pass the Baton

Growing up, all the men in my family were pole-vaulters except myself (the Shadrach strength and speed genes skipped me!), but I did enjoy cheering them on at track meets. One far-off memory I have is a Friday night conference meet in Dallas that featured the world-record-holding Lincoln High School mile-relay team. It was standing room only for this final event of the evening, everyone hoping that maybe the four Lincoln runners would set a new record in front of a hometown crowd.

As the gun sounded, Lincoln's first leg sprinted to the front and maintained his lead around the track before handing it to the second leg, who increased their lead even more. As the third man received the baton and raced around the 440-yard track, the thousands of cheering fans just knew they were witnessing history being made that night. With a huge lead, the third leg came cruising into the handoff zone to pass the baton off to the anchorman, the final and fastest leg of the team. As the fourth man started his sprint and held back his hand for the baton, disaster struck. Even though they had practiced the handoff thousands of times, that night there was a bobble, and the baton fell to the ground. Everyone in the stands froze as we watched the runner lean down to pick it up, only to see him accidentally kick it into the infield instead. Now the young man was on all fours, crawling toward the baton while the paralyzed crowd was hyperventilating!

By the time he got the baton, stood up, and ran back to the track, every runner had passed him. Starting from a dead standstill, Lincoln's anchorman put it into a gear no one knew existed. With his adrenaline pumping wildly (along with ours!), we watched him catch and pass the last man, then the second to the last and the next and the next, until finally, with a photo finish at the tape, he beat the lead runner and actually won the race!

The disbelieving crowd erupted with an ear-shattering cheer, realizing that we actually *had* seen history being made but certainly not in the way we'd expected. It was no doubt a night to remember and learn from.

I don't know who led you to Christ, who followed you up, who discipled you, or who instilled global vision in you. Or maybe you're a spiritual orphan who had to scrounge around and figure out all these things on your own, with no one really there to pass the baton to you in a solid, effective way. Whether or not there's been a person or ministry to hand off the necessary knowledge, skills, character, and vision to help you run (and win) this race, it does not excuse you from now picking up the baton and running with all of your heart, soul, and mind. Regardless of your past, the purpose of this book is to hopefully provide a good baton pass to you, sharing some basic principles that anyone can take and apply to life and ministry.

By now you've realized the Great Commission is not a spectator sport. You need to come out of the stands and onto the track, finding the race that God has for you. In fact, Hebrews 12:1-2 exhorts us to get up, strip down, dig in, and move out: "Therefore, since we have so great a cloud of witnesses surrounding us, let us also lay aside every encumbrance and the sin which so easily entangles us, and let us run with endurance the race that is set before us, fixing our eyes on Jesus, the author and perfecter of faith, who for the joy set before Him endured the cross, despising the shame, and has sat down at the right hand of the throne of God" (NASB).

Think about it. Not only are Moses, Abraham, Paul, and Timothy our witnesses, but also the pioneer student world changers like Samuel Mills, Hudson Taylor, and Grace Wilder. Men and women who ripped out every stronghold of sin in their life, every attachment to this world that might choke out their spiritual power, in order to run the race. Each of them took the baton and ran their leg, and now you're down on the track and the baton has been passed to you. What will you do with it? Let it fall to the ground and crawl back up into spectator seats? Or run the race God has set before you with such determination and tenacity that nothing could stop you? It's your life, your race, your baton, your opportunity; an opportunity of a lifetime.

→ WHAT CAN ONE STUDENT DO?

I know of a student who didn't quite have this vision yet. He indulged himself in the party life and continually mocked the Christians who witnessed to him at every turn. At the end of his freshman year, John decided to transfer to Cornell, an Ivy League school he'd heard could *really* supply the kind of night-life he was looking for without all the pesky religious nuts trying to constantly convert him. When he arrived on campus that fall, who was there to help him unload, unpack, and get him settled into his dorm room but a group of men from a local campus ministry! He could run, but he couldn't hide, as these students persisted in inviting John to their weekly meetings.

Finally, to get them off his back, John agreed to come to one of their little gatherings but showed up late so as not to appear too interested. As he slipped in through a side door, he was surprised to see a packed-out auditorium, each student intently listening to every word that the lecturer, a British sports hero, was saying. As John started to tiptoe to the back, the speaker suddenly cried out, "Young man!" John turned, thinking he had been caught. "Are you seeking great things for yourself?" the loud voice boomed. John stood speechless, unable to move, now in a staredown with this hulk of a man at the podium. "Seek them not!" the speaker added, "Seek first the kingdom of God!"

John finally regained his composure, then quickly lost himself in the back of the crowd. However, he could not sleep that night, wondering if the visiting speaker was calling him out or if God Himself was trying to give him a message. The next morning, John tracked down the British guest and set up an appointment to talk. The speaker, he learned, was J.E.K. Studd of England, who was giving away their family fortune and turning down lucrative sports contracts to help his brother, C.T., and others go to China to be missionaries. Studd's deep conviction about sacrificing all for Christ and His worldwide mission cut John to the core. That very day, John humbled himself, repented, and turned his life over to the God he always knew was patiently waiting for him to get to the end of his rope.

Soon after, John was invited to a Christian summer project in Massachusetts to study the Bible and grow in Christ. He attended with about 250 other guys, not realizing the Lord had another big step for him to take. Midway through the project, a group challenge was issued for them to dedicate their lives to the purpose of reaching the world's unevangelized, asking each man to sign a declaration stating their intent. John was one of 100 men who put their names on the document, making a covenant with God to exchange their lives to do whatever they could to see the world come to Christ.

Because John had been impacted by a visiting missions speaker during his undergraduate days, he volunteered to travel from campus to campus challenging students to embrace Christ's global cause. He never actually became a cross-cultural missionary himself, but over the next sixty years he traveled the world, recruiting over 100,000 students to finish the job of world evangelization. After winning the Nobel Peace Prize in 1946 as one of the greatest missionary statesmen in all of history, John reflected: "Across the years this work among students, first in one's own country and then throughout the world, was always my first love." At the end of his life, looking back at the different people and events that shaped him, he could not forget the short appointment he had sixty years earlier, while still in college, with the visiting British sports hero turned mobilizer. He paused, looked at his biographer, and stated,

"It was the decisive hour of my life."

John R. Mott may have started out as just a rebellious sophomore at Cornell University in 1885, but God awakened in him a heart for reaching students to reach the world, and in so doing, spearheaded the greatest mobilization effort in all of history, the Student Volunteer Movement. Right now, trying to type these words through my tears, I ask you the same questions I am asking myself. What difference can one college student make? What is the potential of one individual sold out to the person and purposes of Jesus Christ? Is this cause worth exchanging *your* life for?

Know this for sure: if you will give yourself as the fuel, God will ignite the flame for worldwide impact. You are responsible for reaching *this* generation of students. Join God in His mission, investing your life as a co-gatherer with Him and reaching people from every corner of the earth to spend eternity worshipping Christ around His throne. Here's a key verse in Revelation that describes our amazing opportunity to partner with God as He completes His history-long endeavor: "After this I looked and there before me was a great multitude that no one could count, from every nation, tribe, people and language, standing before the throne and in front of the Lamb. They were wearing white robes and were holding palm branches in their hands. And they cried out in a loud voice: 'Salvation belongs to our God, who sits on the throne, and to the Lamb'" (Revelation 7:9-10).

This passage tells us what to pray for and work toward in life, always keeping our eyes focused on that day. It is the glorious culmination of all history, and the final exam as to what we gave ourselves to during our brief stay on this planet. Decide *now* that you will not be at the throne that day alone and empty-handed, but instead you will be followed by a throng of individuals who came to college simply as students but left as world changers...as a result of *your* life and ministry.

Are you ready to give yourself
totally to Him and His purposes?
Could this be the decisive hour of *your* life?
The baton is passed to you.
Take it and run!

REFLECTION QUESTIONS:

→ After reading these inspirational stories about the potential of just one college student taking the Lord and the Great Commission seriously, what is the potential of your life? What do you think God wants to do through you, starting now, on this campus?

→ Is there anything at all that is holding you back from making an unreserved commitment to Jesus Christ and to spending your life making disciples? Are you willing to let go of it?

→ In John's story at the end, he looked back on his time in college and identified "the decisive hour of [his] life" that changed everything for him. Have you had that hour yet? If so, describe it.

→ Describe in your own words what the "fuel" and the "flame" are and how that concept has affected you. Stop and pray, asking God to use your life to impact your campus for Christ—and the world.

Steve Shadrach came to Christ at age 18 through Athletes in Action and Fellowship of Christian Athletes. He attended the University of Arkansas, joining a fraternity and getting involved with Cru, Navigators, and University Baptist Church (UBC). He worked at Kanakuk Kamps during the summers as a counselor and head counselor. After graduation, he attended Southwestern Baptist Seminary and finished at Dallas Theological Seminary. After marrying his sweetheart, Carol, they moved back to Fayetteville, Arkansas, where Steve became the Collegiate Pastor at UBC. While living and ministering next to the U of A campus, he also began the Kaleo Summer Training Projects, brought *Perspectives on the World Christian Movement* to Arkansas, began the Student Mobilization (StuMo) campus ministry, and along with Todd Ahrend, launched The Traveling Team ministry. In 2004, Steve became Director of Mobilization for the U.S. Center for World Mission, then began the Center for Mission Mobilization (CMM) with John Patton with the goal of engaging, equipping, and connecting believers worldwide to their most strategic role in completing the Great Commission. Two of the CMM's key resource ministries are Support Raising Solutions and Campus Ministry Today. Steve has a Masters in Biblical Studies from Dallas Seminary and a Doctorate in Church and Para-Church Executive Leadership from Denver Seminary. He and Carol have five grown children and eight grandchildren, and they continue to minister to college students near the Arkansas campus. He is the author of six books, including *The God Ask* and *The Heart of the Campus*.

Paul Worcester is the son of a pastor and church planter, and he got involved with the Baptist Campus Ministry at University of Oklahoma, being trained under the leadership of Max Barnett. In 2009, he and his wife Christy started and developed a Christian Challenge ministry at California State University, Chico. Since then hundreds of students have indicated decisions to become followers of Jesus, with many growing as disciples and learning to multiply their faith. Paul is the author of *Tips for Starting a College Ministry*, *Do More With Less Time*, and the coauthor of the new edition of *The Fuel* *and The Flame: Igniting Your Life and Campus for Jesus Christ* with Steve Shadrach. He has a passion for equipping and encouraging fellow collegiate leaders to make disciples on campus through his writing, speaking, consulting, and social media. Paul is on the team behind Campus Ministry Today, Collegiate Collective and CollegeMinistry.com. Paul just launched Campus Multiplication Network which provides training and coaching for collegiate ministry leaders who desire to accelerate evangelistic momentum, multiply disciples, and plant new ministries. His prayer is that God will use this network of leaders to plant new ministries on colleges until there is no campus left without a multiplying gospel movement. Paul and Christy have two children, and they love to play sports and get to the beach to surf when they can.

there's more
ONLINE

*find tools and
documents mentioned
throughout this book*

THEFUELAND
THEFLAME.COM

hosted by Campus Ministry Today

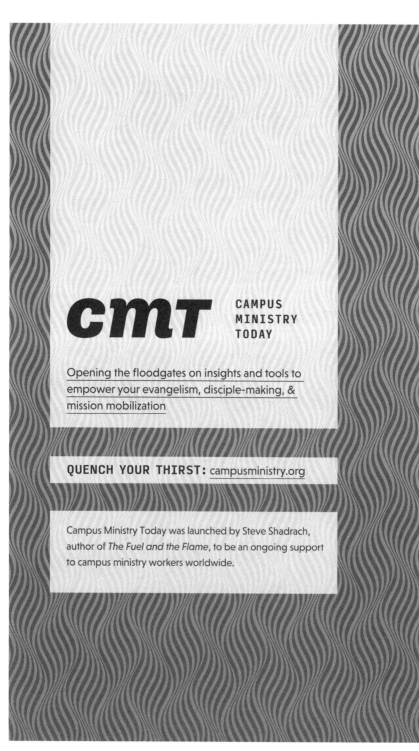

CMT

CAMPUS MINISTRY TODAY

Opening the floodgates on insights and tools to empower your evangelism, disciple-making, & mission mobilization

QUENCH YOUR THIRST: campusministry.org

Campus Ministry Today was launched by Steve Shadrach, author of *The Fuel and the Flame*, to be an ongoing support to campus ministry workers worldwide.

We've made support raising training **fun, interactive, and team-focused.**

SRS Bootcamp

SUPPORT RAISING SOLUTIONS

Developed by the founder of SRS and the author of The God Ask, SRS Bootcamp will equip you with a real plan, hands-on experience, and resources to get to your ministry assignment quickly and fully funded.

*Find a Bootcamp near you
and register today!*

SupportRaisingSolutions.org/**Bootcamp**

Support Raising Solutions is a ministry of the Center for Mission Mobilization. mobilization.org

Free SRS resources

Stay fully funded wherever
God's mission leads you.

Get practical tips and insights on a broad range of real world
support raising topics delivered to your inbox monthly.

Subscribe today at SupportRaisingSolutions.org

Follow us and join the support raising conversation.

SupportRaisingSolutions

 SUPPORT
RAISING
SOLUTIONS™

MULTI-PLY YOUR-SELF

x100

If you become a missionary, you'll add a much-needed laborer to the harvest field. But consider the millions of believers already living next door to the unreached. They are a vast, untapped mission force.

Help raise up a new generation of missionaries from Asia, Africa, Latin America, Europe, and the Middle East.

Become a frontier mobilizer.

mobilization.org/join + 800 595 4881

CENTER FOR MISSION MOBILIZATION